THE
STAINED
GLASS
WINDOW

THE STAINED GLASS WINDOW

molly malvern painter

TATE PUBLISHING & *Enterprises*

Published by Tate Publishing & Enterprises, LLC
127 E. Trade Center Terrace | Mustang, Oklahoma 73064 USA
1.888.361.9473 | www.tatepublishing.com

Tate Publishing is committed to excellence in the publishing industry. The company reflects the philosophy established by the founders, based on Psalm 68:11,
"The Lord gave the word and great was the company of those who published it."

Book design copyright © 2010 by Tate Publishing, LLC. All rights reserved.
Cover design by Amber Gulilat
Interior design by Stefanie Rane

Published in the United States of America

ISBN: 978-1-61663-685-2
1. Biography & Autobiography, Personal Memoirs
2. Biography & Autobiography, Religious
10.10.11

For
Dara

ACKNOWLEDGMENTS

I would like to thank my mother. I love and admire you.

I want to thank Susan and Chris Gahan. Susan, this ministry could not have been birthed without you. Mere words will never be enough to thank you both for all you have done for me.

I would like to thank Marjorie and Nicky Ard for their support. Marjorie, I thank you for being the prayer warrior of the ministry. This ministry could not move forward with confidence without the discernment and confirmation of the Holy Spirit. Thank you for keeping our concerns before the throne room of God.

Katie Altobellis, this ministry would not have survived without your belief that God had a call upon my life. Thank you for your continued support, and Katie, this book would not have been what it is without your keen sense of guidance and editing skills. As far as I am concerned, you have co-authored this book.

I would like to thank Horizon Sites. You were put specifically in my path to help "bring the heavens down to earth, one rung at a time" through our Web-based outreach. Mike Womble, thank you for your pastoral care, concern, and patience with me as I have strived to walk through with Jesus. Knowing of your belief in *Jesuswithoutthejunk* and our desire to reach souls with the simple and clear truth has tremendously bolstered my confidence.

I want to thank all of the individuals who have given unto me, whether you were aware of it or not, you helped me fulfill the call of God upon my life so that others might see we have a Father in heaven who is real. In particular, Louise Torchio, I thank you for giving this ministry its name, *Jesuswithout-*

thejunk. Also, Jennier Philligin, thank you for being our hands and eyes.

Father, I love you with every breath I take. I have told you many times that no one would ever believe what you have done through my life. I am trying by the writing of this book to give them a *brief overview,* and I know it is in your hands which souls you will touch with my story. I will see you when you are ready for me, and until then, I pray to fulfill the call you have ordained for me.

TABLE OF CONTENTS

Foreword 11

Preface 15

Part One 21

The Stained Glass Windows 23

Oh, Yes! I'm the Great Pretender 27

Ten Long, Beautiful Nails 35

My Godforsaken Hair 40

The Green Nerve Medicine 48

Livin' On Love 54

Jesus Freaks 59

Breaking Up Is Hard to Do 66

Pick Yourself Up; Dust Yourself Off—Time to Move! 75

Eighteen, My MGB, and Money, Honey 81

"Mr. Blue Eyes" and Midnight at the Oasis 87

Long Lost Love and Death 97

Part Two 107

"Do You Take This Woman, Finally?" 109

Give Me a Pill So I'll Feel Better! 119

Eighty-Five Pairs of Shoes on the Wall 124

I'll Be Happy When 132

Good-bye to Diets 136

Breaking Up Again 140

D-i-v-o-r-c-e 145

Dara and Me 153

Married Life, Again! 161

The Icing on the Cake 171

I Am Not a Liar, Honest Injun and Suicide 177

Dr. Jekyll and Molly Hyde 180

Ten Beautiful Nails, Finally! 184

Part Three 193

Get Nailed 195

My Little Sanctuary 201

The Wild Stallion Gets Roped 207

Would You Die For Me? 218

Two or More 225

"Let Go" 232

"My People Are Starving" 245

Jesus First, Others Second 264

Stand Down 278

The Willow Tree Figurine 287

Control 298

Jesuswithoutthejunk 305

The Face of Christ 314

Epilogue 317

Afterword 321

For More Information 323

FOREWORD

When God puts someone in your life to tell you who he is, listen.

I was introduced to Molly Painter about five years ago. We met at a salon where she worked. I did not know it at the time, but the Lord led me there. I had been warned about Molly early on and told to watch out for her because all she did was talk about the Lord. I laughed and said, "That's okay; she will not bother me. I will just nod my head and act like I care what she is talking about."

To make a long story short, she ended up asking me to attend her Bible study group. I did not know the Lord then and did not intend to get to know him. From time to time in my life, I had prayed to the Lord when I needed something— just in case. I had never believed in anything I could not see, including God and the devil. After all, if there was a hell, I believed it existed here on earth, and I had been there more than once. Where had God been when I needed him most? I had given up on the Lord long ago.

Frankly, I was miffed when she asked me to join her meeting. I accepted her offer out of a misplaced sense of guilt, and I knew it would be a one-shot deal and I would never be back. It was an offer that saved my life. Little did I know what the Lord had planned.

During the course of the meeting, which probably lasted a couple of hours, I heard things, experienced things, and felt things to which I had never been accustomed in my life. When she spoke about the things of God, something in me stirred. I felt exhilarated, and I wanted more.

Being in her presence that night was indescribably peaceful and euphoric. I did not know much about who the Lord was, but he let me know that very night. The Lord God's hand rests firmly upon Molly Painter, his breath is in her ear, and he speaks through her. That meeting was nearly four years ago. My point in telling you briefly about my early meeting with Molly is to tell you that God put her in my life to prove to me that he is real. I am a witness to some of the things she tells of here, and I have been around her enough to know that supernatural occurrences happen when anyone is around her.

I challenge you to read this book from cover to cover because you are about to embark on a journey that will change your perspective on who you think the Lord is and what you think he is capable of doing. Some of you already know. A number of you will know that what is described in these pages is the truth. Some readers will be appalled and mortified by instances that occurred in Molly's life; disbelief will fill others' hearts. Still, a great many will be able to identify because of what has happened in their own lives. Know that you are not alone.

Molly writes with unashamed frankness about things most would never admit to doing or going through. She shares chapters in her life that include agonizing and unbearable episodes that would have taken a lesser person under. However, she understands with remarkable clarity the calling on her life and why the Lord has placed her here. She had to go through these things in order to let others know what the power of God can do for them in their lives and, first and foremost, that God is real. Her life has truly been one of sacrifice and obedience.

Thank you, Molly, good and faithful servant of the Lord. This book was not an easy task, but what you write here will undeniably bring hope to the multitudes.

In closing, my advice to those of you who will read Molly's story is this: When God puts someone in your life to tell you who he is, listen.

Katie Altobellis, a follower of Christ

PREFACE

The time was Christmas 2006. Everything I thought I had known—everything I thought was my life, things I had grown up with—was turned inside out and upside down.

The previous summer I had written a play—*Get Nailed.* It was unlike anything I had ever done. The play received accolades from two local college teachers and feeling it had merit, they provided the funding that allowed me to take it to a local stage to raise money for needy families that Christmas. It was a very entertaining rendition of my ugly life—satirical, yet poignant in its ability to reach others. It detailed how Satan tried to destroy my life through drinking, addictions, abortions, and numerous other setbacks.

Three days before the play was to be performed, I proclaimed a fast and listened for any guidance from heaven. The Holy Spirit spoke to me and asked, "Are you ready to lay your life down for my children?"

Without thinking anything of it, my reply was, "Well, of course I am ready to lay my life down for you, Lord, and your children." Then, upon further reflection, and as I pondered the question, I thought, *Come on, it's not as if God would really ask me to lay my life down—not in this day and age ... would he?*

The big night came after just one dress rehearsal—I use the term dress rehearsal loosely—and I just knew I was headed for Broadway! I had done benefits in the past that were successful, but that night my pride took a big hit. The play did not turn out the way I thought it would in terms of attendance, but soon I discovered it turned out exactly the way God wanted it to. I had always told God I would go and do what he told me, even if it were just for one person, and that night he tested the very words I had vowed to him.

After the play, I hit a wall. In the days following, I could hardly function. My daughter noticed a big change and kept asking me what was wrong. My speech was slurred, and at times, I could hardly manage to get words to form. It was very odd. Nothing like this had happened to me before.

On New Year's Eve, I called everyone in my family and told them how much I loved them. I went to sleep that night as usual and awoke the next morning not really cognizant of my surroundings. Then, little by little, what happened started to flood back. The Spirit of the Lord had taken me to heaven to have a big meeting. This was not the first time something like this had happened, but this time was deadly serious.

I was sitting at a table talking to someone, unable to make out the form or the exact person. I begged him not to send me back down to earth, desperately pleading my case. I stated, "I have already lived through hell on earth. Please don't make me go back."

The response I received was calm, clear, and to the point: "You have to go back to fulfill your mission."

My mission is this: I am to get to the nations the truth of Jesus Christ's resurrection, teaching others what the Holy Spirit has taught me in a simple and clear way. I am not everyone's cup of tea—or coffee, my favorite—but for those who will listen, my story could be life-changing. I am a cut to the chase type of person with no holds barred. Time is late; I am too old, and there are souls caught in the balance. Many people are in the dark about who God really is. There are many voices saying so many things that great confusion is taking place. I am here to shed light in this area so people can gain the victory right here and right now from a living Savior. I have literally walked through years of schooling in the Holy Ghost to discover the truth beyond any shadow of doubt. I have come to answer for you the question, "Is God really real?"

In the seventh grade, I read a book called *Black Like Me*. It is the story of a man who actually dyed his skin using a drug so he could appear to be black. He was able to infiltrate the black and white community while walking in another man's shoes. I have done the same thing to an extent. I was born and raised a Presbyterian, went to a Methodist church with my high school sweetheart, got married in an Episcopal church, and later joined a Baptist church trying to work my way to heaven. I also attended several charismatic churches in my quest to seek the truth. In addition, I have walked through many things one can experience on earth so I can turn around and help others, whether they are Christians or not, with a message of hope.

I was sick and tired of being sick and tired. I needed something else—something more and something different than I had. I found it where I didn't expect. I have been pulled through the tunnel of life so I can turn around and help pull you out, whoever you are.

One by one, God has sent people to me so that I can minister to them. A girl asked me one time, "How can you possibly know so much about everyone and their hurts and pains?"

My reply was simple: "Because I have lived through the same things." I didn't ask to. It was my destiny.

My life has been saved only—and I repeat only—for the ones it is supposed to touch with the healing, delivering power, and love of Christ. It will be hard at times for you to believe what God has done in and through my life, but this is my attempt to tell you. I have had two complete strangers prophesy over me, telling me about a book I was to write for the nations. This is *the* book.

I always imagined if I ever wrote a book that it would be thicker than *Gone With the Wind*. I want you to understand this book is by no means the whole ball of wax. I will start by giving you an *overview* of some of the things I have experienced on this earth. I refer to it as "The List." People are shocked, amazed, horrified, and repulsed. Nevertheless, they are affected in some way, whether good or bad. If, after reading it, you don't think I have a basis for telling you anything, then you are not one of the ones I am supposed to reach. On the other hand, if you are someone the Lord is going to reach with my story, you will find what you are about to read amazing.

The List

- Married twice
- Verbally and physically abused
- Diagnosed a manic-depressive and later with bi-polar disorder
- I have lived in eighteen different homes in my life.
- Bank manager at twenty-four years old
- I have had twenty-six separate jobs.
- Five abortions
- Shock treatments
- Counseling (two psychiatrists and two psychologists)
- Panic attacks (agoraphobia)
- Hypochondriac
- Hysterectomy (at thirty-four years old)
- D and C
- Gallbladder removed
- Cesarean

- Laparoscopy
- I have had extensive dental work done which provided the pain pills I became addicted to.
- Lying and conning doctors to get what I wanted
- Alcoholic
- Smoked dope
- Smoked three packs of cigarettes a day
- I had two cars repossessed and turned another one in voluntarily.
- Filed bankruptcy
- Owned a business I started with only $88.29
- Attempted suicide
- Physically hurt myself
- I have had weight problems, having been over 200 pounds four times in my life.
- Had money, been broke, and everything else in between
- Have had more sex than I care to remember

By the time I was thirty-nine years old, I was sick and tired of life. I had tried everything I knew to be successful and happy. I had exhausted every avenue that was open to me.

One evening, I looked up to heaven, raised my right hand in the air, pointed at God—where I thought he would be—and said, "If you are really real, you are going to have to help me 'cause I don't want to live down here like this anymore. I would rather you take me home now." I added, "I will be damned to hell if my daughter's life is going to end up like mine." Then sealing my fate, I said, "Give me a hunger and thirst for your Word that I cannot satiate with anything else but you."

My statement was plain, simple, and to the point. By this time, the queen of BS was tired of it all. My big mouth was tired of running on and on, and I needed some help. In order to bring you the whole truth of how I came through the tunnel, I need to take you to what I like to call the PJ days—pre-Jesus.

I have to go back to events that happened in my life that built the foundation for what my life has come to be. I want this story to contribute to the process of justice that is going to break forth in order to expose the devil for who he is and expose God for who he really is.

Satan entered my life and soul when I was six years old. What followed was more than I thought I deserved and more than I had bargained for. If I had not raised my hand to heaven that fateful day, I would not be alive today. If just one person reads this book and discovers what I discovered along the way in my walk with God, then it will have been worth it all. I am called to be transparent with my life, and while I am not dying to air my dirty laundry, I am determined to be obedient to what God is telling me to do. I humble myself before heaven so that others can be set free.

> *The accolades of man are for but a moment in time. The praises of God are for eternity.*
>
> *Molly Malvern Painter*

PART ONE

THE STAINED GLASS WINDOWS

My sister and mother asked me to take a trip with them to our hometown of St. Albans, West Virginia in October of 2007. It was the first time I had been there or anywhere else in years. The trip wasn't going to cost me anything. All I had to do was get in the car and go along for the ride. I believed I was being given an opportunity to have a rest, but what I didn't realize was this was a destiny moment in my life, and I would have to go.

I was (and continue to be) self-employed and felt like I could not take time off from working, so I hesitated at the offer. I had an ache in the pit of my stomach and really didn't want to make the trip. It took some convincing for me to say yes. My younger brother called me (and he rarely calls me) and said I should go. When I told my daughter of the trip, she heartily said, "Go!" I felt like I was being coerced into making this trip when I would rather have stayed home. But several nights later, I had a dream that squashed any indecisiveness on my part about making the journey. In the dream, I was sitting next to my mother and several others, whose faces were blurred, on a church pew. I saw a multitude of colored lights beaming from what I knew deep within to be one of the stained glass windows in the sanctuary of the church where I had grown up. The morning after this dream, the answer—

whether or not to make this trip—was moot, so I reluctantly packed my belongings. I knew I physically would have to sit in the church sanctuary with my mother to receive something I needed. I had no idea what the outcome would be, but this type of circumstance had happened to me once before, years earlier, so I knew I *had* to be obedient to follow through.

As our car made its way through my hometown to my aunt's house where we were going to stay, the streets seemed quite a bit narrower than they had been. The houses seemed closer together, and things in general were not as large and looming to me as they had been when I was young. The town had become a worn and faded memory, much like an old picture that yellows with age. My mother and sister believed we were all going there for just a visit, but what they didn't know was I was only going because I knew I had to. The only thing on my heart as we made our way to my aunt's house was, *What in the sanctuary do I need?*

We got all settled in and I felt anxious. *What in the world was I to discover that could only be given to me by being here?* We had been in town for a couple of days—seeing relatives, going out to eat, and shopping—but all that I could think of was the sanctuary.

Finally, the day came. We dressed up and headed for the First Presbyterian Church of St. Albans. The church was magnificent in its splendor. The stained glass windows were, and still are, the most beautiful ones I have ever seen. I carried that church and the memory of the stained glass windows in my heart all through the years as if they were a secret treasure only to be pulled out and remembered when I needed to recall an easier time in my life.

My heart was racing as we made our way into the sanctuary that morning. I sat down right beside my mother, as if it was destined to be that way. All of a sudden, I was taken back in time to the Sundays I would sit beside my mother as a child, falling asleep on her shoulder as I stared at the stained glass windows while the pastor brought the weekly message. Those windows held the key to something for me, but what was the secret that had to be unlocked?

I sat there that morning, awaiting my revelation. Clearly, I was positioned correctly, so why wasn't something happening? The service started, and I waited … and waited. Nothing happened. Time had erased from my memory what was etched on the windows. I sat there, and I looked at each one, studying it for the answer—the reason I was supposed to be there. One window contained the picture of a woman who was prostrate on the ground, holding onto the cross of Christ with both arms as if her very life depended on it. My gaze then turned to the next one. There was a huge angel hovering over shepherds in the field, as if telling them of the Christ child who was born in Bethlehem to save us all. What was I was supposed to get from those pictures? Yes, they were beautiful. Yes, the colors and the detail were amazing, but what was I missing, and why did I have to be in that sanctuary?

There was no earth-shattering, out-of-body experience. The service continued without any fanfare, and then it was over. My heart sank. I knew I had been called there, but why? I wanted to make certain I had a copy of the windows, so I had my sister take pictures of them after the service.

My childhood home was a big, old, white two-story house that was situated on the corner lot right across the alleyway (as I called it) from the church. After I moved from St. Albans, it was torn down several years later, making room for additional parking. We walked across the paved lot as we left, and I made a joke about our car being parked in our old living room, but it really wasn't funny to me. I was back in my hometown and didn't want to be there, yet I had made the trip because I felt I was supposed to … but why? We drove out of the church lot that day to have lunch with relatives; I felt forlorn.

Later that afternoon, I went back to my aunt's house, undressed, and lay on the bed thinking about the church and the stained glass windows. I knew the streaming, somewhat blurred, multicolored lights in my dream had something I needed. Prior to this visit, I had not been back in that church since my grandmother's funeral. I vividly recall *something* drawing me there. I had entered the church by way of the side doors that sad day and went inside to sit. It was at a time in my life when I desperately needed some answers, and that church was always the place I felt better and more at ease—peaceful.

I thought Jesus lived there, but how could he help me with my life? I sat, recalling the mud pies I made as a child on the steps of the fellowship hall, each one precise. As I got older, I sat on the ledge that surrounded the church and would watch the cars drive past. Everyone noticed me. Cars would honk with familiar faces, hands waving in the air. Why did I feel the need to go sit in the sanctuary? I had taken time off from work to go back to my hometown and my grandmother's funeral, but the days had quickly passed, and now it was time to go back to the life I hated.

Sitting there in the quiet that day didn't give me an answer. What was it? Why had I felt so compelled to go sit there? Why did I feel something would take place there that day to change my wreck of a life? Did I think someone was going to come in there and save me? I was lost and I needed help. I wanted to go back and start my life over from the beginning. I was dying inside. Wasn't there anyone who could help me? I recall walking out of the church that day feeling empty, lost, alone, and most of all, scared of what was to come. *Someone please help me …*

I was feeling a sense of *why* as I fell off to sleep that afternoon after the service. I knew I hadn't come back to my hometown for nothing, but I had no clue the reason for this trip after all these years. Would the multicolored lights beaming from the stained glass window in my dream ever become clear to me?

OH, YES! I'M THE GREAT PRETENDER

I was born Molly Malvern on September 11, 1955 to Walter Lee and Martha McDermit Painter. All I thought about when I was young was growing up, getting married, and having a family just like the ones on TV. I would lie on the dining room floor of my house with my hands resting on my chin, while looking at the album cover of *The Platters' Greatest Hits*. I would listen to each song over and over while memorizing and singing every word, dreaming of being in love—just like the girls on TV.

I didn't grow up in a rural town or in poverty; although as I look back, I know there were times when we needed money. The first memory I have of my life was standing in my crib, throwing a bottle across the room out of anger because my mother wouldn't pick me up. I was eighteen months old. I am the third of four children; I have two older brothers and a younger sister.

There was an elderly woman by the name of Miss Tib who lived around the corner, in an upstairs apartment, from my house. She would come over and baby-sit from time to time when my parents went out for the night or when they left town to go on a business trip. She was a wonderful storyteller, and at bedtime she would tuck my sister and me in bed, position her chair in the middle of the room, and proceed to tell us a story.

If we didn't fall asleep after the first one, we would beg and beg her to tell us another one. I loved to hear her voice as she would recount *Cinderella* or *Jack and the Beanstalk*. I would drift off to sleep, having been lulled into a happy, dreamy state. I didn't mind my parents not being there so much when she was with us.

When Miss Tib's brother—he became known as my "Uncle Walter"—came to visit in the summer, I was given the responsibility of getting up each morning when the clock struck six to administer the medicine he had to take. I could walk to her apartment through my backyard or the "secret passageway," as I imagined it to be. Miss Tib was an extension of my family. She treated me like a friend and related to me on my level, making me feel I was more adult than I really was.

That is the way everyone treated me. When I went to her house, she would give me her undivided attention. We would do fun things like make cinnamon rolls, but she also turned our time into a learning experience by teaching me such things as basic Spanish phrases. I felt worldly!

However, when four o'clock would come, time would stand still. It was time for *The Edge of Night*. We never missed an episode. For one half hour, I would have to be quiet. I did not particularly care for those times, and I would get restless while sitting there, wanting to go home, but for the most part, I loved being with Miss Tib.

Her house was the house I went to when I packed my little cardboard suitcase and ran away from home. I heard the little boys in the neighborhood talking about running away from home, and that put a notion into my head. I threatened my mom about running away from home for days, and the next time something didn't go my way, I left. I really didn't want to, but I had no choice! I was a rebellious child early on. I was headstrong.

I would watch girls on TV washing their hair and twirling it up in towels. At three years old, I hounded my mother so much about letting me wash my own hair that she finally gave in. She said she figured that if I had any soap left in it, she could wash it out later. I would see or hear something that someone would do, and I would strive to imitate it.

I would eavesdrop on my mother and her friends when they had adult conversations in the kitchen that were not intended for little ears; I had learned that from the neighborhood boys. Later, I would entertain my mother by imitating their gestures and mannerisms, making her laugh. I loved to see my mother laugh.

The neighborhood where I grew up was full of boys. I had been told time and again I needed a little girl to play with, but I really didn't like playing with dolls; give me rough-and-tumble boy games! The day did come, as if someone had overheard the statements made by everyone around me, when a new little girl moved into the neighborhood.

She moved in down the street and around the corner right beside my aunt and uncle. Her mother was a widow. I would listen to the adults around me and they seemed to feel sorry for them. She had an older brother around the same age as my oldest brother. Something inside of me felt funny when I would go over to my new friend's house to play but I didn't know what it was.

She seemed to have every make and model of Barbie doll, clothes, and shoes you could buy. She owned a Barbie house, car, and pool. She also had all of the 101 *Dalmatians* games with the ever-popular song, "Cruella De Vil," which we played over and over. I will never forget the line in the song that said, "If she doesn't get you, no evil thing will." If I had to play with dolls and girl things, at least it was interesting.

As I continued to go over there to play, her older brother tried to become more familiar with me by trying to touch my breasts. I would hit him to try to make him stop. It was extremely annoying. I knew in my heart it wasn't a game, but

I had been around so many boys I think I just chalked it up to boys being boys, never thinking it would go beyond that. I just tried to ignore him. He also tried to fondle my younger sister, but he did not try it as often with her.

I continued to go back over there thinking *this time*, things would be different and he would leave me alone. One day I went over to play. Her mother let me inside and said to go on upstairs. She beckoned me into the bathroom, stating she was in there. I slowly walked down the hall, opened the bathroom door, there she was with her brother, and he was sitting on the toilet. It was gross. They were laughing and I turned around and said, "When you get done, I will be outside." I left hurriedly from the house, not even saying goodbye to her mother.

I let some time pass before I went over there again. Summer had arrived and there wasn't anyone in the neighborhood this one particular day to play with, so I walked around the corner over to her house to try and see if things were any different in regard to the icky situation there. I knocked on the door and asked her brother if she was home. He invited me in and told me he would go get her. He told me to go into this little side room and wait for her. I had a funny feeling about it all, and it caught me off guard because the door to this room was always kept shut.

At any rate, I went in, and he followed several minutes later, making some lame excuse about her not being home, stating she would be back later. I felt this heat flood over my entire body, and I sensed this dreadful, bad thing was about to happen. All of a sudden, he started pushing me into a corner. I was trapped. He started saying vile, nasty things and started to pull down his pants. He wanted me to fondle him. He wanted me to pull down my pants as well. I was scared to death. I felt sick inside. I wanted to scream out for help but my voice faltered and I found myself speechless.

I had never been around people who behaved this way, and I tried to pretend it wasn't happening. I had no idea what to do. I thought about trying to pretend to throw up; I thought about trying to run. I just had no clue what to do. I told him to give me just a second and then I would do what he asked. I just wanted to be out of there and go home. I started thinking about my family, and I wondered what they were doing at that exact moment; I wanted to be there with them. I hated this. I hated him. He told me to stop stalling.

I made believe I was looking at some seashells that were lined up on the floor against the wall trying to buy some time until I could figure out what to do. They always brought back tons of them each year from their trips to Daytona Beach. He kept persisting and he cornered me, preventing me from getting out the door. He was not going to let me go. I knew I was in serious trouble. Then, for some reason, I told him I would touch him and made other promises I did not fully intend to keep—if he would move away from the door. After much effort on my part, I bolted out the door. I still vividly remember him yelling after me as I made my getaway. I ran home as fast as I could. I was sick inside. I was scared to death, but I had escaped! I couldn't believe it—I did it. I got free. I ran up to my room to hide.

I dared not tell anyone. What would Mom and Dad do to me if they knew what had happened? Would they be mad? Would they punish me? Would they even talk to me again? Fear gripped me. I felt nasty and dirty on the inside. I felt as if something had gotten into me. From that moment on, things in my life changed; I was never the same again. I didn't go over to my girlfriend's house after that. When we played, we played around the neighborhood.

My little sister and I slept in the same bed when we were young, and one night for some unknown reason, I told her what happened. I made her promise, threatening her with her very life if she told anyone. From that moment, when I thought she was going to start to tell Mom or Dad about it, I would change the subject really quickly or give her the "hairy eyeball" with darts of "you better not tell" in my gaze. I kicked myself for telling her. The time for family vacation had arrived. We were going to Hinton, West Virginia. There was a woman who owned two cabins that we rented for the week. They were situated on a golf course which had a huge swimming pool. Then down a pathway we could walk to the river and go fishing. It had everything we needed to have a wonderful time. My grandmother was going with us that year, so I was excited. There were other relatives going as well, but they were going to meet us at the campsite. We packed up our belongings, our dog Hokey and as we drove out of town, I felt as if a cloud had lifted from my heart. Vacation was a welcome relief since fear had come to be the ruler over my heart for the past several weeks.

We were at the dinner table one evening, and all of a sudden, my sister blurted out that this boy had pulled down his pants and tried to make me pull mine down. She recounted the details, which I had so carefully described to her, in front of everyone. Then, she proceeded to tell my mom and dad that he had also tried to touch her breasts. There was dead silence in the room. My mom and dad were standing at the kitchen sink, and they both turned around and said, "What did you say?"

Due to the other family that had gone with us on vacation, the conversation was tabled for the time being, but I knew there was going to be a big powwow about this before it was all over. It was just a matter of time, and it would be whenever my dad said it was going to be; because of this, I dreaded the rest of my vacation.

The time came to pack up and go home, and I felt like something was going to happen on the ride back. I was scared. I begged Dad to let me ride back with the other family, but— oh, no—my two older brothers were sent with them, and my dad insisted my sister and I were going in the car with him and my mother alone. My heart raced wildly because I knew I was in trouble. There was no laughing or joking in the car.

Then the bomb hit. My dad said, "Molly, I want you to tell me what happened between you and this boy, and tell me what he did to your sister." I started to cry; I was so scared. When my dad talked, you listened, and when you answered him, it was, "Yes, sir."

I thought it would never end, and I had no clue what my punishment would be. My dad was clearly upset, and my mother was quiet. It was a nightmare. As soon as my dad pulled up beside our house and parked the car, he marched right over to the boy's house. He told this boy's mother that her son needed to be locked up. Of course, my aunt and uncle, who lived right beside them, took their side because they pitied this family who had no father.

Everyone but my dad swept the situation under the rug. The thought process was, *Ignore the behavior, and it will go away.* The attitude was, *Poor, poor fellow. He doesn't have a father to look after him.*

Heads were turned, and nothing was ever done. My punishment? I was forbidden to go over to her house again.

This was the beginning of my deep, dark sexual thoughts and the beginning of crippling fear. It was the beginning of my desire to always stay home where I felt safe. Whatever was on him or in him jumped on me. My stomach ached all the time, and I did not sleep well. I would get up and go downstairs to the refrigerator two or three times a night. Sometimes, Dad would hear me and tell me to get back upstairs and get in bed. My life, starting at six years old, was never the same again. Time went on, and I started thinking things I shouldn't have been thinking at that age. We, as children, were consumed in the neighborhood with playing moms and dads. We took it a step further, went into the woods, and pulled our pants down. I think we thought we were having sex. It felt good. We all were exposed to too much and were obsessed with our bodies. My feelings were young, yet tainted and sexual in nature. I felt dirty when we would go play in the woods. Then, we would go back to just playing silly childhood games. When we did, my heart would lighten, and I would actually feel better. We never talked about what we would do in those woods.

I complained so much that Mom finally took me to the doctor. I had to have X-rays to determine the source of the problem. The results came back and nothing showed up. There were moments of rest from time to time from the black cloud of darkness that hovered over me, but it would come back every time something good—or any big change—was coming in my life. I couldn't describe how I felt, but it was icky. If I mentioned anything negative about how I was feeling, everyone around me would dismiss it. After all, my mother had taken me to get X-rays, and nothing wrong was discovered. Nothing was wrong that you could touch or see—nothing. Yet everything in me was crying, and I was scared to death. I was inside this body; no one else was. Something wasn't right. I just didn't know what it was. From that moment on, I withdrew inside to protect myself.

Mom and Dad would go away, and I would hate it. I would make a fuss over it even if it were for just an evening. They went out to dinner at a friend's house, and I didn't stop calling there for Mom. My older brother had been left in charge, and naturally, they left the number for him. I found it and just kept calling. They phoned my older brother and told him to get rid of the number. I already knew he was going to take the number from me, so I had taken a key and scratched it on the headboard of their bed. I was never at peace until they were home.

TEN LONG,
BEAUTIFUL NAILS

I had other friends besides the neighborhood gang. I called them my Sunday school friends. These friends were not nasty and didn't talk dirty. I felt a lighter sense of being when I was around them. I felt clean in my thinking.

My church was a treasure locked in my heart, around which I had made a fortress where there were no outside influences to make me feel bad. I felt protected when I was there—no soap operas, no touching me in places that shouldn't be touched, no molestation tactics. The feelings of guilt and shame would leave momentarily when I was in Sunday school and church.

Occasions at church were a big deal to me. I was always filled with excitement and anticipation, looking forward to the day I would get to sport my new Easter outfit there. Mom always had fresh flowers delivered the day before for us to wear. Easter morning was like looking at a field of different kinds of beautiful flowers; it was breathtaking. The anticipation alone was worth it all. Then, after church, we would head home for hunting eggs and gorging on Easter baskets full of candy.

I would attend Vacation Bible School every summer for two weeks. Knowing it would be out of the norm and there might be new kids there, I would get very anxious inside—almost scared to go. My cousin, who was two years older, would stop by and walk me over there, which was a great comfort. After I would get settled in and knew what to expect, I would calm down and enjoy my time there. There would be a project laid before us the first day, and we would have two weeks in which to complete it. I took solace in the fact of knowing I only had to attend for a few hours each morning. I was right across the alley from my safe haven, and I would remind myself I was in *my* fortress—Jesus' home.

Christmas was the most favorite time of all for me. I didn't really know why, but everyone seemed so happy, and that feeling was euphoric. Christmas plays were performed in front of packed out crowds. I didn't really even understand much about how Jesus came to earth through the Virgin Mary. But one thing I did know was that Mary and Joseph were Jesus' parents, and it was a big deal to be chosen to play those two roles.

Candy was given out after the play was performed. Then, I would rush out the back door of the church, over the alley, through the backyard, and into the back door of my house. I would race through the kitchen to the dining room. There, planted on the Christmas tree so carefully by our uncle, were money envelopes for each of us. What a surprise it always was! Special occasions became an escape for me. I could put away the dark feelings that were always looming.

My dad didn't attend church with us, but he wanted us there. One Sunday after church, evidently he became bored and decided to play a joke on me. He always asked me if I knew how lucky I was. My response was always the same, "Yes, sir."

He would then reply, "Well, I hope you do."

But this day he added, "I think I'm just going to sell you and let you live with someone else so you can see how lucky you are, but I don't know if anyone will want to buy you."

He laughed and joked around and then got up and made a sign. The sign said, "For Sale." He hung it around my neck and made me sit on the front porch. I cried and cried. I begged my mom to let me get up, but my dad told her to leave me out there so I could learn to appreciate what I had.

Cars drove by and my dad would yell at them and ask if they wanted to buy me. Naturally, I was humiliated. Finally, my mom said that it was enough. I ran upstairs to my room and cried and cried that afternoon. I said over and over, "I hate my daddy. I hate my daddy." I fell into an exhausted sleep. Sleep became a place where I could hide from everything and everyone.

Of course, he came upstairs to my bedroom and apologized later. What he thought was a harmless little antic, coupled with what had already happened, was more than my little mind and emotions could take.

The lesson my dad thought he was going to teach me backfired that day. There were many feelings wrapped up in me that kept getting pushed down inside. I started to gorge on sweets; I became obsessed with them. I started, little by little, to put on extra weight. Food became an outlet for me.

The time came for me to begin the first grade. I was petrified at the thought of having to go; I didn't want to leave my house. There were so many new strangers I would have to meet. *Can't I just stay home another year?* I thought. We had a big tree in the backyard, and I would grab hold of it and cry. The school was just down the street and over the hill, but something inside of me was afraid.

Mom would calmly talk to me to get me to go. She would finally say, "Molly Malvern, you have to go school." Then, I knew I had pushed her as far as I could, and I would let go of the tree and whimper as I left our yard. I would be okay once I got there, but getting there was the issue. Fear utterly gripped my mind.

My mother always had a calm and soothing demeanor and had a voice that was like cream washing over you. Every night, she would tuck my sister and me into bed and hear our prayers, and then she would rub my forehead until I fell asleep. She would softly sing, as I would doze off. Yes, I was spoiled on top of it all, but I knew she loved me.

———————

November 22, 1963 rang with a shot. JFK was assassinated. My parents were away in Biloxi, Mississippi on a business trip. Not only was I separated from my parents, but also something bad was going on in the world, and I was too young to comprehend it all. I hated it. I was scared to death. I sat at our dining room table with the daily newspaper, looking at the pictures of him being shot. I was crying because I wanted my mom and dad to come home, but they were too far for me to call, and my stomach ached.

My mom thought it would be a good idea for me to join the Brownies so I could meet some other girls my age. My cousin helped talk me into it. I was apprehensive, but I got to have a uniform, so I joined. I loved my leader. I was always quick to take to heart anything she said. We learned one day about helping our mothers around the house. I had never been made to do anything at home, so I came home that day and looked for the one thing that could help my mother. I proceeded to clean out our spice cabinet, which was a catchall for any kind of condiment, spice, or canned good. She always said she needed to clean it out, so I came to her rescue. Helping her made me feel good, especially when I could do it and surprise her. Then I would wait for the accolades to pour on me. I loved her praises, which always made me feel so good inside.

I got a little older, and the time came for Girl Scouts. I attended for a while, but quit. I had no desire to involve myself in extracurricular activities; I just wanted to stay home and watch TV. My weight caused me to withdraw to a dark place, which began a pattern of starting and quitting anything I did not want to do.

Every once in a while, my cousin and I would spend a Saturday night with our grandmother, with the understanding we had to go to Sunday school. I would reluctantly agree to the stipulation knowing it was the price to be paid. My grandmother was very witty, which made her fun to be around. Boy, could she entertain us! Her upstairs bedrooms overlooked a parking lot where people would meet and park. We would all shuffle up the stairs snacks in hand when it would get dark, keep the lights turned off, and sit there and wait for people to show up. I really don't know what we thought we were going to see, but it was the anticipation of catching someone red-handed in the act of adultery. I really wasn't even certain what adultery was but I loved being with my grandmother. My cousin and I would wake up on Sunday mornings to the scent of homemade doughnuts. They were such a treat! Then, off we would go.

It was in her house where I first looked in the back of movie magazines. Contained in the last few pages of each magazine were advertisements selling a variety of products. My eyes would grow as big as saucers while scanning the pages. It was the first time I discovered I could have "10 Long, Beautiful Fingernails" for the low, low price of $4.99 plus shipping and handling. From the very moment I spotted that ad, I was determined to have long, beautiful nails.

MY GODFORSAKEN HAIR

I will never forget my hard, long summer at the tender age of eleven. I was starting to mature, and I was very heavy. The kids in the neighborhood had been calling me "fatty" for some time by now. I tried to compete with all the boys, proving I was just as good as they were. I could pass a football just like them, run like them and I would pride myself in being able to pick them up, swing them around, and hurl them in the yard.

My sister would tell everyone, "If you don't be nice to me, my sister will sit on you." I pretended it didn't hurt me, but it cut me like a knife.

I didn't like the way I looked when I put on a dress, so I began to hate going to Sunday school. My older brother had already been given permission to make his own choice about attending church or not. When would my time come? *Couldn't it be now?*

I woke up one particular morning and just flat out did not want to go. I settled in my heart that no one was going to make me either. I was always coming up with excuses to try to get out of going, and I could get very creative. That morning, I would have done about anything not to have to go. I tried to fake oversleeping, but I heard Dad say, "Molly, get up for Sunday school."

Then all of a sudden, a light went off in my head, and I thought, *I will pretend to be sick.*

I proceeded to put powder all over my face in an attempt to look as though I was pale and weak. I figured this was the perfect, ingenious idea that would allow me to stay home. I got up and walked very slowly—of course, I was very weak—into my parents' bedroom. I announced to them I was sick and that I did not feel good. I pointed out, "Look at how pale my face is."

Then, the unexpected happened. My dad sat up and took a closer look at me and actually asked me if I had powder on my face. I hung my head in shame and frustration, admitting I did. He immediately said, "Get dressed for Sunday school."

How did he know I had put powder on my face? How did he figure out that quickly that I was not sick? That was my dad, however. He always seemed to be ahead of the game; he knew everything and then some.

My dad had big football plans for my brothers, and they got what seemed to be all of his attention. I longed for it as well, but in his mind, I was a girl, and I had a mother for all of the girl things. I would try to imitate my two older brothers to try to gain his attention. I would compete with boys at anything they did. I wanted to show him I could be as good and fast as any boy. I could pass a mean football! My dad would be sitting on the front porch watching me pass, and my sister would kick the football over the telephone lines. He would make the comment, "If only you were boys." We loved the attention, but in the end, I was not a boy.

That was about the same time The Beatles landed in America. Of course, everyone was crazy about them. Mom had made me take piano lessons with my sister, but when I saw Ringo beat those drums, I wanted to be a drummer. I had my hair cut short and got some shoes like they wore——and a new Beatle was born in St. Albans, unbeknownst to Paul, John, George and Ringo.

When we went on summer vacation that year, all the kids got together and dreamed up the idea of having a talent show. We decided we would imitate the Beatles and guess who was going to be Ringo? The adults helped us prepare the songs, construct a stage, and the video camera was readied. I was equipped with white plastic storage containers that were turned upside down, and I had sticks from the woods ready to beat my drums.

What a night! We had a curtain blocking us from the audience of family and friends, and we were shuttled in behind the curtain while everyone screamed. Who said *Ed Sullivan* was the only venue in town? This was my first taste of limelight and I loved it!

The following fall our school pictures were taken, and when I saw them, I looked at myself and started to cry. I thought I kind of looked tough for a girl, so I began to let my hair grow out. My weight issue had become an increasing concern to my dad. Mom would try to soothe Dad by telling him she had discussed my weight with her friends, and they had said, "It's just baby fat and it will fall off." It couldn't fall off fast enough for my dad.

I was struggling with two different people inside. One was loud, obnoxious, overweight, and ready to play football and fight any boy in the neighborhood. I would wear oversized hoodies to cover up my heaviness. Hoodies also gave me a sense of comfort, as if I were wearing a security blanket, soothing and protecting myself.

Then I was trying to be the young lady my mother wanted me to be, taking piano lessons for refinement while hiding in my heart the desire to play the drums. There was a hellish struggle going on inside of me. I didn't know what to do, and I didn't know which way to go.

Everything came to a head the following family vacation. My hair was long, thick, and full. I started using it to hide my face, thinking it would help hide my body as well. My dad would tell me repeatedly to get my hair out of my face, and the subject of a diet had even popped up around our house.

Friends of my parents and their two girls, who I thought were thin and pretty, went with us that summer on vacation. One evening during the vacation, our family stayed home to eat while the other family went out. All of a sudden, my dad yelled at me, "Get that godforsaken hair out of your face. I am tired of looking at you."

He went on and on about it. My family members froze in their chairs as I listened to his ridicule. The tears started to flow down my cheeks. He said, "Stop that crying."

I couldn't stop crying, so he said, "Go to your room. I have had just about enough of you. I don't want to look at you anymore."

My mom said, "That is enough."

I went to bed sobbing, vowing how much I hated him. My mother came in later that night—she was always the peacemaker—to soothe my fragile heart. The next day, Dad ended up apologizing for the things he had said the night before. I was numb as I listened to him as he kissed me on the cheek.

I had so much locked up inside of me that my emotions started manifesting in very odd ways. My aunt and cousin would come to pick me up at my house, and we would ride around town and sometimes stop by the Dairy Queen. I would hang out the window, screaming and yelling at people walking by. Then to top it all off, I would force myself to laugh so hard and loud I would practically go into hysteria. My aunt and cousin would laugh and laugh. The louder they laughed, the more I performed. I loved going with them. I felt as though I had a volcano inside of me that could only be eased by this obnoxious behavior. Then as quickly as it would overtake me, great relief would come once I would get it out. I would be exhausted by the time they would drop me off at home.

Since dieting was becoming an issue, my aunt—who was always on a diet—suggested we start going for walks to lose weight. Off my aunt, cousin, and I would go—down the main highway of the town. I had convinced Mom how good it would be for me to go. We would get started, and they would both egg me on to perform for them. I don't know why, but I started pretending to act as if I were retarded while walking down the road. They just laughed. The more they laughed, the more I performed. I would not exhibit this kind of behavior around just anybody though. I only behaved this way around people who I knew liked it. At the end of our times together, I would plead with both of them not to tell my mother or dad; they would have killed me if they had known what I was doing. My mom was trying to raise me to be a proper young lady, but as soon as I was out of her sight, something inside of me took over. Neither of my parents had any clue this side of me existed. I was becoming increasingly afraid that my aunt or cousin would tell.

After our walks, I would go home and pig out for all the hard work I had just done. However, after these outings, I would momentarily go back to being a quieter person with a more loving, quiet attitude. I would make a promise to myself, while in my room alone, that I would never do those things again, but a little time would pass, and I would be eager to go out again. In the back of my mind, I thought one day I might grow out it. I was in a constant state of being up and down as the masks I wore started to develop.

My room was not only my safe haven, but my house was the house where it seemed that young and old alike congregated. We had a piano in the dining room, along with several different musical instruments. My parents would have parties, and someone was always playing the piano, a guitar, mandolin, or ukulele.

On a regular night, though, you could always find everyone seated in our kitchen. We had a big round captain's table with chairs in there where many problems were discussed, confidences made, and good times had. It was a place of comfort for all. My mom and dad would sit there in the evenings, drinking their highball drinks while my dad sang and played on his guitar. My mother thought he hung the moon. I was used to hearing adults talk about many things that I probably shouldn't have heard. One evening as I stood in the doorway almost ready to go into the kitchen, I stopped to listen to my dad talking about his parents.

That same night as my mom sat on the edge of my bed, I asked her about what I had heard. She told me some details of abuse in my dad's childhood that were heartbreaking; which caused him to hate his parents. On top of the resentment I harbored in my heart towards my dad, I then began to feel sorry for him. She ended with the story of how his sister had raped him during his high school years. He would tell me over and over how I reminded him of this sister. Somehow, I began to justify my dad and his behavior toward me.

I had only seen my dad's parents a couple of times in my short life, but every time we left their presence, he would be hurt—vowing never to see them again. I got this bright idea that if I could just go talk to his parents, I could heal their relationship. In turn, my dad wouldn't hurt so much. It was summer so I unrelentingly begged Dad to let me go visit. He couldn't figure out why I would want to go stay with them, but he finally gave in to me. The call was made, arrangements were set, and I was off to spend a week with the grandparents I barely knew.

I arrived safely, got all settled in, and waited for the right time to approach my grandmother. We were having dinner, and she started telling me what a hard life she had. She began to cry. She told me she did the best she could to raise seven children, as she sobbed. What could I say then? I felt sorry for her. Of course, my attempt to heal their relationship had failed. I came home with a deep sorrow in my heart for my dad and his parents. I wished I could have fixed them all. I began to understand why my dad would always ask the question, "Do you know how lucky you are?"

There were two sides to my dad, and one of them was golden for many. He was always helping someone less fortunate than himself. While growing up, I would tag along with Dad occasionally to a place called the Choo Choo Inn where he would drop in to have a beer with "the boys." There was a little boy who hung around there whose name was Poncho. He appeared very unloved, needy and his clothes seemed old. My dad would ask his mother, who lived next door, if he could come to our home to have dinner and play with my sister and me. I couldn't understand why he would have to come home with us, and my dad would explain that he didn't have a father or a lot of money. Dad asked us to be nice to him so we did, but for some reason, I was always relieved when he would go home. I didn't want a stranger coming into my safe haven.

Dad and I didn't really talk much about anything important—ever. We would talk *around* things and life. He saw a lot of himself and his older sister in me, which I do not think he liked; this caused an even greater division between us. Due to this, I do not really think he liked looking at me at times. I had become closemouthed about a lot of things that I was feeling and didn't understand. I talked to my mom somewhat, but I never really opened up to her totally. I became the protector of my own heart by not revealing what I felt, and I became the fixer of my life.

A new light dawned, and my life started to change around the seventh grade. My mom and I were sitting at the kitchen table one evening, and I was explaining to her that I didn't feel like I had any friends—a sad but true tale it was. She told me that if I was nice to people, they would be nice to me. I told her I would try. I turned over a new leaf by making an effort to come out of my protective shell to reach out to people in a friendly way. This was something new for me, and slowly I started making new friends.

There was not a defining moment in my life that caused me to settle down in my behavior, but as I got older, I would watch others intently. They weren't loudmouthed, so I stopped being so loudmouthed. My aunt and cousin still tried to egg me on in front of others to be the loud, crass person they knew was inside of me, knowing it would embarrass me. I didn't want to behave that way anymore, which caused me to stop wanting to be around them any longer. I didn't feel good when I was with them, so I withdrew from them. Making fun of others wasn't funny to me any longer. I wanted something different. I wanted a change.

THE GREEN NERVE MEDICINE

In the summer before the eighth grade, my baby fat started to fall off. It was like magic! I had started reaching out to others the previous year and I had new friends. I was allowed to get contact lenses in lieu of my glasses, opting for green ones to match my eyes—the same color of my dad's.

Then what seemed impossible became possible: I was invited to my first homecoming dance! I will never forget the boy who asked me. He was a head shorter than I was, but I really liked him. I gave my dad specific instructions for the big night. I said, "Stay in the kitchen with Mom, and I will bring him in to meet you. And whatever you do, don't stand up when he comes in the room. He is short, and I don't want him to be embarrassed by your height." I went over the instructions time and again to make certain he knew what to do.

Mom had taken me to a seamstress and had a dress made for me. Of course it was green to match my eyes. I bought a pair of "baby doll" shoes, which were all the rage, to go with the dress. I got up early and primped all day long, taking extra time with my hair and makeup. I made certain to wear green eye shadow to match everything else. Truly, I was becoming a green-eyed monster, which was one of the names my dad liked to call me.

It seemed like the clock didn't move that day. Finally, I heard the knock at the door. I opened the door, and there he stood. I had never seen him in anything but school clothes, but there he stood with a suit on and his hair all coiffed. I know both of our faces were beet red as we nervously said hello to one another. He handed me my first corsage. I thanked him as I took it, telling him how beautiful it was, and I said, "Come and meet my mom and dad."

I walked slowly down the hall and turned to go into the kitchen where my parents sat. I caught a glimpse out of the right corner of my eye, and there was my dad—in all of his splendor—kneeling on the floor. He came walking up on his knees with his hand held out in a gesture of greeting to meet my date. I was humiliated. My date was humiliated. My dad laughed and laughed.

I lost even more weight the summer before the ninth grade. I was feeling so much better about myself, though there seemed to be an ever-present lurking I couldn't shake off.

There was a nearby Catholic school that only taught students through the eighth grade, so our school received some of their rising ninth graders that year. There were a couple of guys in the group that were just to die for, as far as their looks went. Everyone was gaga over them.

One day between classes, several girls rushed up to me talking so fast I could hardly understand what they were saying. They went on and on about how this one particular guy liked me; I was shocked, yet I was thrilled and excited. I wondered why he would like me. I wasn't out to get a guy, but there were girls around me who were constantly thinking about guys. I was very shy and naïve, but I thought for a couple of minutes and decided to just wait and see what happened.

From that moment on, everything changed. This particular fellow and I had several classes together, and I would catch him staring at me. A few days passed, and he asked if he could start walking me to classes. Timidly I said, "Okay."

I really didn't know what to make of all of it yet, but I went along. He ended up telling me that one of the things he liked about me was the way I was always changing my hair and overall look. For years I had loved trying new hairstyles and makeup, and going to school didn't stop that. I would go to great lengths to look my very best each day.

Overnight, I became a part of the in-crowd. What a boost to my lack of self-confidence! I really wasn't ready for a grown-up relationship and all that dating encompassed, but a few in my class were seeing older guys and car dating.

My dad really didn't like the fact that I had one single boyfriend who wanted constantly to come over to my house. Seeing one another at school and going to an occasional dance was one thing, but coming to my house was something different. I really wasn't ready for going steady—a deep "thing"—but I just didn't know how to say no.

My dad would limit our time together, which was actually fine with me. I was relieved when he would leave and go home. I didn't want to feel pressured by any boy. It made me feel icky inside. This one relationship was responsible for hurling me into popularity, and I liked it, so I was not going to give it up. But I was still a fearful, dark, and withdrawn individual, never revealing to anyone how I truly felt. I believed that somehow I would grow out of it. I started perfecting a mask—pretending to be happy. I was being invited to do things by friends and meeting my boyfriend at others' homes. I would go, but I still wanted to be in the comfort zone of my own house where I felt safe. Again, the excitement of being popular helped spur me on to do well and kept me pretending constantly that I was happy. I rarely missed school unless I just was too sick to get there.

We had the option of taking two elective classes in the ninth grade. Everyone I was around said drama class was an easy class, and since I had no clue what direction I was going in my life, I opted for drama—why not? What I discovered was that class was anything but easy. I loved it! You know…the whole *Edge of Night* thing.

We were asked by our drama teacher to write a play, so I went home and huddled up in my room. Much to my amazement, a play started spilling out onto the pages in front of me. I turned it in, thankful that it had come so easily and didn't think anymore about it. The teacher walked into class several days later, stood in front of her desk, and announced that only two times in her career had she ever given anyone an A plus on an assignment. She went on to say that someone in class had written a play that had earned one of those. She looked at me and said, "Molly, come up and get your A plus!"

I was dumbfounded. I had also just received an A plus on a literature paper in my English class. The top three plays were performed in the school auditorium. Kids in my class started looking at me as though I was not just a blonde without a brain.

I had drifted through life up to this point just having to do schoolwork for grades, but I found out I had a passion for the arts. I also knew I loved to do hair, makeup, and fingernails. We had a big front porch, and I would go out there with a sketchpad my grandmother had given to me; I drew, passing the time on rainy afternoons. I discovered I could draw objects, and I was good at profiles. I drew an exact copy of Paul McCartney's profile on the front of my piano sheet music "Yesterday."

But as far as determining what I was going to be when I grew up—well, those things were just not talked about when it came to my sister and me. My dad always thought we would get married, I guess, and have families with husbands to take care of us. It never occurred to him to prepare us for the world. Since I hadn't grown up talking about goals or what I would do in this life, I had no clear, set direction. My parents were pleased that I was making good grades, but there was no talk about developing my artistic abilities and making them work for me.

My parents' best friends were a dentist and his wife. Things were tossed around the kitchen table concerning my future, like becoming a dental hygienist. I had been blessed with beautiful teeth just like my dad's. The comment was made that I could work four days a week while making good money, and the field was in demand, so I could get a job no matter where I lived. It seemed okay, I guess, but I wasn't really thrilled about the idea of putting my hands in someone else's mouth. I had answered phones in the dental office one summer while they went on vacation, but that was all I knew about dentistry. *I could like working in the dental field,* I supposed, but my heart was drawn to the arts. My passions were plays, hair, makeup, fingernails, and movies, but how do you make a living doing that?

I met a girl at school who moved to my hometown from Texas. Her parents knew my uncle, and that gave us an immediate connection. We became fast friends. I lovingly referred to her as "Texas" in the beginning of our friendship. She was very smart and her intellect drove me to want to do better in school. My life was as happy at this point as it had ever been.

The ninth grade school year was coming to an end, and I felt sad, yet anxious at what was to come. Every year there was an annual talent show in which everyone could participate. "Romeo and Juliet" was popular at the time, and I decided I would showcase my piano talents by playing the theme song— "A Time for Us"—on the school's baby grand piano. I was also involved in a dance routine with five other girls. We were going to imitate the Temptations while lip-synching "Cloud Nine." I thought I was the cat's meow.

Things always became lax at the end of the year, and I was allowed by my science teacher to go to the auditorium to practice my piano piece. In my mind, I was Liberace, and I would play away, preparing for the big night. I would have barely stopped my piece when I would hear thunderous applause of nearby classes. I would just sit and soak up the glory with a big grin on my face.

The night came for the talent show. I was so nervous that I ended up sneaking a couple of swigs of Mom's nerve medicine that was green in color. *Hello!* Green nerve medicine, as I came to call it, was the answer to all of my fears. Boy, did I feel better inside! That was the beginning of my discovery that life was better drugged. It was my secret. No one else knew.

Even though I had tried hard to mask my fear, it was a colossal factor in my life, as if it were a person. As a result, I wanted to have a great big tube attached to me filled with liquid nerve medicine. I would take swigs every now and again, filling the bottle back up with water to hide the fact I had taken some. I was addicted.

Mom finally asked me if I had been taking her green nerve medicine. I told her I would take it when I got really nervous. She replied, "You have nothing to be nervous about." She had never really taken it much. She only kept it on hand after her last miscarriage. I was caught, and that put an end to my liquid courage. It didn't put an end to my desire for it though; I had no fear when I took it.

LIVIN' ON LOVE

Ever since I could remember, I had been told how pretty my mother was and that my dad was very handsome. As I became older, there were moments that my dad, for this reason or that, would have a couple of highballs and spout out something hurtful. For instance, one evening he said, "I just need to put all four of you children in a gunny sack and throw you off of the Coal River Bridge." Of course, he would apologize the next day, and it would be forgotten, but I never forgave him for those remarks. I would just try to push them out of my mind.

The summer before the tenth grade was another good summer. The boy who became my best friend lived right up the street from me. He had been one of the neighborhood bullies but had grown up to be a really neat guy. We had mended our childish ways and would sit up nights—if we didn't have dates—talking about our lives and loves. We told one another most everything. I trusted him as much as I had trusted anyone.

My brother had been the senior class president and one of the football captains in high school. He made excellent grades, was good-looking, and had tons of friends who were usually hanging out at our house. Everyone talked as if I could just ride on his coattails when I got to high school.

What did I know? I was glad he was my brother. I had a crush on his best friend and thought I had fallen in love with him. He was three years older than I was, but I could just tell that he had begun the year before to start thinking about me in the same way. I would dream of us getting married and living on love. *Who needed money when you could live on love?* Ever since I was a little girl, I had also dreamed of becoming a majorette. I would watch the majorettes coming down the street in front of the marching band when there was a town parade. I watched them at halftime during football games strutting up and down the football field. I had tried out in junior high school but didn't make the squad. My dad said he could have called a favor in, and I could have been selected, but he wanted me to try to get this on my own merit. Everyone assured me, from the ninth grade on, that I was a shoo-in for majorette. They would tell me that I would be *everything* when I got to high school. Therefore, I just bided my time.

During the summer nights, the neighborhood gang would all gather around the front porch trying to come up with something to do. The subject of the dead kept popping up, and someone mentioned we should try to see if we could conjure up a spirit from the other side. We became consumed with having a séance. We wanted to talk to the dead and find out what death was about. Many names came up to seek first, but we all finally decided on Amelia Earhart. We talked incessantly about her and the plane that had gone down. How spooky was her story? Where did she go? Where was she? Was she really alive somewhere else and just hiding out? These were questions that we all wanted answered. We thought we would be the ones to find her after all the years she had been missing. I was the one who always believed that nothing was impossible. Our mission was settled, and the troops rallied, but we needed someone to help guide us.

It was common knowledge in my family that my great-grandmother had been born with a veil over her face. Stories circulated around—at least among the people I was around—that having a veil over your face when you were born was the sign of a special gift—a sixth sense of some sort. For some reason, we thought my grandmother would also possess some sort of other worldly power as well. She just so happened to be visiting our house the night the troops were rounded up and ready to find Amelia Earhart. We begged her to help us that night, and she agreed.

She took her place at the head of the captain's table in our dining room and proceeded to tell us the story of a woman named Mrs. Blake. As the story goes, this woman was known everywhere for her special gifts, which included hearing from the dead. She would place a specially made horn to her ear that would enable her to hear from dead spirits. People traveled far and wide to get this woman's advice about their finances and lives. We were all sitting there with bated breath, enthralled by the story. Yes, as we looked at each other, we knew we had definitely made the right choice by having such a well-learned person lead us.

We prepared for the séance. We placed a candle in the middle of the table, since we didn't have a crystal ball, secured more chairs, and began. We turned out all of the lights, grabbed each other's hands to make a circle, and then began to call to spirits by name. All of a sudden, a bowl fell off the living room mantel. It visibly shook my grandmother. She jumped up, and she said she would never participate again.

Well, that pretty much burst our bubble. Being the troopers that we were, we weren't about to give up so easily, but we soon discovered that without our leader, we just didn't feel anything. We sat around the table several more times over the course of the summer, but it was never the same without my grandmother. We needed the veil power—whatever that meant!

Ouija boards were also very enticing to us, as were Magic Eight Balls—the latter a popular Christmas item that seemed to be advertised over and over again on TV. They could actually give you answers to your life right on the spot. Of course, I always shook my Eight Ball until it gave me the correct answer, which always had to be "Yes."

That summer I had my first real, older romance with my brother's best friend. There was a party at our house one Saturday evening, and there must have been close to a hundred people of all ages there. I had on a one-piece slinky jumpsuit with heels—something just like Cher wore. I overheard guys ask, "When did she grow up?"

I knew he was going to be there that evening, and my cap was set on him. He had gotten a football scholarship at NC State beginning in August, but due to his dad's job, he was moving to Georgia, so I wouldn't see him much anymore. However, I thought I had found the love of my life. We held hands for the first time and kissed and kissed that night, but that is as far as it went. The next day, he left, and my heart broke. We kept in touch with letters once he moved, but it wasn't the same as him being there. After just looking at him and dreaming of him for so long, we had finally gotten together. It was exciting yet depressing, all at the same time.

I was young but had always acted so mature that I could convince anyone of anything. What an actress I was! I convinced him that I loved him and would stay true to him. I pledged my undying love forever through the letters I wrote. I would sit with Mom at the kitchen table and convince her I could graduate early so we could get married. She said that I had to think about what we would live on for money, and my response was, "Mom, we can live on love."

She replied, "Molly, you have to live on something other than love." I dismissed the remark, knowing she was wrong.

He too had been very popular in high school and had told others to watch out for me and make sure that I was all right. I just wanted to get married and not go to high school, but I knew I had to go. I was in love, and that is all I cared about.

I wasn't in a hurry to let the summer pass. Overall, it was one of the best summers I had ever experienced, but I seemed to sense on a deeper level it would be the last summer the troops would congregate together on the front porch thinking up things to do. And for that I was sad.

I had been told over and over that my way was paved for me in the upcoming school year, but I started to become anxious about it all. The closer school came to starting, the more my stomach seemed to ache again. Would the ache ever go away?

JESUS FREAKS

The night before high school started, my stomach was doubled over in fear. I had started to run to the bathroom, out of control. What was going on? I was so drained the following morning I couldn't make it to the first day of school. I stayed home and during the day, the ache subsided. The second night, it started again. My mom tried to talk to me in her calm voice. She called the nurse who lived across the street from us, and she brought me something to help my diarrhea. I would try to talk to myself, knowing that something deeper was going on. The familiar ache in my stomach had reappeared several weeks earlier out of nowhere. Finally, I knew I had to go to school and managed to get there on the fourth day, shaking inside every step of the way.

My best girlfriend from Texas had become a proclaimed born-again Christian. Everything to her was about Jesus—everything. She would sit with a group of kids on the front lawn of the high school at noon, and they had their lunches and their Bibles. It was really weird. Chatter was going on around school about how weird they were, and I listened. My girlfriend had invited me to be a part of the group, but I didn't want to be labeled weird.

I knew who God was; I had grown up in Sunday school and church. Who did she think she was anyway? What gave her the cornerstone on God? You were only supposed to read the Bible in church, weren't you? Why did they have to be so in your face with religion? No, thank you. I had to get on with my life. It was the beginning of the end of our friendship. I didn't want to be called a Jesus freak. Besides, I had coattails to ride on, and my goal was to be everything I could in high school.

Due to the fact I had missed the first three days of school, I couldn't be nominated for some popular contests in which I was interested. You had to be physically present to be nominated for anything; no absentee nominations were allowed. Missing those first three days literally began to change my life. My heart was broken. I went home and went to bed right after school those first days. I felt there was some sort of unseen force that didn't like me and had tried to scare me from attending school, knowing what was in front of me and keeping me from attaining goals.

I managed to finish the first week of school, knowing something different was going on, but couldn't put my finger on it. The second week of school began, and after gym class, I was standing in the girls' locker room fixing my hair. Some girls I knew rushed in there and said there were black people lined up and down the hall, waiting for me to come out. They said they were going to harm me. I was completely baffled and had no idea where this was coming from. The only kids I knew were the ones I had grown up in school with, and I was well-liked by them. Who were these people? Why was this happening to me? I stared in the mirror looking at myself, scared to death and not knowing what to do.

The bell for the next class had just rung. I had the presence of mind to tell my friends to go quickly and get the principal. I had no choice but to leave, so I walked out of the locker room, and these black kids, who I didn't even know, started kicking me. The principal came running down the hall and shuttled me into his office. He proceeded to call my dad who had to come and pick me up. I was expelled for three days until things could settle down. The principal said they had picked me out of the crowd because of my brother's popularity and that it had nothing to do with me personally, so home I went. I could not believe this had happened, especially after I had just gotten used to going to school.

My older brother was away at school but found out through my parents what had happened. He got in touch with a black friend of his named Paul Hurst. He was the current senior class president and a football captain. They decided that Paul would walk me from class to class for as long as it took to get others off my back. He met me at my locker in the mornings, and we would walk down the hall together, which let everyone know to keep their hands off me. God bless you, Paul, wherever you are. The black and white issue had never been an issue with me personally, but it certainly was becoming one in our school and around the country. Why couldn't we all just get along? What was the big deal?

Things eventually subsided. I became withdrawn, but I still had great passion in my heart to do more at school. It seemed out of my grasp, and I had no guidance. At home I was on and ready to do anything, but around school I was very shy.

Constantly I fought the feelings inside of me that crippled my behavior. I felt as though two people lived inside of me. Whenever something good was going to happen, something always tried to stop it. Majorette tryouts weren't until the end of the school year. I thought if I could just hold on until then, things were certain to turn around in my life. Wasn't I supposed to be *everything?*

I was still corresponding with my long-distance boyfriend. Absence made my heart grow fonder, and it gave me something onto which I could hold. Upper-class girls knew whom I was dating, and I became friends with them as well. They thought he was cool, so it just reinforced the way I felt about him. The only reason I went to homecoming that year was because he didn't want me missing out on high school life, but I wasn't really that interested in going.

Carrying on a long-distance romance by mail was harmless, yet somehow magical and romantic. Girls would ask me to go out running around with them, but I didn't have any interest in it. Besides, the ones who asked me didn't have boyfriends, and I had one, even though he was at college. After a while, people quit asking me to do anything or go out with them anymore because they knew my answer would be no. I just felt more comforted and at ease when I was at home among my family.

I had been approached and urged over and over again by the cheerleaders to try out. They told me if I would just show up, I would be chosen. They had all been close friends with my brother and his best friend, my boyfriend, and said I would make a great cheerleader. Had they heard me scream when I was young? I was nice and said, "No, thank you," because I just had to be a majorette.

I went to majorette tryouts but much to my dismay, I was not selected. I was so scared of rejection that I didn't even go to school the next day. That hurled me into a deeper state of depression. I felt I was merely existing, and I did nothing more than I had to on a day-by-day basis. It was unbearable. In the back of my mind, I knew I would have one more chance to try out. It was a glimmer of hope I kept locked away in my heart—my secret place where my dreams and hopes were stored. Two or three more majorettes would be selected at the end of the eleventh grade to compensate for ones who would be graduating, if I could just hold on mentally until then.

My Spanish teacher showed us a film one day about the Peace Corps, and I was deeply touched by what I saw. I wrote a letter I planned to submit in an effort to join them. I took it home to read to my mom. She was standing at the stove cooking dinner with her back turned away from me and listened as I read. I finished the letter, and she said in her calm voice, "Molly, why would you go halfway around the world to help someone when you can help people right here? If you can just help the people around you, you will be doing a lot for humankind."

She ended the conversation that night by stating I didn't have to try to save the whole world, but something in me wanted to. I wanted to help others and save them all. From that moment on, I just pushed the notion of the Peace Corps deep down inside, along with every other feeling that was not being allowed to manifest. I thought, *Now what am I going to do?* Once again, I felt shot down with no clear purpose, feeling as if I was just drifting.

Others around me were talking of college and life goals. I had a friend who kept saying she was going to graduate early and go to Ohio State where her sister was. She was about six feet tall and very bright. Maybe, I thought, I could graduate early too. But what would I do?

We had neighbors across the street who had a basketball court in their backyard. Anyone was always welcome to come over to play. I would go over there sometimes in the evening to shoot hoops. We had played over there as children, and it always took me back to an easier time—when things didn't seem to be so complicated. I loved shooting hoops. It helped me clear my thoughts.

One evening I jumped up in the air and stepped down on my ankle, twisting it. Several hours later, it ballooned up so big that I thought I had broken it. I woke up in the middle of the night in excruciating pain. My sister-in-law happened to be there and gave me a Darvon. Well, let me tell you, it not only took the pain away from my ankle, but it took the hell away from my heart. I didn't know what it was, but I wanted some more! Who cared about green nerve medicine? I wanted her to give me some more of those! She ended up giving me a couple more and then said, "No more."

As my ankle started to heal, I would hit it on the end of my bed so it would appear to get worse. I wanted some more pills. I had become very clouded and dark at the age of sixteen. I was still able to put up a front and a fake persona, so much so, that no one knew what was inside my mind and heart. The sick feelings and thoughts I had as a child were starting to resurface and take over.

The popularity I had attained for that brief time in the ninth grade started to wane within a two-year period. At the same time, what it had done for me was give me something that made me feel good about myself. I liked being the winner; I just didn't know how to get it back. Every time I tried something, the door would shut in my face, and I started to hate my life.

Summer finally came again, giving me a break from all the disappointments I suffered in high school. The fair pulled into our town each year, bringing excitement. There was always a "Miss Town Fair" crowned. That summer I decided to run for the title. Every girl was sponsored by a woman's league of some sort. The goal was to see who could raise the most money, by selling tickets to the fair, by having car washes, spaghetti dinners, bake sales, or anything else we could think of that was legal to raise funds. The money collected would be donated for different projects in town, and the most money raised determined the winner.

I rallied the younger troops in the neighborhood together, and it was all out warfare to see who could raise the most money. We all worked hard. It was exciting and gave me something to think of instead of myself. I was awarded second runner-up at the culmination of the fair. I wasn't a majorette, but I got to ride in a convertible in the parade that summer with them marching right behind me. I loved it.

I still kept in touch with my long-distance boyfriend, but it was a stretch. My dad had flown me down to his parents' house in Georgia the previous spring for Easter break. Both sets of families wanted us to get married, but I didn't feel much of anything for him any longer.

I had achieved what I had set out to do by having an older guy fall for me, and I just wanted to shrink back and be a sixteen-year-old. I no longer wanted all of the pressure of a deep, older relationship. It was really over for me in my heart but not in his or my families' hearts. I had successfully convinced everyone previously that we could just get married. Was I going to have to follow through with my declarations? How was I going to get out of this?

BREAKING UP IS
HARD TO DO

I had all summer to mentally bolster my courage for the new school year, and I thought I was up to the task. I had become very thin; I hardly ate anything anymore. I recall my dad saying, "That's just about enough. You've lost enough weight."

Make up your mind! I guess he wouldn't need a wheelbarrow for me anymore. When I was little, I would doze off in front of the TV, and he would pick me up and carry me to bed. He would whisper in my ear, "If you don't lose some weight, I am going to have to get a wheelbarrow to carry you upstairs." He had threatened me with that statement and made a joke of it for years when I was younger. Now he was telling me what I wanted to hear, and I was getting his attention. I had been thin before, but this time he took notice.

It wasn't far into the year when I noticed a new guy in school. I asked around and found out his name was David. He was a year younger than I was in school but only six months younger in age, and everyone liked him. I fell head over heels in love with him from the first moment I laid eyes on him. I thought he was not only cute, but he was cool in the way he walked, talked, and in his overall demeanor. Several girls I knew dated younger guys, so I really didn't think anything of it, but then it hit me: I had a boyfriend who was expecting me to marry him. Let's face it—everyone was counting on me marrying him. How was I going to get out of this? I didn't know then, but my heart was already lost, and I knew the end was in store for my college man. I was on the road to love, and I wasn't getting off.

David heard I had a boyfriend at college and when he point-blank asked me about it, I lied right to his face and told him I was no longer seeing him. That's all the explanation it took for us to become an item. We only saw each other at school, so I was safe for the time being, but I knew something was going to have to give. I liked having someone at school I could see everyday. I wanted someone to do things with. The plan was already forged, but I didn't know what to do about my college boyfriend yet. The problem of what to do was solved for me by my sister. One of her friends confided to her that David and I were dating. She confronted me with it, and I confessed to her that yes, we were. I then explained to her that I didn't love my college boyfriend any longer. I swore her to secrecy, but true to form, she spilled the beans to my mom.

Christmas vacation had finally arrived but this year, there was a glitch that would have to be overcome. My so-called college boyfriend called and said he was going to give me an early Christmas present and drive from Georgia to West Virginia to stay with my family for a week. The pressure was on. What was I going to do?

I can tell you that the few days following my sister's confession hadn't been pleasant. When my parents found out about David and me, they were furious. The person they thought was going to be their son-in-law wasn't going to be after all, and they really didn't care for who I was seeing then. Why were they so mad? Nothing they said changed my mind. They tried everything to make me see their point of view, but I didn't care. I didn't want to hear it. I will never forget the night my college boyfriend arrived. He leaned over to kiss me, and when I didn't really kiss him hello after months of not being together, he put two and two together. He sat around like a wounded puppy for days, playing the song "Precious and Few" over and over. It was awful for everyone in the house.

Why was everyone on his side? Couldn't they see that we were worlds apart? I wondered what my parents would have said if they had known he tried to pressure me into having sex with him the last time we had been together. What would they say then? I can tell you what my dad would have done. He would have packed his bags for him and sent him back to Georgia. I never told anyone about what he had tried to make me do; I was too scared. The week of Christmas that year was the longest week I had ever endured. The clock couldn't tick off the minutes fast enough.

Granted, the way I dumped him was wrong, but everyone was blaming me for hurting him. The anger I tried to suppress inside was getting worse. Sometimes I thought I would explode. The anger had started when I was little but it seemed over time to become a time bomb inside of me; I never knew when it would go off. My mom said that when I was little, I would throw myself down on the floor and kick, scream, and cry—sometimes pretend to cry—until I got my way. Usually, she stood right there and gave in to whatever I wanted, but one time, I recall her leaving me there to have my tantrum. She said she finally just got tired of it and said, "I'll be downstairs when you get finished."

I was still treading on thin ice with my parents over my decision to dump my college boyfriend. One Friday night, David dropped me off after a date. We were outside kissing goodnight, and my dad flew out of the house, calling me a whore. He commanded me to come into the house and forbid me to see David anymore. I ran inside and up the stairs crying, and I flung myself on my bed. My sister-in-law happened to be there that evening, she ran upstairs, came into my room,

THE STAINED GLASS WINDOW

and tried to console me. Over and over I kept repeating, "I hate my dad for doing this."

My dad had begun to travel for work, and it seemed that he was away from home a lot more in recent months. He would come home on the weekends and then leave again for the whole week. For me, it became a relief when he would leave.

Sunday morning came. I didn't go to church anymore, and it was time for him to leave again for the week. I had gotten up very early—I was worn out from crying—and had come downstairs, turned on the TV, and fallen asleep on the couch. He came in the den, kissed me, and told me he was sorry for what he had said and done. He told me how much he loved me. I heard him, but I didn't care; I hated him for calling me a whore.

David's birthday rolled around, and he invited me to his house to have cake and ice cream. He came to pick me up, and we went to his house to celebrate. His mom brought out the cake, and I wouldn't eat any. I withdrew and made a total fool of myself, not even knowing why I was behaving that way. I had a stronghold about eating in front of people for fear they were judging me. Weight had become such a big issue to me that I wasn't going to eat the cake. It is not that I didn't want the cake; I wanted to take it home, hide, and eat it.

The time together at his house was fine except for the cake part, but on the way home, he started talking about how strange I had acted, and I got defensive. I immediately went into a rage. I started shaking I was so mad. I took the piece of cake his mother had given me to take home, and I threw it on the sidewalk saying, "Here, have your dumb birthday cake!"

Then as quickly as the anger would come, the remorse would start to flow. I couldn't bear the thought of his rejection, so I started to cry and made an excuse—that I was having a hard time with my monthly cycle—for the reason I lashed out.

I had started to tell little white lies to cover up any bad behavior I might have had. That one was the one that popped into my head, and I wasn't even close to my cycle. He seemed somewhat soothed by my explanation, but I am certain that I ruined his birthday.

He had been pressing me for quite some time to have intercourse. I just kept skirting the issue, telling him we would sometime but that I wasn't ready. He would tell me of his other friends who were having sex, as if that should make a difference. He wanted to know when. *When?* I had not had sex with my college boyfriend, and I really had no intention of having sex with David, no matter how much I thought I loved him. I had been raised to believe that good girls didn't do that until they were married, but there were other reasons I didn't want to. I didn't want any man to touch me, but I was too scared to stand up for myself and just say no—for fear of his rejection.

My dad left my mom in the midst of all of this, which turned my world upside down. I will never forget looking out the front door the morning after he left. I felt like the Jolly Green Giant had socked me in the stomach. I called my childhood friend from up the street, and he came down and tried to comfort me. He stayed and cooked dinner that night for my mom, my sister, and me. How were my mom, my sister, and I supposed to live? Who was going to support us? Everyone had always said, "You are just like your father." I guessed that somehow, I was going to have to take care of us, but I had no clue how. Divorce was something I had only heard of remotely. I felt ashamed as if I now had a scarlet letter on my chest. I hated it and I hated my dad for leaving.

Several months earlier, someone had sent my mother an anonymous note saying that my dad was "keeping house" somewhere else. She confronted my dad with it, and he told her, "The boys at the Choo Choo Inn are just trying to get me into trouble." At the time she believed him. Mom asked me why I felt so bad about my dad leaving since I was not the one who had been left. I didn't know, but I was scared of what was going to happen to us. He had always been our provider and protector. My thinking was that my two older brothers were gone and out of the house. I was the next in line and I felt like he had left me to clean up his mess.

———

My mom had raised me not to cuss, drink, or smoke. She did not want me to ever go out in public with a cigarette hanging out of my mouth. After Dad left she would sit up late at night to watch Johnny Carson. She would fix herself a tea party of crackers, cheese, and a coke and relax at the end of her day. I started to sit up with her at nights feeling I was keeping her company. Things around the house became more lax. She let me smoke my very first cigarette with her. I felt very mature. I was just relieved that Dad wasn't there anymore and would dread the thought of him coming home.

I liked the high cigarettes gave me in the beginning. They also gave me a boost of energy. When I discovered something that gave me a rush or a high, I desired it all the more.

I opened the doors to my heart wide after Dad left because I just didn't care about anything anymore. It seemed like the question of David and I fornicating was hanging in the air like a dark cloud when we were together. Why did it always have to boil down to sex? Finally, feeling like he would break up with me if I didn't relent, I gave in. We had already been drinking Boone's Farm together when we would go out on dates, which was a big deal for me. Most of the time he would have his older brother buy it for us. I started doing all of the things that I thought nice girls didn't or shouldn't do.

If I didn't want to go to school, I would make up an excuse and Mom wouldn't make me. I was depressed. Things were deep and dark inside of me, and I had no clue what was happening. The house I had grown up in that had been my safe haven—even if parts of it weren't real—was becoming a tomb in my heart.

I didn't want to go to school. Tryouts for majorette were coming up again, but I had already decided to graduate early. I had no clue what I wanted to do, but thoughts of no school at all sounded good to me. I sat at the kitchen table and convinced my mother—again—that graduating early would be a good idea for me. She was in the midst of her crisis and was devastated by my dad not being there. She was a one-woman man all the way and had never planned to divorce. She was an excellent wife and mother who had raised four children, treating each one of us as if we were an only child. My mother was the glue that held our family together.

She agreed that if I wanted to graduate early, then I should; she wanted me to be happy. The decision about my future was made within minutes, but nothing was ever said about what I would do from that moment forward. I thought that maybe I could work at the department store which was owned by my parents' friends. I really didn't know and I really didn't care.

Suddenly though, as if by some unseen force, my becoming a majorette was prearranged. My boyfriend and several of his friends who were majorettes rushed up to me one morning at school stating it was all set. The band director was going to select me to be on the majorette squad if I were to try out. Well, *this* was a new twist—my dream! My mind started to soar with the possibilities this could bring. My popularity would come back. I would have lots of friends, and I would try to do better in school.

All that was required of me was to show up. I went to the gym, and the band director came up to me and asked me if I was going to graduate early. I told him I had signed up, but I wasn't going to now. The woman in charge of graduation somehow found out I was trying out for majorette. She promptly marched over to the band director's office and told him I could not be selected because I was due to graduate; it sealed my fate. I was devastated.

That was the beginning of the end of any sort of restoration. It was awful, and I hated her for stopping my dream from coming to pass. She said I had to go through with graduation, even if I didn't want to. I was on the roster, and it couldn't be changed. To top it all off, at the very last minute I discovered that I would have to come back the following year and attend high school for half days because I lacked a course I needed. I had to walk through the motions of graduation that year, but the funny thing is that I didn't formally graduate until the following school year. I let life come at me and didn't question anything that happened.

I existed through the rest of high school; I became increasingly unhappy. It was decided after I graduated from high school that my mom, sister, and I would move from St. Albans to Richmond, Virginia where my dad had an investment business. Mom and Dad had been trying to work things out and Mom thought it would be better for us to be close to Dad. She would have a better chance of restoring her marriage and she also knew it would be monetarily better for all of us. I was hopping mad inside but I had no other choice but to go along.

My last date with David came all too quickly. The Saturday night before we moved, David and I rode uptown to get a pizza. I knew I was leaving, and I was heartsick about it, but what could I do? I felt somewhere deep inside that he was kind of anxious about me moving. Did he have someone else waiting in the wings?

On the way home, we started to argue. He mentioned us seeing other people, and then I knew. What about promises to love each other forever? What about him being the first boy I had ever had sex with? Didn't that mean anything to him? Was I to be tossed aside now like trash? I threatened to jump out of the car if he broke up with me. I told him that I would kill myself if he did. I opened the door and pretended to start to jump out of the car. Then I started hitting myself. The rage within me was getting worse. I hated myself. I hated my life. I hated my dad. Things were happening on the inside of me that I just could not explain. *Leave my high school sweetheart? Leave my hometown? My life—what life?* Long-distance romances at our age were doomed; I had already learned that. He came to see us off when the movers had packed up all of our things. I walked into my empty bedroom and looked inside my empty closet. I walked around the house I loved. It had never occurred to me that I would have to leave my home, which had become a safe haven for me.

So many memories were bad yet good—my church, the stained glass windows I had etched on my heart, the basketball court, my grandmother and extended relatives whom I loved. I hated leaving, but I wasn't in charge. There was a tearful good-bye as I slid into the backseat of the car. How would I ever recover?

PICK YOURSELF UP;
DUST YOURSELF OFF—
TIME TO MOVE!

I had moved to a new city, a new home, and—from what everyone in my family kept telling me—I was embarking on the chance at a new life. We moved to a fairly new home that was very nice. It came equipped with its own fountain in the backyard that lit up at night with the flip of a switch! I loved it. There was a glimmer of hope deep inside of me that believed things could be better. I thought that maybe this could be a new beginning and that I could make a fresh start. No one knew me, and they didn't know the rage inside of me. I had a clean slate and a second chance. I was going to try to see if I could control my anger and temper. The darkness that hung over me didn't seem to be there anymore; maybe it was gone forever. Maybe I had left it in St. Albans! I picked myself up, dusted myself off, and started all over again. I kept going and my thought was, if I buried my past deep enough, no one would be able to unearth my secrets.

There seemed to be many opportunities in Richmond. To me, it was like moving from Hooterville to Hollywood in terms of size. We had come to Richmond on vacation several years earlier, but I had no idea I would end up living here.

My sister and I knew virtually no one. My dad introduced us to one of his employees' sons. The oldest one ended up taking me for a ride one day, but he was too touchy-feely with me, and I didn't like it. Besides, I had left my heart in St. Albans along with my virginity to David. My heart was still with him. I had always equated happiness with men, and I was lonely. My thoughts were not of fulfilling a destiny or striving after a passion. They were about the fact that I did not have a guy to adore me. When I didn't have a boyfriend I felt less than a girl.

My dad's business would have social functions from time to time and Mom, my sister, and I would be invited to attend. At one of them I met another fellow that I really liked. He had a wonderful personality and sort of reminded me of my old college boyfriend in the way he could command everyone's attention through laughter. It just seemed that we were being thrown together. He was flirty with me, slyly pursuing me, but there was never a concrete date made.

One evening there was a crowd of people hanging out at my older brother's home. Everyone was going to bed, but he said, "Why don't we sit up a little longer and listen to some music?" One kiss led to another and another, and soon, we were doing more than kissing. We ended up—reluctantly on my part—having sex. In the heat of the moment, I gave in to him, thinking it would bind him to me. It turned out that I made a fool out of myself; I ended up being a one-night stand for him. The conquest had been made, the flirting stopped, and nothing more ever became of us.

By the time I realized that I had been duped, I started becoming nauseated in the mornings, and I just knew I was pregnant. I went to my mom and told her what I thought was going on. A pregnancy test was performed, and—yes—I was indeed pregnant. We hadn't lived in Richmond long and the conclusion was that it was David's baby, and I didn't dispute it. I gave pause about keeping the baby, but after several conversations with family—(which did not include my dad)—it was determined the best recourse would be to abort the fetus.

A decision was made that I would be taken to Washington, DC. Arrangements were made through my older brother and his wife. I recall the shock of it all; I was numb to everything being said. I felt like I was a robot. The program of what I was to do had been keyed into the computer, and now I would walk through the motions of an abortion on autopilot.

There were so many women there. We were sitting in a huge, gray room where there was no sunshine present, and we were lined up in rows. No one spoke. Heads were low, and people were dozing off to sleep. Someone would appear at the door with a clipboard in hand to shake everyone out of complacency. A mark would be made with a pen, and a name would be called.

I was ushered from room to room and counseled to make certain I knew what I was doing. As I was questioned and grilled, I felt uncomfortable having a stranger delve into my personal life and feelings. I answered each question in the way I thought they wanted me to, so I would quickly be able to put this nightmare behind me.

Yes, I knew it was a mistake, and I would never do it again. Yes, I would use birth control and take account of my body. Yes, I would be good. Yes. Yes. Yes was my answer to every question, over and over. I smiled and answered, "Yes." *Now let's move on, please. No one said anything about you making me cry.* I already hurt enough.

Finally, the actual abortion was explained, beginning from the time you undressed and put on a white gown to the procedure of opening your legs, going up through your uterus, and sucking the fetus out with a suction tube.

I knew this wasn't right, but—thank goodness—this was just a fetus and not a live baby. The abortion was performed, and I was shuttled home to recuperate for several days. Without any fanfare, it was shoved under the rug and never spoken of again. I secretly made a vow to myself that I wouldn't ever be in that position again. It was time to pick up and move on—again.

I was soon to be eighteen, and I replaced the memories of my "you know what" with dreams of a new car but not just any car. I wanted a little convertible just like one I saw in an Elvis movie at the Alban Theater. I could just picture myself riding down the road with the top down and with a scarf around my hair—the ends of it flying in the wind. Now *that* would make me feel better!

There was a car dealership on Broad Street in Richmond that sold British Leland cars. My dad was very willing at that time to do most anything for my sister and me. He told me that if I had a job and would agree to make the monthly payments on a car, he would take out a loan and pay the yearly insurance.

Whatever it took to make that car happen, I would have agreed to. I wasn't working or doing anything else, so my dad literally bought me a job in a bank where his company had their business account. I was hired as a drive-through teller. I liked being the banker when we played Monopoly, so it sounded good to me. *Maybe it will be fun,* I thought.

September 11 came—my birthday! I was so excited. I just knew I was going to get a car. Not only was I getting a car, but I was getting *the* car, just like in the movies. I had it all planned out in my mind. My dad was taking Mom, my sister, and me to dinner to the best restaurant in town. When he came to pick us up, he said he had some bad news.

He said, "I don't want you to get upset—*who, me?*—but I was not able to get the car for you. Due to your age and the fact that the car you want is a sports car, I wasn't able to get you covered with the insurance company." What about the picture I saw in my mind of me riding down the road in my convertible?

The twenty-minute drive to the restaurant that night seemed like an eternity. How could this have happened? I was already in a deep, dark place, and to top it all off, I had to give up my dream car. We pulled up to the restaurant parking lot and drove around, scouting for a place to park. I lifted my head up off my chest, looked outside the window, and noticed a car just like the one I wanted.

I said, "See, Dad? That is just like the one I want."

He said, "Well, let me park, and we'll go take a look at it." His response caught me off guard. My dad was not usually so attentive to my whims. The question of my having a car had been settled, so why would he buy into this little discussion any further?

We proceeded to walk over to the car, which was parked in front of the restaurant. Out of the corner of my eye, I glimpsed a huge card with a bow on it in the passenger's seat. It was for me! What a thrill! *Look out, Elvis—here I come!* I couldn't believe it. I was all shook up!

He had gone to the car dealership after all and purchased the car. Dad said, "The car is a stick shift." I didn't know how to drive a stick shift! But, who cared? I would learn. We went inside to have dinner, and my dad was grinning from ear to ear. In one fell swoop, all had been forgiven. Who says you can't buy love?

We all walked out of the restaurant—my stomach filled with filet mignon, birthday cake, and a glass of champagne to top it off. I was eighteen, I was thin, my dad loved me, and I had a convertible. What more could a girl ask for?

Dad said, "Hop in. Let's put the top down and take it for a spin." I asked him if he could drive a stick, and he said it had been a while, but he thought he could remember. The gears kind of grinded into position as we started out, but once going, the sound became a lot smoother. We didn't say much on the trip home. I tried to make small talk to say thank you for making one of my dreams manifest, but the words just wouldn't seem to come. I sat there beside my father and would look at him from time to time. My heart was saddened that I couldn't think of much to say to him. I didn't really hate him and I wanted to tell him how much I loved him. I wanted to open up to the man who I called my dad. I felt a sense of deep sadness for the life he had lived. He seemed to try so hard for me at times, but I just couldn't bring myself to talk to him. It was as if there was an impenetrable wall between us. The worst part of it was that we both knew it.

EIGHTEEN, MY MGB,
AND MONEY, HONEY

I was thin, I was eighteen, and I drove a burnt orange MGB. It was euphoric!

Suddenly, out of nowhere, reality hit. I had to fulfill my promise of working to make money so I could pay for my dream car. This would be my first "big girl" nine-to-five, Monday through Friday, everyday job. *Yuck!* The ache resurfaced.

I stopped and looked at what I was facing. I had a grown-up job I really didn't want that had been planned in an instant to fulfill a promise I had made. I had thrust myself into something just to make money. Emotionally I was not ready for any of this, but I was going to have to pretend it was all right. I worked alongside a guy who had just graduated from the University of Richmond. He was the bank president's nephew, so everyone thought highly of him. I discovered he had a girlfriend and was making a career of the financial business. I sat beside him for eight hours a day; he, in turn, discovered that I was new in town and didn't know many people. We became buddies in a sense; we would make light conversation, and he asked me one day if I would be interested in having a blind date for the upcoming homecoming game, dance, and festivities that were to take place over the course of a weekend. I had never had a blind date but had heard many people had, so thinking it might be a good way to meet some other people, I said yes.

The Friday night affair was at his frat house. My blind date came to pick me up, met my mother—not my dad—and we headed for University of Richmond fraternity row. He seemed nice, and I thought, *Well, maybe I will meet the love of my life through him. Who knows?*

We arrived at the frat house, and we could hear the live band as we got out of his car. As soon as my foot stepped across the doorframe, I noticed a girl sitting on a guy's lap. She yelled, "Molly Painter, from St. Albans, West Virginia! How are you?"

Was I that renowned? When I saw the friend from high school, all that flooded over me was that I missed my home and David. My date went to get me a drink, and I didn't stop until I couldn't swallow anymore. I professed undying love to my date as he nursed me through the evening, listening to me ramble on about my life. The more he said, "Molly, there is no way you could love me," the more I tried to convince him that there was such a thing as love at first sight.

He took me home that night—we didn't have sex—and I stumbled up the steps to bed and crashed. I managed to get it together the next day, hangover and all, for the game and the dinner afterward. I was very quiet but kept noticing another guy stare at me all day and evening. My date was a gentleman—very attentive but I had already spotted someone else.

I walked into work the following Monday, and my co-worker just started laughing. He said, "I heard you had a very interesting weekend!"

I said, "Ha ha. I don't want to talk about it."

Then he said, "If you are not too in love with your blind date, there is another guy who would like to date you."

As quickly as I had conned my blind date into dating me steadily, I broke it off so I could date this other fellow. We dated several times, but nothing much ever happened. However, I was back in the saddle again and hot on the trail for a guy. It hadn't been long since my abortion. I was always looking for someone. I couldn't bear to be alone. What could possibly be worse?

There was a pretty cute construction guy who was refurbishing the building where I worked, and he was right under my nose. I didn't have to make any effort at all to play up to him. He got up his nerve and asked me out; I accepted, of course.

We went out on a couple of dates and by the fourth date we were in bed. Once wouldn't hurt, would it? Immediately, I brought up the subject of marriage. We had nothing in common, but it didn't matter to me. I told myself I would just mold myself into what he wanted, he would love me, and it would just work out. I wanted to get married and I didn't give any consideration to anything except my desire of being a bride and wearing a beautiful gown.

My mother was reluctant about the whole concept of this union but she went along with my whims to keep peace. My dad grilled me on the phone about our combined income and then stated it wasn't even enough to live on. I resented him for laughing about it. I was going to get married and be happy no matter what anyone said.

One evening I invited him and his mother over for dinner so everyone could meet. I had been home long enough to change into some sweat clothes, pull back my hair and didn't bother to retouch my nine hour makeup. *After all, he was already caught and* I thought, *Why should I have to dress up? I'll look good on my wedding day.* I heard a knock on the door and there stood my fiancé and his mother.

She came in and noticed a picture of me hanging on the wall. She turned to me and asked, "Where is the pretty girl I see in this picture?"

What kind of remark was that? I'm tired, I thought, *and besides, I'll do that later on when we are married.*

We went parking several nights later to talk, and he started to cry. He said he just didn't love me. He went on to tell me that he really loved the girl he had broken up with before me, so I had no choice but to break up with him. Secretly, I was relieved. Besides, I still loved David.

A few weeks later, I got up to go to work. I went into the bathroom, and all of a sudden, a wave of nausea hit. I went to the doctor and a pregnancy test was administered. Two days later, I called the doctor's office to discover I was pregnant yet again. After my last abortion, I had vowed to myself I wouldn't become pregnant again until I was married. I was so mad at myself. I always made promises when I did something bad, that I would do better. I felt I had no choice but to have another abortion. I had to take time off from the bank, and I ended up telling the secretary the truth about why I had to take a few days off. She sat at her desk and cried. I went downtown, this time by myself, to have my second abortion.

My mother was put out with me, and I knew it. My dad didn't know. I don't know what he would have said or done. I was slightly chastised by the workers in the abortion clinic, but they didn't have to scold me; I already felt bad enough. As I sat there waiting to go into the procedure room, I thought to myself, *After this abortion, I am going to turn over a new leaf.* I promised myself there would be no more sex outside of marriage. I would stay on birth control, prepared for the heated moments if and when they arose. No, they wouldn't, because I wouldn't let them, so I really didn't even need birth control, but I would use it anyway ... maybe.

I told myself I wouldn't even date again. I sat there thinking, *I am just through with men.* Thoughts of becoming a nun crossed my mind. That's what I needed, a nunnery! I wouldn't need birth control for that!

———————

When I went back to work, I was determined to buckle down, focus on work, and behave myself. The new account representative I worked with at the bank strode slowly over to me one day as I was pouring a cup of coffee minding my own business. She stated she had had a dream. In her dream, she said she saw a girl with green eyes and blonde hair. She continued, "I think that is telling me that my son is going to marry a girl of that description." That *did* describe me somewhat, but was I the only girl on the planet who had those features? My co-worker overheard and started to laugh. Everyone thought she was nutty. But it really wasn't funny to me. Taking what she told me to heart, I thought, *Well, maybe this is the one.* It wasn't as if she had a crystal ball or anything, but a dream? Well, I could buy into that.

Since I was a drive-through teller, her son started coming to the drive-through quite a lot to make his deposits. Little by little, we started carrying on light conversation. Then one day, he drove up with a red rose included in his deposit and asked me if I would like to go out and have a pizza. He was really cute and had what I called "a life." He had aspirations. He was going to make something out of himself. He was interesting, and it was refreshing to be around someone who had a clear direction to follow. I really liked that because I was such a drifter, and the image he projected attracted me. I wanted a clear path, but I didn't know how to get one. I was definitely attracted to him, but I had an ache in my stomach that I couldn't describe or ignore.

We dated for a month or so, and he stated he wanted to marry me. Of course, I ended up breaking the promise I made to myself in regard to having sex. My intention was to be abstinent, but the guys I dated all wanted sex. His mother had been drilling me at work about us, and quite frankly, that helped sour the relationship for me. The more I got to know her, the more something about her scared me. The way she looked at me with those eyes of hers was unnerving. The expression on her face was very odd. I just couldn't imagine my life with her in it. The ache was becoming stronger, and I just couldn't commit to him forever, so it was adieu.

I wanted to put all of the aching, the pain, and the abortions out of my heart. This was not what I had planned in my mind about my happiness. Where was my Romeo?

"MR. BLUE EYES" AND MIDNIGHT AT THE OASIS

Romeo, wherefore art thou? Ever since I could remember, I had been a hopeless romantic. I didn't ask to be this way; it is as if I was predisposed to be like this. I longed for the true passions of love, happiness, and—above all—to be settled inside, and I desperately looked in every nook and cranny but couldn't seem to find what I was looking for.

My sister and I were out driving one day in my relatively new car, and it overheated. We were stopped at a four-way intersection, and there were three gas stations staring me in the face. Hmm, which one would I pull into? "Eeny, meeny, miney, moe"! I drove into the closest one I could get to before my car blew up.

I pulled into one of the gas pump lanes, and out from the garage walked the cutest guy I had ever seen. I was frantic about the car and said, "Please, can you help me? My car is almost brand new and is overheating!"

He said, "Let me take a look." He walked around to the front and lifted the hood. Then he said, "Could you come here for a minute?"

I looked at my sister with a questioning expression, then opened the door, got out of the car, and went to stand beside him. He looked at me and pointed to something under the hood, as if I would understand what he was talking about. I could hardly take my eyes off his gorgeous blue eyes long enough to pay attention to what he was even saying. Who cared what was wrong with it? He turned and pointed to the car he was working on in one of the bays. He said, "There is my car. It is an MG Midget."

Was this a sign? We both had MGs! I knew he wasn't a dream, but he sure looked like one. He made an adjustment and assured me that everything would be fine. I had no idea what his name was or if I would see him again, but I was determined to find out. As I drove out of there that night, I told my sister, "I am going to marry him."

I went into work the next day. This time I wasn't performing a dance routine to "Cloud Nine"; I felt like I was floating on cloud nine! Immediately, I started rambling to my co-worker—the one who had introduced me to my first blind date—about the guy at the gas station. I didn't know how I was going to hook up with him, but the wheels were turning. He said he would talk to his girlfriend, make some inquiries, and try to discover the name of the mystery gas attendant.

He came into work the next day and startled me with some information. He had talked to his girlfriend the night before about what had happened to me. He continued, "You are not going to believe this."

His girlfriend told him that her sister had come home that very night, saying her boyfriend's brother had met a girl at the gas station where he worked, and she drove an orange MGB. What were the chances of that?

After some networking, phone numbers were exchanged, and he called me several days later. It really—for the first time in a long time—felt right. It didn't feel conjured up just for the sake of being with someone ... anyone. "Mr. Blue Eyes" was six months younger than I was, just like my high school sweetheart. Do, do, do, do. It seemed to me like our meeting was more than coincidence. He was not only handsome, but he was funny. He was also very cool. Our first evening together was heavenly. I made a point of buying a new outfit for the date; I wanted to look extra special. He asked me out to dinner and a movie.

We went to a Chinese restaurant to eat. He asked me if I wanted a drink. I told him I would love one, but I was underage. He said, "Don't worry, they will serve us."

Nervously, I ordered a Singapore Sling, and much to my amazement, the waitress appeared with one on her tray several minutes later. I had discovered a long time ago that drinking helped calm me down, and it gave me liquid courage. It wasn't as good as green nerve medicine, having a lot more calories, but it was a close second. I was so nervous that night my hands were shaking, but with each passing sip, my inhibitions melted right away.

I ordered a dish but I didn't like eating in front of others, so I got a doggie bag to go. Besides, I didn't have my toothbrush with me, and all I could imagine was food being caught between my teeth. I was not going to ruin my perfect façade.

We headed for the movie theater to see *Blazing Saddles*. I don't think I had ever seen anyone pass gas on a movie screen prior to seeing this movie. It reminded me of a time I'd been watching TV with my ninth-grade boyfriend and a commercial came on about Kotex feminine pads. I was humiliated then, and I was humiliated now. Thank goodness, it was dark in the theater.

I leaned over at one point and tried to kiss him, but clearly he was not interested. It made me feel rejected. I had become very forward. He said, "Not here." After the movie, we ended up at his best friend's house, and he kissed me for the first time in the front yard under a big oak tree. I was in love.

I decided I was not going to tell him about my past. What he didn't know wouldn't hurt him. I wasn't going to spill the beans and ruin my chances at true love.

I was unaware that he had been seeing a girl who was away at college. After our first two dates, he said he had to take care of some business before we went out again. He proceeded to tell me there was another girl. I felt jealous that he had been in contact with her, but he was adamant that he had to break it off with her before we could see one another again. I was nervous about the trip he was going to make; I wondered if she would try to hold on to him. His mind was made up though, so I tried to be mature—and understanding. He went the following weekend to break up with her. Yes, there were tears, but he was clear to her that he didn't love her.

After that, we were stuck together like glue. My whole family liked him. They remarked that he reminded them of my dad. He seemed to know everyone in town, and was well-liked. I was at his house, or he was at mine. We both thought we were in love. Physically, things remained light for a while, and I kept my guard up. Then of course, sex became an issue as it always had. I knew we were headed for intercourse. I lied to him and told him I was a virgin. I only meant to have sex with him one time, feeling we would be married someday, but that didn't last for long.

Sex continued. I had stopped taking birth control because I hadn't needed it for a long while. My thinking was, *Why take birth control if I am not going to have sex?* I didn't like the way it made me feel, and I started to gain weight each time I took it. So I became pregnant for the third time.

I could truly see us being married with a baby. I had it all figured out in my mind—my dad could help us, and we would tie the knot. I would finally get married. I just knew we would be in a married, blissful state. For a brief moment in time, he did entertain the thought of marrying me. I had tried and tried over and over to convince him that this was the thing to do. He never said much at those times though.

We told my family. My dad said he was going to marry me under no uncertain terms; his family said something different. Unbeknownst to me, he went to see my dad and told him he was not going to marry me. My dad called to tell me, and it was as if someone had taken a dagger and thrust it through my heart. There would be no marriage, no husband, and—once again—there was not going to be a baby. Let's see, how many now? That would be abortion number three.

I was not going to a cattle clinic this time, made to feel like I was some kind of slut. This time, I had the abortion the white-collar way, and I went to a physician's office. A check was dropped off in the mail slot of our home with the intention that we were never to see one another again.

My mother was there for support, but I know she was thoroughly put out with me. After the abortion was performed, I watched the doctor intently as he stood at his sink examining the fetus. Without a doubt, I just knew he had determined the sex of the aborted baby. I never said a word, and he never commented. My mother took care of me afterward but didn't say much about the whole affair.

Messages began to go back and forth between our common friends, and gradually "Mr. Blue Eyes" and I started sneaking around, seeing one another. Several months passed, and we slipped right back into hot and steamy sex—behind the backs of everyone.

As all of this was occurring, I went from the bank job to contemplating the notion of going to college. I thought maybe I would finally become a dental hygienist. I convinced my dad this was the career path I wanted to take. He said that if I chose to continue my education, he would sell my MGB because he was not willing to make the payments. I cleaned up the car, and it sold immediately. I had to have some sort of transportation, so I bought a brand-new VW, got a part-time job at a clothing store, and enrolled in a local college. Dad said if I did well enough to graduate, he would send me away to a four-year institution to complete my studies.

I was back on speaking terms with my boyfriend's family, and he of course, had begun to come back around my house again. But I knew Dad wouldn't like it. I never told him so *mum* was the word. Things were kind of cool between everyone, but I had convinced Mom that I really did love him. So after a while, the past was ignored, never to be spoken of again. Eventually everyone seemed to fall in step with what we wanted.

My boyfriend had gone away to college, and I missed him horribly. I hated school, I hated my life, and I felt lonely. I continued to harbor deep, dark, unexplainable things inside of me that pulled me down into an unbearable pit. I couldn't seem to pull myself out of bed every morning to attend classes, so I just quit. Now what?

I was at a six-month dental checkup and started to pour my heart out to my dentist regarding my life. He said, "Why don't you come and work for me? I will train you and pay you at the same time." I felt that perhaps this could turn out to be something good—a turning point for me.

I purchased several cute uniforms, said goodbye to work clothes and began in the dental field, working four days a week. The dentist who had seemed so kind, caring, and friendly was the hardest person to work for I had ever encountered. From the moment I began to work there, our relationship changed. I couldn't seem to do enough and was clearly getting on his nerves. He was short-tempered in the office and wasn't at all what he had appeared to be.

My family loved going to him and always looked forward to their dental visits. They could hardly believe what I was saying when I recounted my feelings about him. It was as if he was a Dr. Jekyll and Mr. Hyde. He would yell around the office. He even yelled at me in front of several patients, sending me to the lab in tears. I asked one of the girls one day about his temper, she just shrugged her shoulders and wouldn't talk about it. After work one day, I caught him lounging in one of the dental chairs, getting tanked up on laughing gas. I was getting ready to go home, and he called me in and apologized for being so mean. I knew I did not like this man, and after three months, I left. It was job-hunting time again!

I answered an ad in the paper and managed to get another job working for a dentist who specialized in root canals. He was an older man, funny, and I came to really like him. He was laid-back, and he let me do my job. The drawback to this position was that I only made seventy-three dollars a week. After three months of working there, he said that I was such a good worker that he gave me a five-dollar-a-week raise. Thank goodness, I lived at home.

My lower stomach started to ache quite often. I didn't miss any work but had told the secretary what was going on. She suggested I go next door to the OBGYN, who was very well-regarded in the community. I really didn't want anyone knowing about my past abortions due to possible judgment, but I strongly felt the need, for safety's sake, to be examined by a specialist. I reluctantly called and made an appointment.

I was young and good-looking, and he seemed to be a nice, hip medical doctor. I went to him once and really liked his manner, but then his nurse called me back for a reexamination. I didn't think anything of it. Maybe he had missed doing something he needed and had to see me again. The second time I went to see him was very different. The nurse took me into a room and had me undress and put on a robe. He walked in with the nurse and then dismissed her, saying he no longer needed her services. To me, doctors were like gods, so I did not question his dismissal of the nurse.

I started to feel rather funny and got all flushed. He asked me to stand up, disrobe, and turn slowly around so he could examine me—I was stark naked! I did as he requested. After what seemed to be an eternity, he got up to leave and told me to get dressed. I was a little stunned.

I walked to the reception desk to take care of my visit. I was told I would not be charged. As I turned to leave, I thought I was going to vomit. Something had just happened that was not the norm for a doctor's visit. He sent word by one of his nurses that he wanted me to come and work for him. As soon as I heard what she said, I knew it was for more than work. I felt sick and violated. No one would have believed me if I had reported him to the medical board, so I dropped it. I was not one to stir the pot, so to speak, so I chalked it up to my ignorance and kept going. I told no one but "Mr. Blue Eyes." I saw the doctor one other time when he was going into his office. I gave him a frozen stare, acknowledging I knew he was up to no good, and I never laid eyes on him again.

I felt lost. I knew I had to earn more than seventy-eight dollars a week, but I had no clue what to do. The title of the song "What's Going On?" sure fit my life. What was wrong with me? By this time, I had already had six jobs, and I had gone to school and quit. I already had three proposals of marriage under my belt and was after the fourth. I had had three abortions and had sex with six different guys. I was getting tired of it all, and I was not even twenty years old yet.

My boyfriend's dad suggested I try to find a job at a savings and loan association. I didn't even know what one of those was but searched the papers and there was an ad for a teller at one. I interviewed, and a job offer was made to me.

Another completely new era of my life was beginning. The best part to this new job was that I was going to get to ditch my everyday uniforms and buy new, professional work clothes. My mom, as usual, came to my financial rescue and we went shopping.

I had become very heavy. I had my hair cut off and wore it in an afro style because *A Star Is Born* had hit the theaters and was all the rage. I always seemed to copy what was the current trend in fashion. I had gotten up to 200 pounds though, and the hairdo was not becoming. I was very unhappy inside, and my outward appearance showed it; I just kept going. Somehow, I was always hopeful that things would get better.

My boyfriend had quit school because he had missed me, and he had come home. It seemed that for months now, our routine was traveling between our two houses, watching TV, and eating. We were in a dreadful rut.

Tent dresses? Well, I loved them! I had been wearing tent dresses in my time off from work. They were comfortable; I could let it all hang out without being convicted by the clothes I wore that I needed to do something about my weight. If I didn't feel the tight pants or see the bulges, then the fat didn't exist in my mind.

He came to pick me up one Saturday, and we went to a local hamburger joint for lunch. We ordered our food, and I sat down with my hamburger, large fries, and large chocolate shake. I unwrapped my meal very carefully. I saw, in my mind's eye, saliva drooling out of the corner of my mouth as I got ready to embark on a food fantasy.

All of a sudden, my boyfriend looked at me and barked, "When are you going to lose some of that weight?"

I remained calm, which was unusual for me. I held my tongue and slowly, calmly wrapped it all back up, and headed for the trashcan. I said, "Take me home."

Our love affair was over. I was devastated, yet in a sort of weird way, relieved. Something had to give. He took me home without much fanfare. We drove up to my home, and I got out of the car, slammed the door, and went inside. We had claimed "Midnight at the Oasis" as our song, but he was no longer my sheik.

I didn't shed one tear as I shut the door behind me. Minutes later, a thought popped into my head: *You're fat, and no one is going to want you like this*. Diet time had arrived.

LONG LOST LOVE
AND DEATH

I continued to search for some type of relationship with my dad, hoping some sort of wisdom or guidance would come from our time together, but we never seemed to be able to communicate. I would always go to see him with hopes that the next time would be the time that we would connect. I would go over to his house, and he would drink, get drunk, and make a fool of himself every single time. By day he was the picture of health and success, but when nighttime came, he fell into a pit. Each time I walked out his front door, I left feeling forlorn; I had a heavy heart because he was so unhappy, but the funny thing is that I was too.

My dad could talk anyone into anything, sell anyone anything, and at the same time, would give or help anyone with anything. However, he always left his family wanting more.

One time when I was at his house and he was smashed, I overheard him tell someone he kept a list of all the money his kids borrowed. I had gone back for more punishment one night and upon leaving, found myself short on cash. I needed gas, and I reluctantly asked if I could borrow five dollars. He looked at me with a sick smirk and said that of course I could. The guilt I had over it was tremendous. I made a point of taking it back to him two days later.

I longed to have a close relationship with Dad like the children on TV programs like the *Brady Bunch*. Neither of us, however, could get beyond any of our shortcomings. Being around my dad didn't make me happy. I held the thought in the back of my mind that when I got married that I would find the happiness I longed for. I would say to myself, "I just want to be happy." I was doing everything in the world to make it happen. I looked for my happiness in everyone—in everything and under every rock.

I had no boyfriend and was doing my best to lose weight and get in shape again so I could acquire a new love. My weight went up and down like a yo-yo. It was a cycle, but—like it or not—that was me. But! I still had the job at the savings and loan and that was a miracle.

I hurt inside and ran to the doctor for this or that with any little pain. If I got depressed, I would make something out of nothing and head for the doctor. My mind-set was, "Just give me a pill, and I'll feel better!"

Sometimes I would leave for lunch and go to the doctor; they would diagnose me with whatever my complaint was. I would then call work from the doctor's office and go home for the afternoon. I just wanted to be in love and be happy. I was bleeding on the inside, but I could not seem to fix myself. I would do better for a while when I had an illness to focus on. I would return to work, put all my efforts into working hard, and receive pats on the back; then "it" would come back again. I felt like something had crawled up inside of me and died. I really needed a *soul* doctor, but they didn't have those. If they did, I didn't know any.

I was depressed and anxious, and I was put on Valium. After all, my dad had been put on Valium when he was my age, and *I was just like my dad.* The doctor diagnosed me with a "bad case of nerves." That was a term doctors used at the time for me because they really didn't know what was wrong. But the more nervous I said I was, the more nervous I became, so the pills just kept on coming. I ate them like candy.

The aunt I had been obnoxious with when I was young was not a well person. She had gone for shock treatments and was temporarily placed in a mental rest home. She had always told me, "You are just like me." She put some weird thoughts in my mind, and at a young age I took them to heart. I started thinking I was like her. Of course, how could I be? I was just like my dad!

I nearly killed myself trying to lose weight. I lost about sixty pounds in a span of three months and headed back to my hometown where I had left my heart. Secretly, I was going to find out what was going on with David. I was going on a fishing trip—a manhunt—to see what I could find. I asked a friend to go along, put a gun under the front seat I had borrowed for protection, and off we headed for the mountains of West Virginia to my grandmother's house. Guess who's coming to Grandma's? David had come to town from college for a friend's bachelor party. He was meeting one of my cousins at my grandmother's house so they could ride together. What luck! When I found out he was coming by, my heart skipped a beat, as it always did at the mention of his name. The last several years of hurt were out the window. Who was the guy who had just dumped me several months earlier because I was fat? Who cares? My high school sweetheart was coming. The way I could shift gears emotionally was utterly remarkable.

I was in the bathroom primping, knowing I was minutes away from seeing David. The one I had cried for at night as I imagined him being with someone else after I moved away. The past was the past. It was a new day and another time. I heard a knock on the door. I could hear voices muttering in the next room. My heart started beating wildly as I wondered what he would think of me now. I had had my hair cut short and straightened. I wondered if he would like it.

The only way I would find out was to take a leap of faith and go into the living room. I took in a deep breath and shook inside the entire time it took me to walk the ten steps to reach him. Our eyes locked. It was all I could do to keep from running into his arms. He commented on my hair immediately, saying he liked it. I sighed with relief. Outward appearance most of the time was very important to me; it was odd that I had let myself get so fat. It was as if I just couldn't help gorging at times.

This was the first time in several years we had seen one another, and I was already, in my mind, planning on us getting married. Anyway, there we were face-to-face. I was nice, polite, and—of course—funny. People loved it when I was funny, so that was what I was going to be. The last time we had been together had been deep, dark, and depressing, and I was going to show him in an instant that I had changed.

I had made plans to go uptown to a club that evening with several other friends, but had made the comment that my friend and I were going to stop first to pick up something to eat. David and I said our good-byes. I walked out the door with the friend who had traveled with me, my heart sinking as I took each step toward the car. I would never again see the one person on earth I longed to be with forever. I knew I had to play this cool and collected. Deep in my soul, I still loved him. He was the only one in my heart and the only one I wanted. I slowly drove to the A&W, which was a drive-in, about ten miles away. Waitresses came to the car to take our order; it was fun to go there. There was nothing like a cold draft root beer from the tap, and I didn't really even like root beer.

All of a sudden, there was a knock at the window. I was talking to my friend, and I assumed it was our order. I turned my ahead around, and there stood David. My heart felt like it was going to burst out of my chest. I rolled down the window and said, "Hi."

He said, "I would rather be with you than go with my bud-dies to the bachelor party. I can see them anytime."

I said, "Are you sure?" He nodded yes.

That was it. He got into the backseat of the car and said he was going with us. My girlfriend knew how much I loved him. She piped up and said, "Why don't I go with the others so you and David can be together for the evening?"

I jumped on the invitation, and she was off with my child-hood friend to go dancing uptown. I was glad to have her go—boy, what a friend I was. It was all about me, and I usually got what I wanted at the expense of others. True to form that night, I got what I had come for.

I was filled with anticipation, knowing I had to tread lightly with him. I was casual, yet attentive. We went to a local hangout and talked. We really didn't even know each other any longer, and the conversation was forced at times. The attrac-tion was definitely there, but I could not be sure there was anything more going on in his mind. He treaded lightly with me as well.

We saw someone we knew from high school, they made a big deal out of us being with one another and asked if we were back together. We quickly both assured him we were just friends. Minute by minute, my heart sank; I felt that he just didn't trust who I was. We left, picked up some beer, and went up to one of the parking places in town. We turned the radio on low, and there was silence for quite some time. We had made small talk up to that point, and then he started asking a lot of questions about me. I felt he was probing for something, and I answered calmly and quietly as he asked. I didn't ask many questions of him as we sat there. I really didn't care to know if he were seeing someone for fear that my heart would get hurt, even though we had no commitment.

I finally piped up and told him that I thought I still loved him. He was shocked. He reached over to kiss me, and it appeared the same feelings were still there. He couldn't believe that I still cared about him. We stayed there talking for several hours, and then I drove him home around midnight. The time between us seemed different than it had been in high school. We decided that we wanted to stay in touch, but there were no commitments made that night. He was very cautious. We said our good-byes. I didn't know if I would ever see him again, but as I drove away, I was singing in my heart, "Heaven ... I'm in heaven!"

He told me he would be in Richmond the following year for a wedding. We got together at that time and were able to see each other again briefly. That visit settled the fact that we would try to see if we could work out what was happening in our hearts.

I was at work one Friday evening getting ready to leave when the phone rang. It was David. He told me that all the guys were in the fraternity house at Marshall, celebrating the end of the semester and he was going to come and see me for the weekend. He also proceeded to tell me that he had gotten a job in Richmond for the upcoming summer with a friend's dad who owned a construction business.

I was elated. Then for some odd reason, I said, "Why don't you let me fly there for the weekend?"

He was emphatic and said no. The plans had been already made. He was going to hitch a ride with some guys who were coming that way. He said, "I love you, and I will see you about two in the morning."

As I hung up the phone, I said, "I love you too."

My mother happened to be at my grandmother's house in St. Albans visiting for the weekend. I was awakened quite abruptly to the phone ringing about six o'clock the next morning. My first thought, as I groped to get my bearings, was it must be David. My sister and I had waited up for him to come until the wee hours of the morning, and then we had fallen asleep. The voice on the other end of the phone was my mother's. The first thing she said to me was, "Molly, sit down. I have something to tell you."

I got a horrible ache in the pit of my stomach. "David was killed on the West Virginia turnpike around the Princeton area early this morning."

She kept talking, but I wasn't listening to what she was really saying. Her speech became muffled. She went on, "He and four others ran head-on into a truck. He was sitting in the front passenger's seat, and he was the only one in the car killed." The only injury he sustained, I discovered later, was a gash on his forehead.

I seemed to be frozen in time as I continued to sit there. David was gone. In an instant, the world I had built in my mind for us to share was over.

My childhood friend had come to Richmond for the summer to work. He was the same one who comforted me during the devastation after my dad left home. He was the first one who I thought to call. He arranged with his work to take time off, as did I, and we headed to our hometown for the funeral. I was in complete shock not feeling anything.

David's dad was the manager of the local funeral home. He had driven to pick up his dead son in one of the hearses David used to wash on the weekends to earn spending money. The thought of it was awful. I shrank back at the funeral home on the night of the visitation, unable to speak to his family. His death was my fault; I was the one to blame—the cause of the sad circumstance that brought everyone together at this time. I couldn't take their rejection of me.

Finally, I took a step forward and managed to speak to his older brother, but I just couldn't bring myself to speak to his parents. I looked their way and smiled, then turned and walked away. If it hadn't been for me, their son would have been alive.

I went to the florist in town, ordered a huge plant, and sent it to their home with a note attached. In it I explained my feelings. I could always put down on a piece of paper exactly what I wanted to say without having to confront anyone; it was my way. Plain and simple, I was a coward. When I returned to Richmond, I went back to work. I would leave at lunchtime and go out driving in my car. The tears would start to flow, and I would stop at a phone booth to call my mom. I would stand there sobbing as I listened to her talk me out of my anguish so that I could return to work for the afternoon. No one could soothe me like my mom.

I didn't want to live. I became very scared, particularly of death. I started sleeping on the couch at night. It was all I could do to keep going from day to day. Then one night, something happened.

My mom, sister, and I lived in a beautiful townhome now. The very first home we moved to in Richmond had been broken into, and my sister had become so distraught that my dad finally moved us to the other side of town.

The neighborhood had been vandalized and thirty-five houses burglarized within the span of several days. Three men and one woman came in and stole my mother's diamond watch, $300, and other minor things. A cousin had come for a visit and was staying there with her baby. The thieves had actually moved the baby from its crib into the bed with its mother without stirring anyone in the house.

All of a sudden, I was awakened, drenched in sweat. I just knew something was wrong. I got up and looked all around. I awoke to all the drawers opened up with clothes hanging out and our bedroom light was on. I cautiously got up to look down the hall, and a dish flew right by my head. I ran across the hall to my mom's room and hid behind her door. Then I turned and ran into her bathroom, locking myself inside.

Seconds later, my sister was banging on the door wanting to come in.

I was frozen with fear; I didn't want to open the door at first, but she kept screaming, saying, "Molly, let me in!" I opened the door and pulled her in, and we stood there screaming our heads off. I had picked up a brush for protection! My mom was asleep in her bed. When I had run past her, I wasn't sure if she was even alive. The screaming woke her up, and she literally followed the burglars out the front door. They had taken off at the sounds of our shrill screams.

We now lived in Fort Knox, baby! When we moved into our townhouse, Dad had someone come and place black bars on the two back windows. On the back door was a decorative bar that covered the whole door from the top to the bottom. On top of that, there was the doorknob lock, of course, and above that, we had a chain lock. At the top and bottom of the door, were extra deadbolts.

At any rate, there I was—asleep on the couch. It was about 2:00 a.m. or a little later. I could hear a constant knocking on the door that seemed to be muffled. Something kept knocking and knocking. I knew it wasn't going to stop unless I answered it. I got up and slowly opened the back door.

I methodically began at the top. I slowly pulled back the deadbolt at the top and the deadbolt at the bottom. Then I unhooked the chain on the door. I opened the door, and there stood David.

He said, "I love you. I'm all right."

I said, "I am so sorry. I love you too."

He said, "There is nothing to be sorry for. I have to go."

He turned slowly and headed off into the air. He appeared exactly the way he had looked to me in life, wearing the same black and white jacket that he usually wore. It was as if he had been sent back to comfort my aching heart. He told me he loved me. He told me he loved me!

I awoke the next morning not recalling the dream at first. Then little by little, it all started to flood back into my mind. Seeing him did something for me nothing or no one else had been able to. I was grief-stricken and wasn't certain how I would pull myself together again but seeing him the way I did, comforted my aching heart. I knew I could continue on this earth knowing he did love me; there was no doubt. Going on without him was horrible, but I held his words in my heart. They gave me something to cling to, and knowing the vision of him was real opened my eyes to life after death. I had always felt there was something more after a person died, and this confirmed it.

This was to be the first of many visions. The next one wouldn't come until years later. I didn't dare tell anyone; what would they think of me? This was different from the games we played or the séances we had at the dining room table. If I tried to tell anyone, they would think I was just overwrought and dreamed it up, but I knew I didn't. That encounter was as real to me as any human encounter I'd ever had.

I had to keep living a life that was really no life at all now, and I would have to live it without David.

PART TWO

"DO YOU TAKE THIS WOMAN, FINALLY?"

My childhood friend—the one who drove me to David's funeral—who was still living in Richmond was having a party, and he thought it would be a good idea for me to come. It had been months since David's death and I was feeling it was time to get on with my life and stop grieving, so I accepted the invitation. I got there and proceeded to drown my sorrows. With each sip I took I began to feel better inside so I just kept on drinking until I was so drunk I could hardly see. I had to go to work the next day, and I knew I wasn't in any shape to drive, but I—Miss Hardhead—wouldn't listen to anyone. Once again, I had cunningly convinced everyone I was okay to drive home.

I wasn't 500 yards down the road when I ended up actually blacking out, having a wreck, and tearing down a fence that surrounded someone's yard. I got scared, jumped out of the car, and somehow made my way back to the party. I told everyone there what had happened, and they immediately took off to the scene, coming to my rescue. Someone grabbed their keys and drove me home. The ones left behind contacted the police and cleaned up the dirty mess I had created.

At the time, I happened to have my car insurance through the parents of "Mr. Blue Eyes," so I called them from work the next day to find out what I needed to do with my wrecked vehicle. Of course, his mom ended up telling her son she had spoken to me on the phone. You will never guess who showed up at my front door. You know it—"Mr. Blue Eyes" himself!

He had just gotten back from a vacation to the beach and came by on the pretense of delivering a shirt he said he had gotten for me while away. He said he couldn't stop thinking of me and wanted to see me. Of course, I perceived immediately he liked the way I looked, but he always did when I was thin. I gave him the cold shoulder for the way he had treated me the last time we were together in regards to my being overweight, said a polite thank-you for the shirt, and closed the door.

A couple of weeks later, my childhood friend told me of another big party he was going to and asked if I wanted to go. I told him I would go, and off we went across town to another party. Once there, I kept drinking until I was wasted again. I danced and danced the night away.

I would get all dolled up, go out, get drunk, and make a complete fool of myself. The party was beginning to wind down, and I had lost track of my friend. I went to the front of the place, hoping he would be looking for me as well, but he wasn't anywhere to be seen.

I found some steps to sit on—fall down on—and began to cry. Someone came from out of nowhere and softly asked me if I needed any help. From what I could discern, which wasn't much, he sounded as if he had a British accent. I did not know this person, but he was nice to me. He seemed to have good manners, being very polite. I literally couldn't see to go any-where, so I had no choice but to trust him. I felt as though I had a blindfold on, stumbling along the path as he led me to his apartment. For an instant, I became scared and blurted out that my boyfriend's mother—even though I didn't have any boyfriend—was waiting up for me. I couldn't call my mother and wake her up with my nonsense. That was out of the question. Besides, she would have killed me. So I continued with my made up story. I told this complete stranger that a woman who hadn't seen me in months was expecting me to call at any moment. Well, he called my bluff and said I could use his phone. I slowly dialed the number to "Mr. Blue Eyes'" mother at two in the morning, knowing this could be the only lifeline I might get if he was a murderer.

She seemed startled to hear from me, yet she was nice and said if I could get there, I could come and crash on her sofa. I hung up the phone, and the man asked me if she was going to come and get me. I thought, *Are you kidding me?*

He asked, "Do you need me to take you there?" I couldn't believe he asked me if I needed a ride. It was a thirty-five minute trek to my side of town, and again, I had gotten myself into a horrible mess and had no choice but to let this stranger help me.

He was very cordial to me on the way home from what I remember, because I dozed in and out of consciousness during the entire ride to my ex-boyfriend's house. I ended up getting there in one piece, and as I stepped out of his car, I thanked him profusely for his help.

In the wee hours of the morning when "Mr. Blue Eyes" came home, he discovered me sleeping on his parents' couch. One thing led to another and we got back together.

————————

There was a customer at the savings and loan where I worked who was rich, cute, drove a 'Vette, had a plane, and he and I had always flirted with one another. His name was Larry. He was just a neat guy. During the last several months, he had issued several invitations to me to come over to his house for a drink, but I never bit the apple.

However, for some reason, one night after work, I took him up on the offer. I lied to my boyfriend about having to stay late for a meeting. I just didn't know about anything anymore. I was justifying interaction with Larry by telling myself I had to make certain "Mr. Blue Eyes" was really the one I wanted to spend the rest of my life with.

My heart still seemed empty. Forever with one person was a long time. I wasn't certain I was really in love with "Mr. Blue Eyes" anymore. The feeling I had was more like, "I got you to crawl back to me and bow down before me. Now the thrill is gone." But he was the closest thing—in my mind—to David. I so desperately wanted the stability of being married and above all, being happy. But I harbored doubts as to whether he was to be my knight in shining armor.

The liaison with Larry lasted about three-and-a-half weeks. I didn't once mention to him that I had a boyfriend. They lived on opposite sides of town and chances were they would never run into one another, so I thought I was safe. Larry had been out of town for a business trip for several days of those three weeks, and upon arriving home, immediately drove to my home. We got in his car and on the way to his house, he stated that while he was away he couldn't get me off his mind. He wanted me to move in with him. He said he would give me anything I wanted. I could quit my job and live with him. The whole idea of it seemed surreal. I really didn't know him at all. I had proved to myself I could get him but I knew inside what I was doing wasn't right. I was really just done with the whole thing, knowing I was wrong for seeing him in the first place. Besides, I was scared of the unknown with no firm commitment. Familiar was more comforting to me. I didn't have the energy or the stamina for a brand-new relationship either. I didn't want to have to rehash all the things a new person would want to know about me. My childhood friend said he got tired of telling girls the same old things about his life, so he just started making stuff up to make it more interesting for himself. I wasn't into that. I was into many things, but not that—that was lying. I made my choice; I threw myself into the relationship with "Mr. Blue Eyes" 100 percent. And as for Larry, he stopped coming to my branch never to be seen again.

Christmas was on the way, and love was in the air. From the way my boyfriend talked to my mom and sister, he was going to ask me to marry him and give me a diamond for Christmas. He made a really big deal out of it. Everyone in my family seemed to be excited, and it made me excited. I was finally going to get what I had always wanted.

Christmas Eve arrived and it seemed magical. "Mr. Blue Eyes" had prearranged a big occasion at his parents' house in front of all of his family and extended relatives. What else could it be but a proposal of marriage? I was scared, elated, and shaking from anticipation. This was going to be it for me. I sat there and carefully unwrapped the present as everyone looked on. I looked at the box and thought it was oddly-shaped to have a ring inside. I opened the lid and there it was. I was stunned. I couldn't speak. It was a diamond all right, but it was a diamond *necklace.*

The look on my face, I am sure, was pure, overwhelmed shock. I could just imagine myself with egg on my face. They were all waiting with bated breath to see my reaction. I am certain it was not the reaction they were expecting, but I wanted *my* way, once again, and I hadn't gotten it.

I wanted a diamond ring. I couldn't believe it wasn't a ring. I sat there for a moment as if I were dead. To him, the necklace meant he was committed to me. It was a big step for him, considering that a few short years earlier he had told my dad he would not marry me when I was pregnant! He was giving it as a token of his commitment to me, but I took it as a slap in the face.

I cannot even imagine what his family was thinking about my reaction as they looked on. They wanted him to wait until he was twenty-seven before getting married anyway. Well, I knew I was not going to wait another three years to get married to him. I composed myself and pretended I was thrilled. I believe they took the shock on my face to be elation, but that was not the case. It took me a couple of days to calm down over it. I had to have several talks at the kitchen table with my mom over what happened, but finally, I came to realize that this diamond necklace was his way of saying he did love me and wanted to marry me. I bit my lip, smiled, and pretended it was okay ... but it really wasn't.

The following spring, we were officially engaged. This, of course, was after much discussion and arguing, mind you. The big night came. He planned a big "pop the question" evening with champagne and candlelight. He gave me the first ring his dad had given his mother. There was a condition issued to me that night concerning this ring, however. If anything ever happened to us, the ring was to be returned to his mother. It was pretty, but I felt like I was engaged to his father. It was as though I were getting second best. It was weird, but I finally got what I thought I wanted.

Arrangements were made, and he bought a townhouse for us to live in prior to our wedding. The understanding was he would live there with his best friend for six months so they could have one more fling at single life and being boys. *Whatever!* I was getting married—finally!

Wedded bliss was going to make me whole and happy. I had imagined getting married since pretending to marry my boyfriend in the first grade and having his dad's high school ring as my wedding band. I had imagined being in love since I had been a child listening to The Platters' *Greatest Hits*. This was what I had always wanted. I imagined showing up at the front door of our townhouse in my negligee and high heels with a drink in hand, meeting my husband after a hard day's work—just like the women did in the movies. There was much to do to prepare, and I was all about it.

I had just been promoted to branch manager at the savings and loan. That I had managed to keep my job there was in itself, I thought, a miracle. I had made strides in my personal convictions—trying to have a good work ethic—and had come out the winner. I think I had more sick time on my record in the beginning than anyone, but when I was there, I was a hard worker.

I had just won the Central Virginia Speech Contest judged by professors from the University of Richmond. I took home first prize, which was one hundred dollars—much to my amazement. No one from my institution—bank, not mental—had won this event in eleven years. It was made clear that the president of the bank wanted the title, and I brought it to him.

Everyone who entered the competition was expected to write a speech about saving money. I knew I couldn't write such a speech, but I knew I could deliver one. I called upon my brother, who was the big writer of the family. I talked him into writing a speech for me, promising him half the winnings if I was declared the winner.

The day came, and we went downtown to the contest. There were ten contestants. I was dressed in my all white "John Travolta" jacket and skirt with an aqua blouse and white high heels. My nerves were so "nervous" that I tanked up on two-and-a-half Valiums (5 mg. each) prior to giving my speech.

Instead of calming me down, my heart raced as I hit the podium. The name of my speech was "Acute Pecuniary Spenditis." The thought process behind it was how you couldn't save money because you had to keep buying something else to match what you already had. People laughed in all the right places, and a cheer went up at the end. The decision was in. I won! I was thrilled. I couldn't believe it.

I was called to the main office to deliver this award-winning speech to the board of directors. The promotion to branch manager came right after I won the speech contest. The victory of the promotion and the contest kept me doing that job better. The icing on the cake was that most of the board members were friends with my soon-to-be father-in-law. All the right components were set in place for me to have complete success in my life.

It appeared to everyone that I was on the way up—finally—but nothing could have been further from the truth. There was a tug-of-war going on inside of me that was becoming harder to keep under control. I felt both good and evil continually struggle within me—so much so that I couldn't let anyone know. I was scared to reveal my inner self to anyone, even family, for fear of what would come forth. People had started to hold me in high regard, and it felt good to be looked upon with respect and accomplishment. I believed I could just BS my way through this life, and somehow the dark feelings would eventually go away. The mask I wore became more cemented the longer I lived inside my own personal hell. My thought was, *Just keep going, and you'll get clear of this.*

The Presbyterian church my now fiancé and I attended sporadically was cold and had metal chairs. I certainly could not picture myself getting married there. We discussed it and decided to get married in an Episcopal church. My soon-to-be husband had been in the All Saints Boys Choir there when he was little, so there would be no charge, and the church itself was majestic. It truly looked like it was out of a movie. Now, *that* was me!

I picked my dress out of a magazine. I knew what I liked, and when I saw this dress, nothing else would do. I went to

Tiffany's in Richmond to buy it. My dad ended up paying for most everything, but not without a lot of arguing and fussing. We had a huge reception that included an ice carving with shrimp, two stocked bars, and a combo played as well. Still, to this day, there are people who say it was the best wedding reception they ever attended. I didn't eat anything at the reception due to excitement and not wanting to pig out in front of others, but believe me, I drank.

There were a bunch of us congregated in the kitchen area talking, laughing and having a high time, but when I slipped on the kitchen floor, falling down in my pretty white suit, someone piped up and suggested it was time I went on my honeymoon. I turned around to look for my dad. I might be drunk but I wasn't that drunk. I wanted to thank him for shouldering the expense of most of the wedding and for everything else he had done. I looked at him with all the love I had in my heart, and he said, "You don't have to say a thing." So, that was it. There were no more words exchanged between us about the wedding or anything else for that matter. I hugged and kissed him good-bye, and we were off. I was finally married!

I was starving as we pulled out of the parking lot to begin our new life together. The first stop we made was McDonald's. We stayed in the honeymoon suite at the hotel where my husband was working and left the next morning for Disney World. I had always wanted to go there—Pretend Cinderella. We drove because I was too scared to fly.

What a trip! We smoked dope on the way and took silly pictures of ourselves. I had managed to weasel out of having sex on our actual wedding night because I was so drunk. I had convinced my husband that we would have our honeymoon night when we got to Disney World. I mean—come on—we had already been having sex for years, and I had already had one abortion with him. I managed to put him off until Florida. I figured I could rise to the occasion by then.

After the sixteen-hour trip, I was faced with the honey-moon night. I can tell you for a fact that I was just not into it. My stomach ached, and I dreaded the thought of having sex with him, all the way there. I found myself trying to talk my way out of it once we arrived. It was awful.

He got upset, but I really didn't care. All of a sudden, I found myself on my honeymoon—*the* honeymoon I had waited for all of my life. I thought to myself, *This is what you wanted.*

I could have done without sex altogether. Well, sometimes I did want sex—just not with him. Something was dreadfully wrong, and I didn't know what it was. I just wanted to be married, safe, and settled. I wanted a normal life. I wanted a happy life, and deep inside I knew I wasn't happy.

GIVE ME A PILL SO
I'LL FEEL BETTER!

My husband managed the property of a local hotel chain, and for the first few weeks of our new marriage, his employers were very lenient with him in terms of the number of hours they made him work each day. That was, however, soon to change. He was eventually sent on a business trip to New York for three weeks.

Several nights into the trip, he called me with a big surprise. He and a couple of co-workers had taken a trip to New Jersey to hit the casinos. He said, "You are never going to believe what happened!"

I said, "What?"

He said, "I won nine hundred dollars!"

Naturally, my immediate thought was, *What's yours is mine.* When I alluded to my share, he said, "*I* won it."

I said something to the effect, "You mean to tell me you are not going to give me any?"

After a few moments, he reluctantly said I could have $250. My feelings were bruised, and I accepted it very sourly. He had an attitude about money that I really didn't like. I brushed it off and pretended it didn't hurt.

The "normal" thing for me to do in my new role as a wife was to imitate *being* a good wife. Something inside of me was fighting against it though. Nonetheless, I was going to make the effort since this had always been my dream.

One day I was talking with his mother on the phone, and she said that when her husband traveled, she would plant flowers or do something new around the house to surprise him upon his return. There was something ingrained in me that made me want to imitate the behaviors of people I saw on TV and in the movies. Therefore, if I heard or saw something that looked or sounded good to me, then I was going to put it into play for my life. I waited for the weekend to come—I didn't do much of anything extracurricular except on weekends—and decided I was going to become an avid horticulturist.

Saturday came and I headed to the nursery. I never went anywhere alone, but there was no one else to go with, so off I went. I knew nothing of flowers but made a purchase of several different types, feeling very grown-up, and headed back home to play the role of a good housewife … just like Donna Reed.

I was squatting in the front yard when my heart started to palpitate and race wildly. I became flushed and sweaty all over. I couldn't catch my breath; I got scared and jumped up, leaving everything all over the yard and ran inside. What was happening to me? Was I dying? Was I having a stroke?

My first thought was to call Mom. I managed to dial the numbers on the phone, and I uttered, "Help me!"

She said, "What's wrong, honey? Try to calm down."

I barely got the words out as I gasped for every breath. She talked calmly, and I listened. I couldn't cry; I could hardly breathe and could hardly hold a thought in my mind.

She said, "Molly, it sounds to me like your nerves."

Nerves? Okay, maybe I wasn't having a stroke. That realization calmed me down, but I wanted to know what was going on with me. A few minutes passed, and she said, "Why don't you come over here and stay with me?"

Okay, I thought, but how was I going to manage to drive a car in my condition? I pleaded with her to come and get me, which she did. It seemed as if hours passed until she arrived. I walked around the house, gasping for every breath until she got there. We packed a few of my things and headed for her house.

I sat in front of her TV, staring at the screen. All I know is there was nothing in my head—nothing. I felt as though my mind was going to float right out of me. All the years of thinking I was going to go crazy—it was really going to happen. My aunt would have been right; I was just like her. I also recalled the comment my dad had made about his grandparents, who both went insane. Thinking that my issue was something feminine, Mom called her gynecologist and made an appointment for me. He checked me over and discovered nothing physically wrong, but he placed me on a small dosage of Valium for several weeks.

I had been on Valium earlier but had stopped taking them because they made me sleepy. I lost any inhibition I had while I was on them and would pig out, causing my weight to balloon up. Then I would have to turn around and lose the weight I had gained. Up and down. Up and down.

All I ever had to do in the past was tell any doctor I was having chest pains, shortness of breath, or—of course, the old standby—that I felt "nervous." They would listen, look at me, and then prescribe a sedative. I knew all the right buzz words to say to get what I wanted to ease my pain. He handed me my prescription and referred me to a colleague of his, who he believed would be better equipped to help me. Now I took Valium as my lifeline, but I could only function at about fifty percent.

Mom and I headed for the next doctor. He was young, handsome, and caring, but even eye candy was not helping me. He listened to me and placed me on an antidepressant. I had never heard of such a thing, but it sounded to me like they were something given to crazy people. Bring it on—just help me! I returned for a follow-up visit to let him know how the pills were working. I told him they only made me feel funny inside. He tried me on a different kind of pill, but that one also made me feel weird as well. The reaction to the medication added to the fact that I already felt I was losing my mind was too much for me to bear. I apparently stymied the man. He threw his hands up in the air as he proclaimed there was nothing else he could do for me. He suggested to my mother that I go to a psychiatrist. He gave us the name of someone who was supposed to be top-notch in his field. I thought, *I really must be crazy.*

When talking with my in-laws on the phone, I would pretend everything was okay, which was exhausting. My husband was still away, and when he would call, I would cry. I didn't want to be labeled crazy. It reminded me of the kids in the neighborhood calling me "fatty." I tried so hard to fake the fact that I was happy, but the darkness that had settled in me was becoming too hard to mask.

I started rapidly losing weight. I could hardly swallow anything for fear of choking on it. I was not well. My mom was doing everything in her power to help me. I couldn't be alone, so I had to sleep with her at night for fear of something happening to me.

My husband had to come home from his business trip one weekend to be in a friend's wedding. I was still staying at Mom's and didn't want to go home, but I knew I didn't have a choice. I wanted to stay with my mother where I felt safe. Was he going to want sex? That was out of the question. I was actually afraid to tell him it had been suggested I go see a psychiatrist, but I knew I had to. After recounting the story of the doctor's visit to my husband, he said he just wanted me to be well; he wanted me "fixed." The weekend flew by. He left to finish his stint in New York, and I went back to Mom's house.

The appointment was made with the new doctor but I had to wait two weeks before he could see me. I was going crazy, and I thought, *How could his office make me wait for two weeks?* I managed to suffer through, and finally the day came for us to go to my next appointment.

I sat across from the first psychiatrist I had ever been around and watched him as he sat, holding a chart and clipboard in his lap. He seemed normal enough. He looked up at me and asked me how I was. I looked at him and asked the only important thing on my heart: "Am I going crazy?"

He looked me square in the eye and said, "People who ask if they are going crazy are not. It's the ones who don't ask that you have to be concerned about."

My answer had come. *Okay, so I am not crazy. I can face and deal with anything else,* I thought to myself as I sat there. The words kept rolling around in my heart, "I am not crazy."

I was not going crazy, so why did I feel like I was? It was as if those few words pulled me back from the pit of hell. My savior sat right across the room from me that day. He is the one who let me know I was going to be all right. He is the one who spoke those comforting words to me when I needed to hear them the most. That day, he started trying me on antidepressants, and counseling began. All I knew was that I was not going to end up miserable like my dad and aunt, and I would do whatever it took to stop it.

EIGHTY-FIVE PAIRS OF SHOES ON THE WALL

Each time I was tried on a new drug that didn't work, I didn't throw it away; I just put the bottle in the linen closet. I was standing at the linen closet folding towels one day and felt as though someone was pulling me back to take a closer look at its contents. I began to count the different bottles of antidepressants that were lined up on a shelf like little soldiers.

I began, "One, two, three, four, five, six," until I reached the number twenty-five. My doctor said these drugs were new drugs on the market, and it was a "process of elimination" until we found the group of ones that matched my physiological makeup. I trusted this man with my life, so I allowed him to use me as a guinea pig. Aside from that, I felt like I had no choice; I needed help. I always kept his emergency number in my wallet in case I ever had a bad reaction to any new drug. One afternoon I felt as if I was going to lose my sanity, which I was trying so desperately to hold on to, so I dialed his number.

He said, "Go buy a package of Sudafed and take one immediately." He assured me the weird, sick feelings I was having would stop. After hanging up with him, Mom and I raced to the local 7-Eleven and bought some Sudafed. I took one, and within fifteen minutes, the weird feelings subsided. From that moment on, I always kept some on me just in case I felt like I was coming unglued.

"My savior" diagnosed me with agoraphobia. I had pure, raw fear that manifested physically in the form of horrible panic attacks. I tried anything that was brought to my attention that I thought might help my condition. I took cold showers, which seemed to help my flesh calm down and lift the depression. He suggested I drive around with a paper bag in my car. That way, if I had a panic attack, I could breathe in and out of it, normalizing the excess of carbon monoxide, which caused me to gasp for each breath I took.

I would *always* drive in the right lane so I could pull off on the side of the road in case the unthinkable happened—I passed out. I felt it was also a safeguard against hitting someone as well. I couldn't bear to be in anything that was enclosed, especially elevators. My chair had to be near the entrance of any establishment I went into, or I would not go in. Fear crippled my life. I was running out of choices for groups of medications to try, and finally, the doctor prescribed something for me called Parnate, which became my deliverer. There were lists of foods and liquids I couldn't ingest—especially any kind of alcohol—while taking this medication. I had become only a social drinker by this time, even though there was a well-stocked bar in our living room. So not being able to drink was no big deal to me by now; anyway, Donna Reed didn't drink! I also fully understood the implications if I did drink while taking these medications, and it scared me into compliance.

Also, knowing I was down to the last type of drug that was even an option for me, I was determined they were going to work. The Parnate made me feel a little anxious, so he also put me on another antidepressant called Ativan, which helped take the edge off. Those two combinations of drugs brought me back to life. I felt numbed into existence but was able to cope without feeling like I was going to fall to pieces, and it was a relief.

Once a week on Wednesday afternoons, I would sit across the room from my psychiatrist and spew the pent-up hell inside of me; the anxiousness would deflate. I would walk down the steps from his office feeling a great sense of relief, which would last for several days. However, by the following Monday, things would be built right back up, and I would hardly be able to wait until Wednesday rolled back around again. Nothing ever changed; I just got older, but I wasn't about to quit going to the man who had helped save my life.

I was trying to run the branch of a savings and loan, but the pressure was starting to become overwhelming. I started to push the envelope, not considering the consequences of taking anything in addition to my meds. Every now and then, I would take a couple of hits off a joint in the evening. If there was anything left come the next morning, I would hide it in the ashtray and take it with me to work. I would drive around at lunch and take a few hits to calm me down.

There was a fireplace in our kitchen, and I wanted to sleep in front of it when nighttime came. I would get all of our bedding and bring it downstairs; we would build a fire, snuggle up, and pretend we were on a camping trip. This was a sweet escape; we even roasted marshmallows. This arrangement also helped keep me out of the bedroom and alleviated the pressure I felt there. Sleeping in front of the fire made me feel like I was on vacation somewhere else. Then morning would hit. As the light would hit the back window and dawn came, the feelings of sickness in the pit of my stomach would return. I hated my life. I wanted to die.

The first Christmas I was married, I ended up throwing the balls off the Christmas tree onto the floor because my husband had to work late again. I was so lonely, and the hours he worked were long. I threw a fit because he had to go to work again. He slapped me in the face because I wouldn't let up. I screamed, turned, ran upstairs to the bedroom, and then threw myself across the bed. How dare he hit me! My pride was wounded, but deep inside, I knew I deserved the slap.

I had such conflicting thoughts about him and the marriage. I wondered if I loved him. I wondered if we should stay married. I felt like he did not deserve all the horrible things I put him through but at the same time, I felt like I should not have to stay with a man who was never at home. I had gotten what I asked for, and I was not going to get divorced as my parents had.

My routine during the week was to come home and throw my clothes all over the bedroom—I felt I was justified because I had worked all day, and I was tired. On top of that, I felt sorry for myself because of the ailment I had. I always told myself I would straighten my bedroom out on the weekend. The truth is I really didn't even want to work. My husband made the comment he didn't want to work either, but someone had to make money in order for us to live. The memory of his mother coming to pack his clothes for our honeymoon floated through my thoughts as I listened to him. I just knew something was not quite the way it should be with any of this.

I had become very somber after the slap in the face, and one evening as I was cleaning up our bedroom, I wondered what was going to happen to me—to us. As I was realigning the shoes against the wall in my closet, I counted them. I didn't stop until I reached eighty-five. I was rather stunned. I wondered why I needed eighty-five pairs of shoes. Oh, well.

I concluded something was going to have to give between us. If my husband was going to have to work all the time, then I was going to try to be a good wife and go where he was. Maybe it would end up being fun. But I knew I had to do something to help our situation. There was a popular lounge in the hotel he managed, and he suggested I come down there on Friday and Saturday nights.

On his suggestion, I called ahead of time from work on Friday evenings, and he would have the chef create a dinner for me. Upon my arrival, I would be escorted to my table, and my husband would join me for dinner. We would sit, eat, and describe to each other what went on during our day. In my mind's eye, things seemed to improve between us. I also started to believe I was living out the TV show *Dallas*. I started going there every Friday and Saturday night, telling myself it was so I could be a supportive wife. *Saturday Night Fever* was a huge hit, and there was great excitement in the air as everyone wanted to learn to disco. I started asking friends and family members to come and join in the fun of it all. I would place an order for a drink—against instructions from my doctor—and sip it throughout the evening. Anyway, I felt it was harmless and I was having fun for a change. I would sit and watch others dance, longing to be on the dance floor myself, but knowing my husband was in charge of the hotel, I knew I had to keep myself in check and behave properly.

They had hired an instructor who was quite handsome to teach disco lessons to anyone who was willing to learn. He would show up in a tuxedo night after night. All the female patrons would swoon at the sight of him. With the urging of my husband, the instructor started asking me to dance. One thing led to another, and over the next several months, we started dancing every Friday and Saturday night as a couple. I learned to dance and loved every step I took.

My sips started turning into gulps, and I started to drink heavily. The more assured I became that I would not die from the medication and alcohol mixture, the more I drank. I built my tolerance level over the course of an evening—up to six double Black Jacks on the rocks. I prided myself in being able to drink nearly any man under the table. Then I would hit the dance floor and dance my heart away, having drunk my sorrows into the deepest sea.

Slowly but surely, I became attached to the dance instructor because of all the attention he was giving me. I was obsessed with going to the hotel on the weekends and dancing the night away with him. I thought of nothing else. I was doing something I loved for the first time in years, and I didn't care who liked it or who didn't like it. I had dance fever.

I had overheard someone talking about the Atkins diet. This no-carbohydrate diet claimed you could eat anything as long as it had no carbohydrates and still lose weight. It was a win-win situation for me. If a new weight loss fad came along— and it seemed as though there was always some new great way to lose weight—I would try it. So, I bit the apple and went on the diet. I recall one evening one of the waitresses on staff stating, "You've lost just about enough weight, haven't you?"

I smirked as I walked by and thought to myself, *Leave me alone. It must be working. I'll just lose a few more pounds.* I would lay on my bed to zip up my size seven jeans, and I loved it.

Happiness for me was at the bottom of a glass while dancing the night away. I was committing adultery with my dance partner in my heart, right in front of my husband's face, convincing him it was harmless. I craved attention. The thinner I got and the more looks men gave me, the more I wanted all of them to fall for me.

In the middle of all of this weekend nightlife, things at work started to heat up as well. I had become friends with an assistant manager at a local commercial bank. He stopped by my office one day to call on me, supposedly since I was a business account of his. I had an office in the lobby of the building I managed as well as an office upstairs that I used when taking loan applications. This was the first time he had been to my office, so I took him on a tour. We walked upstairs, went into my office, sat down, and started to make small talk. I was feeling very funny about the whole thing and was trying to maintain a professional demeanor when he suddenly blurted out that he had been on his boat with his wife the previous weekend, and all he could think of was me. He kept talking and said, "I want to leave my wife for you if you will have me."

My pride and self-worth were definitely being stroked. I had to go to his bank every day to make the deposit for my office, and I would always make certain that I was dressed fit to kill. I had played a flirtatious game with him, but that was all it was to me. I never anticipated a declaration of undying love, but it was certainly exciting.

I showed him my ring and said quite sheepishly, "I am married." I thought, *I can't have an affair with you. Besides, my heart is with the dance instructor.*

When push came to shove, I would only fantasize about other men. When they proclaimed they wanted me, the bubble would burst, shaking me into reality. I had egged him on, and he had taken the bait. He left that day and asked, "Would you think about it?" I told him I would, but I knew I had to make haste and end this flirtation. I sat in a stunned daze the rest of the afternoon, wondering what kind of person I was to drive a man to want to leave his wife.

I began to hate going to work each day. All of the pressure of my life was just too much, coupled with the responsibility of managing an office of a bank. I wasn't happy, and I was in a mess. I made the decision after talking it over with my husband that I needed to find another job. My whole life seemed to be a sham. My customers and others around me always thought of me as Miss Twenty-Four Hour Smile, but I was exhausted and unhappy. My husband said, "If that is what will make you happy, then do it."

The phrase that had been instilled in me from my childhood by my dad was, " If you are not happy, then quit." I hated to give up the title and the admiration showered on me by everyone I was around, but I was drowning and had to try to save myself. This was the only thing I knew to do. I was under the constant care of a doctor, but this situation seemed even beyond his realm of expertise, so I scoured the papers for another job without telling anyone of my decision.

I found a new job I thought might be the answer. I went to work as a teller at another financial institution. It was less pay but less pressure. I dreaded telling my in-laws I had resigned. They had such a high opinion of my position that it was hard for me to be "less than" in their eyes. I will never forget the disappointed looks on the faces of those who had admired me, even my dad.

Several weeks into my new position, I was sitting behind the counter and I felt as if a bucket of ice-cold water had been thrown on me. It suddenly occurred to me how good I had had life and the status that had gone with being a manager, but this time it was too late. I couldn't go back. I was stuck. I got what I had asked for once again, and I knew I had made a huge mistake.

I'LL BE HAPPY WHEN ...

Get married, have a family, grow older, retire, and then die was my thinking.

Years earlier my husband had made it clear he didn't want children. I had always believed if we were married and in love, I could change his mind. I had gotten what I wanted most of the time, and I figured I would get my way on this.

I became pregnant. I was very thin again and liked the way I looked. I was still carrying on my dance fever life, having a ball. I thought I could be pregnant and still be a hip chick. However, every Friday and Saturday night as I would leave the hotel, I would start thinking, *I just don't know if I want to have a baby.* I couldn't bear the thought of having to stop the only thing that had really made me happy in order to be a mother. I felt like I was in another life when I was at the hotel, and I didn't want to give that up for a life of the unknown.

I got scared and decided to abort the fetus. I just couldn't go on with the pregnancy. A lie was conjured up; we told everyone I had a miscarriage. I would always promise myself I would do life better and cleaner by not having another abortion—that I would get away from the heavy, dark funk that loomed over my life, but that time never seemed to come.

After the abortion, I was placed on birth control, and I was back to nightlife again. Push came to shove, and the dance instructor and I devised a plan to rendezvous one Monday. He was to call, and I would meet him wherever he said. I was in bed the morning of our clandestine meeting with a dark cloud hanging over my life. Thoughts of guilt and shame were rolling over in my mind as I lay there. I watched the clock and waited for the call that, much to my relief, never came. I rolled over, took my meds, and went back to sleep.

By this time, I was also on a mild sleeping pill. The psychiatrist I was seeing didn't help, really. Medication didn't help. Drugs didn't help. Alcohol didn't help. Sex didn't help—when I had to have it. Not even all of the attention from the many men I was around helped. I would get from one day to the next tanked up on meds, living for the next moment in my life. *I'll be happy when ...*

We were asked by my husband's employers to babysit their three children while they went to Las Vegas to attend a hotel convention. A week away from my surroundings was a welcome relief. I eyed a book lying on the table by L. Ron Hubbard entitled *Dianetics.* The book explained how you could think yourself into being happy. Maybe *this* was my answer! I began trying to speak and think myself happy, but after several weeks of putting forth a good effort and not receiving a quick fix, I gave up. I would get my hands on something new and try it, only to be left disappointed and in a worse state of hopelessness than when I began.

My dance fever lifestyle started to phase itself out as my husband was moved to manage another property location. However, I wasn't ready to let go of the only thing that had made me happy so easily. I had my dance instructor come to the new place, but it wasn't the same. It was as if something was trying to stop all of this extra weekend nightlife. As much as I tried and tried to hang on to it, my best manipulation didn't work this time.

The psychiatrist I had been seeing for about three years suggested I start seeing his wife, who was a psychologist. I had no idea what a psychologist was. I didn't really like the thought of leaving his care, but I had come to a crossroad with his counseling, so I was open to his suggestion.

I began therapy with a woman doctor. From our very first meeting, I knew we would not get along at all. I would walk into the room and she would quietly stare at me until I would say something. In other words, it had been determined that she was going to try a different tact with me. She always made certain to remind me to leave my check on the desk beside the door as she said, "Our time is up." That made me resent her. Wasn't I more important than a dollar bill?

––––––––––

Once again I stopped taking birth control and became pregnant. This time, however, I was determined the pregnancy would not be aborted. I was going to have this baby, come hell or high water, and no one was going to stop me—even myself. I stood at the top of the stairs crying, telling my husband, "I am not going to have another abortion." Somewhere in the back of my mind, I thought having this baby would help me get on a stable footing, and I just wanted someone in my life who loved me unconditionally.

I dreaded telling my new doctor I was pregnant, but knowing I would eventually start to show, I had no choice. I told her the news, and the scowl that appeared on her face after hearing my news made it obvious she was not happy with this new development in my life. I left her office that day and made the decision to stop all counseling.

Having something tangible on which to focus started helping me overcome the inner darkness I had always known. I knew I was not going to be able to enjoy pregnancy if I had to face her sour attitude week after week. I had a knot in my stomach every time I had to go see her, and the familiar ache had returned as well. This, coupled with her attitude about money, only added fuel to the fire, and I was going to put this fire out.

I went one day specifically to tell her I was going to quit therapy and did not intend to return. I did not beat around the bush. I told her bluntly and boldly that after I left that day, I would not be back to see her again. She was clearly taken aback but said she wanted to see me for at least three more sessions so we could wrap up. I reluctantly consented.

When we met again, in the middle of the session, she said, "You should not be having a baby. You are not fit to have a baby."

I left there that day, went home to my husband, sat on the steps, and just sobbed. He told me to call her and tell her that I would not be coming back, and that is what I did. After four abortions already, I did not want to hear I was unfit. I really hated her. Who was she to tell me that I couldn't have a baby?

GOOD-BYE TO DIETS

I threw caution to the wind and chucked all diets. I was finally going to have a baby. I made an appointment with an OB-GYN. This particular doctor happened to be a friend of my husband's and they frequented the same gun club. He told me that I would be able to stay on my medication—thank God. He let me know all was well with my pregnancy, and I was relieved to hear that.

Even though I was nauseous for the first three months, for the first time, my heart and mind were at peace. I felt good; I felt relieved, and I felt happy. I was getting all the attention I wanted, and I was able to focus on something other than myself. I stopped drinking and smoking. Giving up smoking was quite an achievement, considering I never did anything without having a cigarette in my mouth. The amazing thing to me was that I was giving things up in my life that I loved—making the sacrifice for someone else. The feeling was euphoric.

I allowed myself carte blanche, and it was not long before I was putting on weight too quickly. The doctor told me I had to stop gaining weight because my blood pressure was getting too high. There was an ever-growing concern about me contracting toxemia, so I started dreading the scheduled appointments for fear of him getting mad at me.

I started to make a more concentrated effort not to eat as much out of fear of becoming sick. I went to my next scheduled doctor's appointment, and much to his amazement, I had lost a quarter of a pound. Believe me—I didn't do it on purpose, but I took the credit. The doctor was elated at my progress, which in turn made me feel good about myself. That afternoon my dad called to see how my appointment went. I told him the big news, and he began to laugh. I said defensively, "What is so funny?"

He said, "Molly, that is like an elephant taking a shave."

The pregnancy continued and the due date of May 18, 1981 was fast approaching. I felt happy, contented and complete inside. I got up one morning and just felt different somehow. I got dressed and went to the hospital to visit my sister who had just given birth to a baby girl. I returned home very tired and got in bed that evening with a big bowl of ice cream. I was propped up in bed, having just licked the last of the Hershey's syrup off the spoon, when I felt an odd kind of cramp.

The teachers at our birthing classes said, "Try not to eat any food after you go into labor, because you will throw it all up." I hated throwing up worse than life itself. Now all I could think of was throwing up all over the place right in the middle of delivery. *Would I choke to death?*

Though not unbearable, the cramps started to come more frequently. We were told we had hours to get to the hospital once they started and not to rush getting there. We timed them, and they seemed to be about five or six minutes apart by early morning. We made the call to the doctor, and he said to meet him at the hospital. I took a shower and got dressed. We put my bag in the car and headed off to have a baby.

The doctor checked me and said I had only dilated a centimeter. He sent me home with a sedative and told me to get some rest. I was told I could stay this way for weeks. The cramps did not stop, and we ended back to the hospital the very next morning.

I was hooked up to a monitor and was told I was definitely in labor, but I had not dilated. They tried everything they could to induce hard labor, but nothing helped. Twenty-four hours passed with no delivery. I had fallen asleep, and upon waking I didn't see my husband in the room. I was told that he had gone home to get some rest.

I was furious. He was tired? All he had been doing was lying in a recliner. I called my sister-in-law and told her I was going to divorce him. I couldn't believe he had left me there alone. I realized that I was not the first woman to have a baby, but this was *my* delivery—my baby—and I was scared. Where was my husband? Where was the rock to lean on? He showed up the next morning at about 6:00 a.m., and the first thing I did was throw up when he walked into the room.

A feeling of dread came over me; I felt that something wasn't quite right. Without knowing why, I started begging the only God I knew to let me have this baby. That was a pretty gutsy thing, considering I had four abortions under my belt. However, I was gutsy when it came to getting what I wanted. *I promise! I promise! I'll do better! I'll take good care of the baby! I promise!*

All of a sudden, the doctor and nurses rushed into the room. They flipped me over on my right side. The baby's heartbeat had dropped to twenty-three beats a minute. Two nurses rushed into the room, huddled in the corner, and started whispering. I saw one of them hand a syringe to the other one.

I said, "What is that for?"

I knew, however, what they were thinking. They thought the baby wasn't going to make it, and they would have to knock me out. I just knew it. Maybe I wasn't going to make it either. One of them said, "Don't worry about what this is for."

My husband was told to get changed and to meet us in the delivery room. Off I went. They placed a blue sheet over my stomach and tested for pain, and the doctor made the incision.

The doctor asked my husband if he wanted to take a look. He stood up, peeked over the sheet, and said, "Molly, it's just like guttin' a deer!"

I thought, *How neat!* as I rolled my eyes.

My husband and I had listened to the girl in the next labor room screaming her head off saying, "Get this baby out of me!"

I already had purposed in my heart I was going to be tough when it came time to deliver my baby. I had listened to many horror stories about childbirth, so I was already scared to death. But deliverance was in front of me, and I was going to have to get through it and be a trooper no matter what the outcome.

My husband and I just *knew* we were going to have a little boy. Secretly, I didn't want to have a little girl because I didn't want her to be like me. I had two nephews, and I knew how to treat boys. I had grown up with two older brothers and had played with all the boys in the neighborhood. The doctor pulled and pulled, only to have the baby keep slipping from his hands. He kept grabbing and pulling, and I thought, *Will it ever be over?* I didn't utter a word and finally, our baby emerged! My husband whispered in my ear, "Molly, he has the biggest penis I have ever seen." The doctor said, "You have a little girl, skeet shooter."

A girl? We looked at each other in shock, and I quickly asked him to check and make certain all her fingers and toes were there. He said, "I think so. Wait, I think she is missing her little toe on her left foot." But after a closer look, we discovered her toe had tucked itself around so you couldn't see it.

The two nurses who had been standing in the corner turned and walked out of the delivery room. For my baby to be healthy at all, I thought, was a true miracle. God had heard my prayer, hadn't he? The long penis turned out to be the umbilical cord, which was wrapped around her neck; that had caused the long labor and difficult arrival. I knew one thing for certain; she was not going to be like me.

BREAKING UP AGAIN ...

About a month before my daughter was born, I was sitting on the couch watching a variety show. Neil Sedaka came on with his daughter, and they sang the most beautiful song together. I had no idea it was his daughter until the end when she was introduced. I watched her speak and move, and she appeared as though she could just eat her daddy up.

I thought to myself, *If I ever had a little girl, I would want her to be as sweet and pretty as this girl seems.* Her name was Dara. That was the name I chose for my daughter. From the moment Dara Ann was placed in my arms, there was a love that emanated from me I had never known before. She was sucking on her index finger, and I thought I would squeeze her to death.

I was now responsible for another human life. Having her in our home was like waking up to Christmas every morning and unwrapping a beautiful gift. The feeling was not what I would call weird, yet it was something that shook me to my very core. I couldn't seem to take my eyes off of her.

I was on pain meds in the hospital and was kept on them for a couple of weeks thereafter. They gave me a super high and made me feel like I could do no wrong. I loved being on them, but as soon as I took my last one, I started feeling very down, even though I was still on my antidepressants. The tendencies I had always possessed were still there; having a baby didn't make them go away. The only thing that had changed about me was that I was a new mother. By now, we had been living in our townhouse for close to three years. We were growing as a family, and we wanted a house. Buying a home was another diversion and gave us something to focus on other than ourselves. With our minds made up, we started searching for just the right one. During our search, we discovered that the house where we had kissed for the very first time (do, do, do, do) under the big oak tree was available. It needed major attention, so we went in and totally redid it. With our new home looking just the way we wanted, what else could we do but have a party. All the stops were pulled out, and we invited everyone we knew. We had many amenities available for our use that were lent to us by the hotel where my husband worked. We had a dance floor brought in and set up in the living room. Two video games were set up on the screened-in porch. We borrowed tables and tablecloths and set up a taco bar in the living room. We had all kinds of liquor and a keg of beer.

Everyone had a good time. All the people we invited got sloshed, including the president of the bank where I now worked. My old dance partner showed up, and we danced a few dances, but the thrill was gone. I even tried to make time with a guy at the bank where I now worked, but thank God, he said, "Molly, you are married."

The house was beautiful, and I was still miserable. I was sitting on the couch in my perfect living room one evening, staring at everything—trying to take it all in. My wedding portrait hung over the fireplace. We had new furniture, and I went in there to contemplate my existence to see if I could gain a new perspective. Everything seemed clean, fresh, and new in there. I wanted that "newness" and "freshness" for myself as well.

I had liked sitting alone on the front porch to draw when I was young. It was a place where I could also go and think my own thoughts. I always came away from those alone moments with a renewed sense of "better," and this night I needed to feel that my life was going to be all right. At some level inside I knew things were bad all the way around in all of our lives, but I honestly didn't know what to do. I couldn't seem to fix the problem. I desperately needed an answer.

My husband came in and said, "Why are you sitting on that couch?"

To him the living room was used only when we had company. I had grown up having the same thing instilled in me, and I understood what he was saying, but it evoked something in me.

I stated, "This couch is just as much my couch as it is your couch. I have every right to sit on it anytime I want."

Things between us were not good. We existed in our glass house, polishing everything for everyone to look at and having them believe there were no smudges. Nothing could have been further from the truth.

"Doing life" set in. You know—working nine to five, just to make a living. I had what most people strive for their whole lives. One morning my mother-in-law and I took a walk. She asked me point-blank why I wasn't happy. My reply was the same whenever asked that question: "I don't know."

She said, "Well, you better get happy, or you are going to lose everything you have."

I said, "I know."

I couldn't seem to stop whatever had me bound, no matter how hard I tried, or what I did.

The conversation with my mother-in-law made me realize that I had to do something. Nothing had been resolved for me by simply having a baby, and if anything, it made things around the house worse. The issue of who worked the hardest always seemed to be hanging in the air. I was still the same person I had been; nothing had changed. The old ways and feelings were cropping back up; they had never left. The new home only helped for a while, and then it was back to the same old routine of life, and I hated it. I hated myself for feeling this way.

My husband's long hours hadn't changed, and when he came home, I expected him to assume his responsibilities as a father and take over caring for the baby. After a long day, I needed a break. All it did was drive a deeper wedge between us.

———————

The name of a Christian psychologist popped up at work. I decided to let him have a shot at me. Something deep in me felt that if this doctor believed in God, then it might make the difference in his ability to help me. Perhaps he could get to the root of me and all the crap inside—what I was feeling and dealing with. If he could help me get well, then my marriage might have a chance of surviving too. I explained to my husband that I was going to try to help myself get happy. He was supportive of this decision and even drove me to some of the sessions.

The panic attacks had started to resurface. I was still taking medication, but it barely seemed to help anymore. I had to continue to check in with my first psychiatrist as well because I discovered my psychologist was not allowed by law to administer medication; he was not a medical doctor. They knew of one another and agreed to work together for my benefit.

After several months of individual sessions, the psychologist suggested I attend group therapy. I winced at the idea because I liked having the undivided, individual attention from the doctor, but I wasn't progressing. In fact I was having a tougher time with the panic attacks but did not know why. He was the doctor, and I had come to him for help, so I hesitantly started group therapy.

I had lost all of my pregnancy weight because I wanted to be a good-looking, fit mother. Then gradually I started eating more, and the weight began piling on. My old habit of getting up in the middle of the night to eat resurfaced. I would wake up to find empty wrappers lying all around and would realize I had been on a nighttime raid. I came up with the bright idea of putting a chain around the refrigerator to keep me from ransacking its contents. It was the only thing I thought would help stop me from eating, but I broke through that too.

Upon arriving home from therapy, my husband would anxiously ask me when it would be over. He wanted to know when I would be well again. *Over?* I had no clue! I would smile, put on my pretend face, and tell him therapy was helping and that I was certain it wouldn't be much longer.

One night I went to "class," as I came to call it, and something inside of me felt different. I arrived that night, walked into the room and noticed everyone in attendance. There were times when, for this reason or another, one or two would not show up. We had become a somewhat close-knit group—in a clingy sort of way. We cared for one another. Everyone had issues; some were worse than others, to be sure. Hearing their stories didn't make my life easier, but it let me know that others suffered too. I was not alone and it wasn't all about me.

All of a sudden, I blurted out, "I don't think I want to be married anymore."

The statement just flew out of my mouth. I felt scared, yet relieved. I had been with my husband for about ten years, off and on, and had been through so much with him I was scared of what would happen without him. I was unhappy and sick of my life. I just wanted to be happy. I didn't know what the consequences would be if we separated. I didn't stop to consider anything, especially my daughter. On the drive home, I thought to myself, *Have these years been a farce?* I held my tongue as I walked into my home that night, keeping the secret in my heart that only others knew.

D-I-V-O-R-C-E

Even though I felt that our marriage was over, I didn't say a word. Coming to the realization of this fact did something inside of me. I became more sullen in my nature for a while. I was content to let things be as they were because of the fear of the unknown. I did my best to hold out, but something in me was pushing me to blurt it out. I had always vowed I would never get divorced and hurt my children, but I just knew this train was bound for inevitable destruction.

I was at home watching *Moonlighting* one evening when things finally came to a head. I called my husband at work to find out when he would be coming home. He said he would have to stay and work late again, and I just blew up. I was sick and tired of him hardly ever being there. We ended our conversation in a very nasty manner. About forty minutes later, he marched through the back door, headed for the bedroom, and proceeded to pack his bags.

He came downstairs into the rec room where I was sitting, walked over to the back door without glancing at me, turned around, and said, "Is there anything you want to say to me before I walk out that door because, Molly, when I leave, I am not coming back."

I continued to stare at the TV set without making a move and said, "No."

I knew he would be back. I would lose weight, and he would come back. It was a pattern we had lived in for so long, why would it be any different now? He slammed the back door and left. I continued to sit there and think it was just a matter of time. Maybe in a week or two he would be back, we would pretend to be in love, and everything would be okay.

Day after day went by and he didn't call or come home. I would wake up in the mornings with the familiar ache I had grown up with as a child. I would wonder what in the world was going on. I was barely able to get up and get dressed. Dara was the only thing that was keeping me going. I would manage go to work, pick up Dara, come home, hunch down in the corner of my room, and wail out to God, "Why did you let this happen to me? Where are you? What am I going to do now? I *hate* you for allowing this to happen to me!" I would continue to scream, "Help me! Where are you?"

I would rage on and on. I would cry and cry until I thought my stomach was going to turn inside out. Dara started sleeping with me at night. We would huddle up together in the king size bed, and I would hold her tight, not certain if it was for her or for me, and she would doze right to sleep. I had to finally explain to her where her daddy was, so I lied to her, telling her that he was away on a business trip but would be coming home soon.

We were asleep in bed one night, and out of the blue, my husband showed up. She was thrilled to see him. I was happy to see him, thinking that maybe he was home to stay. But he had only come home to pick up some of his things, and out the door he went. He was oblivious to Dara. He left us both there crying that night as he walked out the door. I tried to soothe her the best way I knew. Emotionally I was still a child myself, but I was going to have to be strong now for the child I had brought into this world. What had I done to her, and what in God's name was going to happen now?

Christmas came several months later. Time and circumstances had emotionally worn out both my husband and me. Our daughter needed us, so he had begun spending time with her again. The spirit of Christmas helped, and we were able to pretend our lives might be fine for the sake of our daughter. We were sitting on the couch in our rec room in front of the fireplace talking late one evening after we had put Dara to bed. I could see that all of this was draining him as well, and he almost stated he would come back to me. However, there was something I could not put my finger on that was keeping him from returning home.

As a last ditch effort we turned to the only pastor we knew. We made separate appointments with him and met for counseling sessions over lunch. My meeting ended up with me blaming my husband and his long work hours for our failed marriage. As I got up to leave, I did so carrying with me the belief that he would convince my husband to come back home. I put all my trust in this one man to put us back together again.

I had to stop therapy because I didn't have anyone to watch my daughter. I thought blurting out my loveless marriage was the answer I needed in order to come to terms with my life, but I soon discovered it was not the answer; I was still a mess. I knew I had to buck up and do something, but I was in such turmoil. Now I was faced with having to turn my focus on my separation from my husband and attend to my daughter, who was not doing well due to the upheaval in our home life.

My husband called stating he wanted to come over and talk to me. He walked in, and the feelings between us were icy. He had a seat and said he had come up with a list of ten things he wanted me to change about myself; if I would, he would come back home. The first thing he wanted me to do was lose weight.

I tried to remain calm, knowing I had to hold my tongue if I wanted him to come back. I agreed to this stipulation. He continued with the next item and then the next. The list he held in his hands brought back to my memory the list my dad kept of all the money his children had borrowed. What was it about lists? Heat started to rise within me like a volcano, and I knew I was going to erupt. After about the fifth thing, I said, "Forget it! What about the things *you* need to work on?"

I was furious. His comments about my need to lose weight, stop counseling, and get "fixed" were nothing short of cruel.

It was downhill after that. I took off the engagement ring—his mother's—and threw it at him as I stood there spouting off at the mouth. Then I said, "And why don't you just put the house on the market and sell that too?"

We had only lived there for about a year and a half. He stormed out the door, and that was that, but I somehow felt that the storm still wasn't over.

———

My husband jumped at the chance to put our house on the market. He promptly brought over a contract for me to sign. I hesitantly signed on the dotted line since I was the one who had opened my big mouth about it. Besides, I didn't think anyone would really buy our house, and if it did sell, I thought it would take a while.

My daughter and I had gone to the movies the following Sunday afternoon. I walked back into the house, and the phone was ringing. It was my mother-in-law. She told me that there had been a cash offer on our home, and I had thirty days to move. The house had only been on the market for three days! I sobbed and sobbed, and she asked me why I was crying. I said, "I don't really want to sell my home. I don't want to move, and I don't want to get divorced."

She said, "Well, it's too late now."

I hung up the phone, sat down at the kitchen table, and cried. I didn't think I was going to be able to stop. Yes, my daughter caught the brunt of my emotions. She started crying too. Dear God, what was I going to do? I didn't want to leave my home—my beautiful home. Where would I go? Who was going to help me?

I had worked for the past five and a half years by this time at the same bank, working my way up to assistant manager. Then an announcement was made that our president had sold the bank to a larger one in town. He made a deal for each of us so that we could keep our jobs, but an equal position wasn't guaranteed. I was transferred to another office as an assistant manager, so I was relieved.

I got along well with the co-workers, but from the get-go, the manager did not care for me. I hadn't worked there long when my husband and I became separated. I would go to work, start crying, go into the break room, and not be able to pull myself together. I couldn't bear the thought of having to pretend to be helpful when my life was going down the toilet, but I tried, only to fall apart.

It was time for my annual review, and I walked into the conference room where my manager and a co-worker were sitting. She had given me a warning previously that my work performance was not up to par, so for the previous ninety days, I had made more of a concentrated effort to do better. They both sat there staring at me and stated I was not going to receive a raise because I just wasn't performing up to expected standards. Here I was thinking that my work ethic had improved considerably, but clearly, they thought differently. My complete work history was spread out before them. I had always had good job performance ratings, excluding my attendance, and now I sat face-to-face with someone who was going to "allow me" to keep my job but not give me a raise. I had counted on that raise.

Most all my life, people liked me, but there were those few and far between who really just couldn't stand the sight of me, and I could feel it. I would always recall the statement my mother had made to me when I would encounter people like this: "If you will be nice, they will be nice." The harder I would try with these few people to be nice, the more they didn't like me.

So there I sat. The thoughts that went through my mind that day were wide-ranging. How dare she be so heartless! I was the girl who had worked her way up to being a branch manager of a large financial institution in my early twenties. I had won an area-wide speech contest and received the accolades of man. I had left my management position due to stress and then started all over again as a teller. I worked my way back up to the position of assistant manager at this new bank and was in the depths of a serious personal crisis. I had heeded the warning and done better, but that didn't matter to her. I knew deep inside that nothing I could say would be enough.

Everything I was putting my hand to was falling apart little by little, piece by piece. The last ninety days had meant nothing to them. I tried not to cry, but one tear slid down my cheek; then they all started to follow. Before I could stop the words, I blurted out, "I have had enough. I need to stay home with my daughter anyway; she needs me and I quit."

I was shaking all over as I cleaned out my desk to leave. I was so furious, but I didn't say one word. It was over, and there was no use trying to say anything else about it. I didn't even know what was going to happen to me as I walked out the door, but one thing was certain in my heart: I could spend some time with my daughter and help her heal. She needed me.

My daughter was still so upset over her daddy leaving. He came over early one evening to get some more of his things, and when he turned to leave and get in his car, Dara ran after him crying and sobbing, asking him not to go. I thought maybe my being with her consistently for a while would help her heal somewhat. But after that incident, I knew I had to do something more. I ended up doing the only thing I knew to do. I took her to the psychologist I had recently stopped seeing. I wanted an opinion on her mental state, from not only a professional standpoint, but I wanted to hear from someone who was not involved in our lives on a day-to-day basis. He saw her alone, and then he talked to us together. He recounted his time with her to me, saying that he told her a story about a family of birds who lived in a tree. The story went like this: There were three birds. The daddy bird flew away, leaving the mommy bird and the baby bird. He said, "What happened then? Can you finish the story?"

She replied, "The daddy bird flies back home with the mommy bird and the baby bird."

Hearing her answer almost did me in. I felt horribly guilty about what I had done to my only living child. I thought of myself as some sort of a monster.

Those days shook me up enough to get me going on the right track again. All I knew was that for right now, I didn't have to work. I could stay home with my daughter. I moved us into an apartment. I was trying to make some kind of a life for us, but I knew I was winging it. I felt like I was at a loss. I just got up and carried on from day to day, but it seemed like it was all a blur. I tried to stay happy in hopes that my ex-husband would see the change in me and come back. I also tried to stay on good terms with his family, who wanted to be around their granddaughter. I put on my happy mask and kept doing what I knew how to do. I had heard of couples reuniting after divorce ... maybe it could happen I thought.

I had received half of the settlement from the sale of our house, but not without a fight on my ex-husband's part. He argued that his money bought the original townhouse we lived in, and therefore, I was not entitled to get anything. I had to go see an attorney because this obviously was not going to be settled between us in a civilized manner. I hated confrontation, but I knew that for my daughter's sake, I needed to fight back. I then had to take him to court for child support. He was not amicably going to hand over anything. We had argued endlessly over an amount for monthly child support. He called the night before we were to appear in court and offered me $225 a month for her support if we would settle out of court.

I said, "If you will give me $250, I will do it." He said, "No." So I said, "I will see you in court."

The judge hit his gavel the next day and said, "Four-hundred-fifty a month support, plus all medical and dental for the welfare of your daughter. In addition, you will pay all expenses of your wife's attorney."

My ex-husband flew out of that courtroom enraged. It was always about the money with him. It was like déjà vu all over again. I had had to argue with my dad about it years earlier, telling him if he ever left my mom, sister, and me, that we would take him for everything he had. He had to end up paying a huge amount of alimony. Why did it always boil down to putting a price tag on love, feelings, and hurt children?

Of course, no one in my now ex-husband's family and none of his friends could understand how this had happened to poor him. The so-called friends I thought were mine turned out not to be. They all sided with him. I was becoming increasingly aware of the fact that I had literally griped him out of the house, yet I also knew it took two to tango. There was his side, and there was my side, and the truth was somewhere in the middle. The year was 1987.

DARA AND ME

It had been almost six months since I quit my bank job, which allowed me to have some quality time with Dara. Wounds began to heal—hers more than mine. I was becoming increasingly aware of the fact I couldn't live without more income. I had child support and a savings account, but that was not enough. I felt stronger as a person and believed I could weather holding down a job and managing a single-parent household now.

I had no real expertise in anything except banking, so it was a natural step to look for a job in the financial sector. I scoured the Sunday newspaper, and—lo and behold—my eye caught an ad for a bank manager. I got all dressed up, went to the interview, and was hired on the spot. It seemed like a miracle to me.

The financial institution I had worked for years earlier had been bought by another firm that hired me. The building I was to manage was the exact same building I had managed previously. It still had some of the same customers I had been privileged to help. It was also there where I had spoken the very last words to David, telling him I loved him. It was really do, do, do, do, once again.

This particular financial institution had twenty-four offices. I ended up running the third largest in deposits, amounting to fifty-three million. I had a good salary, a company American

Express credit card, and I was riding high. I felt rejuvenated and ready to go back into the merry-go-round of life.

Things went well for me there. As I said, I knew banking inside and out, and I really put my nose to the grindstone. I performed so well that the vice president stood up at a meeting several years later and stated that if anyone needed to know how to run a branch office, I was the one to call, because apparently I was the only one who knew how to run one. If anyone were to look at me, they would think I had it made. I held a prestigious job, I made an excellent salary, and I had a beautiful daughter. I seemed to have it all. I was certainly back on top of my game.

I had only signed a six-month lease at the apartment complex where we lived. I felt that before the money in my savings account dwindled away, we needed to invest in something of our own. I wanted a stable home for my daughter, and providing one for her would ease my conscience. She depended on me, so the most coherent thing I did at that time in my life was buy us a townhouse. We moved again to a nice, established neighborhood. A family lived up the street that included a girl Dara's age. My daughter seemed thrilled to have a playmate and someone else to spend time with.

The upheaval in my life and home and in my daughter's life had taken precedence in my mind. However, the monotony of my new life caused dark feelings to resurface once again. On the flip side though, I felt euphoric due to my new station in life.

An old love interest discovered I was the manager of a bank and newly divorced. He was hot on the phone to call me, asking me to lunch. This same man rejected my advances during the party my ex-husband and I had thrown at our new home, but things were different now. He came to my office, and the girls nearly passed out at the sight of him. We were both kind of nervous as we got in his car to go. As we left, he turned to me and asked me if I was hungry. I said, "Not really."

He said sheepishly, "Well, what do you want to do? Go to a motel room?"

Without hesitating, I said, "Yes."

He came over a couple of times to the townhouse, but as it turned out, we really didn't have anything in common. The big love affair I imagined we were going to embark on really wasn't anything at all. I had gotten my way though and had finally made my conquest.

Every time Dara spent the weekend with her dad, I hit the bars. I would go to the most popular dance place in the city, meet a guy, get wasted, and then take him home and go to bed with him. The next morning I would invariably wake up with a horrible pill and alcohol hangover. I had been doing this long enough by now to know how to somehow manage and get it together by the time my daughter returned home.

Unfortunately, my ex-husband and I played the "he said, she said" game, and our daughter was caught in the middle. Both of us were very immature. She stopped telling either of us anything in regard to one another.

I had put Dara in daycare for several months, but then my sister piped up and said that if I paid her, she would pick her up after school and keep her until I picked her up after work. I felt like this would give Dara a more normal footing, and at the same time, I didn't feel so guilty about what I had done to her. My sister had two children, and one was a girl four days older than Dara. Dara and her cousin were like twins. Even with everything that was going in her home life, Dara had as normal a childhood as I could provide for her, and I *did* try. She was in the first grade by this time, and I had given her a picture of her daddy and myself in a little frame to take to school with her so she wouldn't think we were going to leave her. I would tell her repeatedly how much her daddy and I loved her and that she was our main concern.

She would still cry for her daddy sometimes at night. I would be holding her in my arms as she would cry, and she would say, "I want to talk to my daddy." I would dial his number and give the receiver to her so she could talk to him. She would be soothed again for a brief time.

Her teacher called one day requesting a conference with me. She said the first thing my daughter would do upon arriving at school was open the lid of her desk, take the picture out, and position it on the corner. Then she would start to cry. This went on for several weeks.

I explained the situation at home, and this gave her some insight and understanding into why Dara was behaving the way she was. Dara was resilient and with the help of her extended family, eventually things got better. After a while, she liked going to school.

The first year was ending, and her teacher wanted to see Dara's father and me for a year-end conference. She suggested that we think about having her repeat first grade. Dara being held back had nothing to do with her grades; it was based on her emotional state, and it was purely a suggestion for us to consider. The teacher stated that she, too, had been held back in the first grade due to home life and that it had given her time to mature and catch up with the other children.

Her dad got all red in the face and stated, "No, I don't agree with her being held back."

I believed the teacher had her best interests at heart. Dara's teacher saw her every day and had even taken her out to dinner one evening. Dara loved her first-grade teacher. Since I had full custody, I went against my ex-husband and had Dara repeat first grade. After what my daughter had been through that year, if this would help her, then so be it. The big surprise for Dara was that she had been assigned to the exact same teacher the following year. One night, as I was tucking her in bed, she asked, "Mommy, I like the first grade. Can I stay in the first grade again next year?"

I started to laugh and said, "Honey, you only get to go through the first grade twice."

We hugged and said prayers—the exact prayers I was raised with—and I felt she was happy again finally, thank God.

Time went on and I was getting restless because of the routine of life. My mom, sister, and I were invited to a wedding in Huntington, West Virginia. I thought that maybe a change in my normal routine could help me gain a new perspective.

I was going to see childhood friends at this wedding, some of whom I hadn't seen in years, and this prospect excited me. I always treated the friends I grew up with as if they were something more than they really were because of childhood memories, but I hadn't kept in touch with any of them for several years. I always thought that I would renew old friendships when my life settled down, but that never seemed to happen; my life never seemed to settle down!

I got all dressed up for the big event and proceeded to get sloppy drunk at the reception. We were staying at the hotel where the reception was, so I was within walking distance of our room. A few hours into the reception, I was spent so I fumbled up to the room, peeled my clothes off, and passed out. I got up in the middle of the night, as was my custom, to raid the fridge. The only problem with that was that there was no fridge in the room.

I stumbled out the door of our hotel room onto the balcony, not knowing where I was or, for that matter, where I was going. I couldn't see, and everything was dark and blurry except for a few city lights sprinkled here and there. The only thing running through my mind was that I needed to get back to my room.

I groped in the darkness, discovered a doorknob I thought was to my room and I entered. I tried to get my eyes to focus somewhat and saw strange people lying all over the floor and on the beds. A heat flush went all over me and I became scared, turned around, and tripped back out the door. I found myself standing on the balcony again and began to cry. I felt I was in a labyrinth and couldn't find my way out. I looked out into the thick night air and begged someone to help me, but who was going to help me? It was the middle of the night, for God's sake!

Anyway, somehow—and I don't even know how—I got back to my room where my mom and sister were. I crashed and fell asleep on the bed. I woke up the next morning feeling like a ton of bricks had hit me, not even knowing where I had been the night before. It was hours later when it all started to flood back into my mind, and when it did, I got a really sick feeling inside. I didn't dare tell anyone. What would they think about me? I took all my antidepressants, got in the car, and slept all the way home. *How had I gotten back to the room?* I wondered.

I wanted a Norman Rockwell life, though I don't recall any drunks in his paintings. I still was waiting for it and it seemed to be taking much longer than I thought it should. I just couldn't seem to make all the pieces fit. The ingredients were there at times, but they never all seemed to come together at once.

One evening, my old dance partner called, wanting to come over to my townhouse and talk to me. Even though I knew I had nothing in common with him, I was lonely and pondered on "us."

A knock came at the door. I was all dressed up and there he stood with a Bible in tow. I invited him in and asked him if he wanted something to drink.

He said, "Coffee, please." *Coffee?* Well, this was a switch! Why does he have that Bible in his hands? He won't put it down! We made some small talk, and then he started preaching Jesus to me. He was not going to budge from that Bible. I couldn't move him from his stance. Nothing moved him.

He definitely was not interested in coming on to me. He kept telling me about Jesus. He kept telling me how his life was turned around now. *Good, but let's get together.*

Well, I thought, *that's nice for you, but I have to get on with my life. I'll do Jesus much later, thank you.* I was not ready to give up everything I loved and go around in a glazed daze with a plastic smile on my face, telling everyone how happy I am in Jesus. No, thank you. And yes, Amy Grant was a cool Christian, but even she wasn't enough to really get me to give up my life for something unknown. Besides, I knew God. I grew up in Sunday school and church. I knew everything—probably more than all of them put together. I wanted them to get out of my face with Jesus.

I had a few more brief encounters with him. I was determined and very hardheaded in my belief that I was going to break through his wall of defense. I was hot on the trail to have a man—any man. I just wanted to get married again, thinking that would be the answer to my unhappiness. The answer was not the Jesus he kept trying to sell me. I wanted to be settled within myself, and I wanted to have a stepdad for Dara. Then I would finally be happy, wouldn't I? We eventually stopped calling one another, and things just fizzled out. He knew my take on the whole Jesus thing, I knew his, and that was that.

It was time to move on and hit the bars! I met a guy one Friday evening who appeared to be out of the norm. He was wearing a suit and tie—that was a change. He drove a great car, and I assumed he had money too. Wrong! Not all that glitters is gold.

After a few brief months of dating, he asked me to marry him. I will never forget sitting at my desk at work talking to my ex-husband's mother. She would call me about Dara, and we would engage in light conversation. One particular day, we did more than just lightly visit. She really made the decision for me about marrying the guy from the bar, even though she didn't know it. She told me my former husband was getting ready to be married again. I said, with a sinking feeling in the pit of my stomach, "Does he love her?"

She said that she thought he did. I had always had a glimmer of hope we would get together again. His impending marriage killed that notion altogether. I shot back, "Well, tell him that I am getting married too."

MARRIED LIFE, AGAIN!

In a moment of jealousy, I had sealed my fate. The question had been asked, and the answer had been blurted out of my very big mouth. My ex was getting married, and I was jealous—plain and simple. He always seemed to be so happy and on top of everything in his life; that made me sick. I wanted that, so I purposed to make it happen for myself again.

There was a lot to do. My fiancé and I took a day off to prepare for my next wedding day. We drove to get our wedding license. He parked the car, and after some hemming and hawing, he finally blurted out, "I have something to tell you."

What now? I thought. He continued, "I have been married before."

What? It took me a few minutes to get over the shock. *He forgot to tell me about a previous marriage?* He talked a mile a minute, going on and on about how the marriage didn't mean anything and it was only something he did because he was young. I thought his tongue was going to get tangled up.

Hello! Talk about an ice-cold bucket of water in the face! That should have been a warning to me to stop what was about to happen, but dumb old me—I said, "It's all right, don't worry. Everything will be fine. Everybody makes mistakes."

I also believe my pride got in the way and would not allow me to just walk away and tell him to get lost. I had already made most of the plans myself; besides, I had already told everyone. What else could I do? Someone was trying to tell me something, but I just wouldn't listen. Deep within, I already knew I shouldn't marry him. The day we were to be married, I stood in my living room and wished for someone to just come over and stop me from what I was about to do. I had heard a story of friends who kidnapped the prospective groom to keep him from certain destruction. *Please someone, kidnap me! Shake me—slap me back to my senses. Help me.*

No one did. My neighbor stopped over to say she was sorry she couldn't go to the wedding. I didn't want to hear that; I wanted her to beg me not to marry this fruit loop. She knew he wasn't quite right. Her husband knew it too. Satan personified walked right through my front door, and I invited him in and married him.

My life was starting to spiral downward again, and I seemed powerless to stop it. Right after we were married, my new husband started to become physically and verbally abusive. He would actually strangle me as we had sex. Out of fear I started sleeping with a knife under my side of the bed, tucked between the mattress and box spring. I remember him asking once where his favorite knife was. Well, it was on standby, ready to stab him.

He would drink nonstop every evening; he would put a pint of rum away every night. I started drinking with him on work nights—which was not my custom—just to drown him out. By the time he was completely sloshed, I had already tucked my daughter in bed for the night. She didn't see that part of our existence. She had always fallen asleep easily. It would take her about fifteen minutes, and she would be out like a light and not wake up.

I had managed to save up about $3,000 in a relatively short period of time while working in my new position. I got up to get dressed to go to work one morning, and I was standing at the dresser putting my jewelry on. My new husband defiantly stated he was going to take $1,000 from my savings account to buy a gun. Something in me winced at that statement. I remained calm as I continued to stare straight ahead in the mirror. I recall taking in a deep breath and then silently thinking, *Well, he is your husband. What's yours is his, and what's his is yours*—though he didn't have anything. I was afraid of him and did not know what he would do if I did not consent to letting him withdraw the money, and I did not want to find out.

He had a friend who belonged to the same gun club as my ex-husband. All of a sudden, he wanted to be an avid shooter. We would go to the club on the weekends when my daughter was with her dad. I found going to the hunt club boring, and I hated it. But I had pretended to like it when I was married to my first husband, and by God, I was going to pretend to like it for my second husband—the devil himself. I always tried to mold myself into what I thought would make others happy. I was doing it for someone I didn't really even like, but the behavior by then was second nature to me. Trying to build this man up from his lack of self-worth and self-esteem took more than I had in my bag of tricks. It wore me out mentally and physically. I hadn't acquired a lot of tools in my years of therapy that would help me with anything he had. I wasn't going to admit I had made a mistake quite yet though. I had developed enough inner strength and nerve by this time in my life to help protect my daughter. No one—and I mean no one—was going to touch her. I knew I was going to have to be tough to weather his antics.

Late one evening he got so drunk he slipped and cut his arm on the wall. I mean, come on—how do you cut your arm on a wall? Nevertheless, he managed to do it. It was a big gash, which was not going to heal without being stitched up.

The hour was late, but I called one of my brothers to come over and watch my daughter while we headed for the emergency room. Evidently he talked about committing suicide to the staff doctor. I had been sitting in the waiting room for what seemed to be several hours. I had made numerous inquiries about the state of my husband's well-being and finally, the doctor came out to talk to me and told me my husband needed help. He said he could have him legally detained if he needed to but that he needed psychiatric help. I knew that by then, but I would never have told him he needed to seek mental help for fear of what he would have done to me.

My husband had previously told me I needed to be on lithium for my mood swings—as if he just picked a drug out of thin air and said I needed to be on it. Like a fool, I did go to see a new psychiatrist, hoping it would shut my husband up. Strangely enough, this doctor did put me on lithium after performing a series of tests. I guess I was having mood swings from living with someone who scared me to death. The doctor asked me in a caring way if I was having problems at home; I lied and told him no. I was scared of what would happen if I told him the truth.

The doctor walked me back to his hospital room. As expected, my husband pleaded and begged me not to put him away. Then the promises started. He would stop drinking, he would go to a psychiatrist, and he would work at getting himself together if I just wouldn't put him away. I fell for his lies and signed him out.

By the time we left the hospital that night, the alcohol was wearing off, and he started to become sober. We got home, my brother left, and we went to bed. We were sitting up in bed laughing about all that had happened. He would try to make me laugh when there was a serious matter at hand. It really wasn't funny to me. I was laughing more out of nervousness than anything else.

About 2:00 in the morning, we heard a loud banging on the door. He got up, went downstairs, and opened the front door. I then heard him calling to me to come downstairs and bring his pants with me. Dara was sound asleep. There were six police officers standing in the middle of my living room, and they handcuffed him to cart him off to a psychiatric hospital. The whole time he was trying to weasel his way out of it, but no amount of slick talk worked this time.

I was humiliated beyond anything I had ever felt before. What in God's name had I done in my life to deserve this jerk? The doctor who examined him earlier that night had him taken to Westbrook, a mental hospital. The doctor told me he was a danger to himself and others and that he didn't need my signature to have him committed. He let me take him home, but he said upon further reflection, he thought better of it. The doctor decided he needed to be locked up.

I was trying to run a large office of a bank, trying to keep my daughter happy and untouched by this man, trying to hold on to what dignity I had left—which by that time really wasn't anything at all—and my "had to have a man" husband was putting this added burden on me. After several days, the date was set for my husband's bond hearing to determine if he was fit to be released. I had been to see him several times before the hearing was to take place. He would sit at a table with a Bible and proceed to tell me how he had given his life to Jesus and was determined to do better. He said he didn't belong there and was actually helping several other men reconstruct their lives.

I took the bait, of course. I was always willing to believe and give anyone the benefit of the doubt about anything they said, especially if they were in the throes of despair holding a Bible. It made me immediately accept what he was saying, so I forgave him for acting like a jerk. I pushed all he had done to me deep down inside. I did not want to have to think about it. Have you ever seen a devil sitting before you holding a Bible?

Due to my position as manager in the same community where the hospital was, the judge said he would release him to me on the stipulation that he seek counseling. He ended up going one time and left halfway through the session; he said he was never going back. In a moment of weakness, he let slip the fact that the psychiatrist told him he needed serious help during his session.

Well, immediately after this intense appointment with the psychiatrist, he wanted to have this wonderful Christmas. He assured me things would be better ... blah, blah, blah. He also promised my daughter that he would take her to Disney World. He went to the train store in town and spent several hundred dollars on a train set, which he put around the Christmas tree. I thought to myself, *I am not into trains, and why are you spending this money?* Trains and guns were *his* toys. What a bunch of crap and lies. It all made me want to vomit, but I tried to stay composed.

I invited his parents to stay with us that Christmas. *Poor little hurt boy. I'll mend you and your family,* or so I thought. It reminded me of trying to mend my dad and his family when I was young. I certainly would to try to fix them all if I could.

My townhouse was two bedrooms with one full and two half baths. His parents arrived and we set them up in our room. We decided to camp out on the floor in my daughter's room. That evening after dinner and after his parents had gone to bed, he stood in the middle of the living room and held a gun to his head. His parents were upstairs in our bedroom listening; I am certain of it. He stated he was going to blow his brains out with the new .357 Magnum he bought himself for Christmas. I looked at him, and the very first thought that crossed my mind was, *Molly, how did you get here?*

The Christmases I had as a child and when previously married were never like this, and this was the last place I wanted to be on earth. I didn't want my daughter to be there either. My next thought was a wish that he would blow his brains out. I just wanted this sick, sick man out of my life and my daughter's life forever. He proceeded to pull my hair and tell me that I needed to get on the floor and put my daughter's toys together. He let me go when he remembered his parents were upstairs. I started to cry. I cried myself to sleep on the couch. It was the worst Christmas I had ever had.

I woke up to him gently nudging me and saying, "Wake up! Merry Christmas!" All of my daughter's toys had magically been put together. He had a grin on his face while he said it. I had to remember his parents were guests in our house, and I had to pretend that it was a very merry Christmas. It was a make-believe existence, but as long as my daughter was happy, I didn't care what happened anymore.

Time marched on and I became pregnant. I know—I couldn't believe it myself. *Maybe if he just had a child of his own to love,* I told myself. I had a knot in my stomach when I found out. I didn't even like having sex with him. The same dull ache was back that I had when I was little and scared.

I knew I did not want to be connected to this man in any way, and having his child would have given us a permanent link for the rest of our lives. I had an abortion. I told my daughter that I had a miscarriage. I wanted Satan incarnate out of my life. Why was it that I could never be happy with what I had? Why did I think I always had to have a man to be happy?

My job performance began to suffer because of the hell I was going through at home. I was barely maintaining at this point; I would call in sick so I could get some peace while he was at work. It would be such a relief. He had talked up the Disney World trip so much to Dara that the following spring, we went. He talked me into taking a second mortgage out on my home, paying off all of his debts, and using the remainder of the money for the trip. I was in a tangled web, going from one mess to the next. We bought a new car right before we left so we could have a nice ride down there. He drove a sports car, so we obviously couldn't take that. We traded in his sports car for a more expensive four-door sedan.

Disney proved to be an unpleasant and destructive trip. I tried to clothe him properly in name-brand clothes, but you can't dress the devil up. We were going to look like a perfect, wonderful little family, but nothing could have been further from the truth.

He thought he looked like a movie star. He wanted to wear a certain pair of white pants this particular day, but I had failed to have them altered. He was furious. He put my daughter out on the balcony and grabbed my arm, almost breaking it, while calling me names. I thought, as he had me in his grasp, *I have enough money in my account to fly Dara and me home,* but I lost my nerve and couldn't do it. Why was I so scared to ditch him there?

He calmed down after what seemed to be an eternity. I regrouped, putting on my perfect façade for Dara, and off we headed for the Magic Kingdom. I will never forget letting Dara buy anything she wanted in Disney World; I wanted that trip to be for her. I wanted to make up for the fact that I had divorced her daddy—to make up for him not coming home. I knew this was not the man I needed to be in Disney World with—or anywhere else for that matter—and he was not the role model I needed my for my daughter. The man I was with was evil—clear and simple. Why in the world couldn't I leave him? The remainder of the trip was uneventful, but we never ate anywhere that did not serve alcohol. It's what kept him calm, so I didn't care. As long as Dara was happy, I thought, *to hell with him.*

The following Thanksgiving, he was planning a hunting trip. He demonstrated so much sorrow in his good-byes it would have made you weep. He could have won an Academy Award for the performance. He told me there were no phones where he would be staying, so I wouldn't be able to reach him. He left the Wednesday before Thanksgiving, and I was relieved to have him go.

The following Saturday morning as I was waking up, something told me to drive by a particular apartment complex in town. My husband mentioned one night during one of his drinking binges where his ex-girlfriend lived. This complex was right on the way to my daughter's dance class, so that day, out of curiosity, I turned in and started looking around for something. Without question, I knew just what that something was. Would you like to take a guess whose car I discovered in the parking lot? That's right. I told my daughter to sit tight; I walked up the steps to a cluster of apartments and started banging on doors. One girl opened her door and kindly asked me to stop. I told her that I was looking for my husband. Who do you think opened the very next door?

Mr. Hunter stood right there, and he knew I had caught him red-handed. He was fuming mad. He tried to blame me for being nosy. His slick, wily talk managed to get him back home, but only because I had hometown friends coming in to stay with us that weekend. I didn't want my friends walking into our crap, so we faked it for them, and I faked it for my daughter.

I also discovered that he had been taking a muscle relaxer. He had a doctor at work who prescribed them for his back problem, and he took them like candy. He was always tanked up on them, on top of all the booze he was drinking.

All the while, my ex-husband seemed to be having a happy life, which made my life seem all the worse. I became jealous of him, his wife, and their life together. I was relieved when it was time for Dara to stay with her father and his wife every other weekend. I felt as though she was in a happier place and that she was safe.

I would work all day, pick my daughter up from my sister's, and then go home and be expected to work around the house until I went to bed. I was never allowed to sit down once I got home. I started staying at my sister's house for a good thirty minutes longer at night so I could rest before I had to face you-know-who—Satan.

I had the presence of mind one day to call the hotline for abuse, inquiring about what I could do to seek help if he started becoming more mentally and physically abusive. I also wanted to know if there was anything I could do on my part to prevent further attacks. They said that they would have to catch him in the act of abusing me before they could do anything. How would that happen? How would I call anyone if he were trying to kill me? That he would do it when my daughter wasn't there—was all I could hope for.

THE ICING ON
THE CAKE

At lunchtime I would go to my office upstairs and put my head on my desk to sleep for thirty or forty minutes. I was totally exhausted. My home life was horrible. I don't know how, but I was able to maintain a professional demeanor with my customers just the same.

I always strived to do the right thing, even at my worst moments, but I knew I was slipping. One of the girls in the office wanted my job, and I noticed her listening to my every conversation, watching my every move, and trying to butter me up more than usual. I had received high accolades for three and a half years from this company and its vice president, but I knew something was in the air. There were some things going on in that institution that were to the detriment of the customers, and there were about five of us who had gotten together to see if we could come up with some alternatives about these particular issues.

One morning my area manager called and said she was coming to see me. In the meantime, another so-called manager friend called me all flustered and said the word on the grapevine was that there were five managers being let go that very day. I got the dreaded ache in my stomach but didn't actually think I was one of them. In the course of our conversation, it was revealed that the only way I could collect unemployment—if it came to that—would be if I were fired. If something weird was in fact going on, I could never depend on my husband for financial help.

I had never been "one of the guys" at this particular bank. They wanted me to play their games, but I couldn't, and they didn't like it. They were a partying crowd, and to be one of the "in crowd" of this institution, you had to party with them. Many times their meetings were held on weeknights, and I couldn't go out with them often because of Dara. Rumor was that they thought I was a goody two-shoes. I had taken my job quite seriously, as far as my work performance, and I treated customers with the utmost respect and honesty. I obviously was doing something right, however, because my branch was successful, and they knew it.

When my area manager arrived that morning, she was all business, and the dread hit my stomach. She asked if she could speak to me for a moment privately. We walked into my office, and she closed the door behind her. I walked around the desk and had a seat in my chair, and she looked frozenly at me and said, "Due to your substandard work performance, we have to terminate your employment effective immediately."

I sat there stunned for a moment or two, and then I asked her point-blank what I had done to deserve this. I went through the facts and figures of what my office had done the last three years, and she just stared at me with an unemotional look. I started to cry. I continued to explain my case, but it was to no avail. I argued that I hadn't done anything wrong to deserve this, and she said coldly, "If you don't resign, we will fire you."

I again reiterated my position—that I had done nothing worth being fired over. That is when she said, "You are fired." Just like that, it was over. I was in shock as I gathered my things to leave. You could hear the silence in the office as I walked out the front door. I got in my car and wondered what in the world I was going to do. This was the place that I had been administered the Meyers-Briggs test, and ironically enough, I was the only one out of the whole institution who was correlated to Abraham Lincoln. I would never have done anything worth this, and I was in a state of shock. As I drove home that day, the dread flooded over me, as I knew I had to confront the devil.

The day I was fired, five other managers were asked to resign as well. They all were able to secure subsequent jobs in banking due to the fact they resigned. I, on the other hand, had been fired. I discovered much later that they were paying my replacement substantially less than what I had been making. It all started to make sense then; money was always the bottom line.

Of course, my husband seemed to be sympathetic. I had no clue what the process was when something like this happened. I had to attend a hearing to determine if I would be awarded unemployment. My former employer was present by speakerphone, and my fate was to be determined by a judge who didn't even know me. I was very nervous about all of it. I felt like a criminal. Both parties presented their cases. At one point in the process, the judge even rolled his eyes in disbelief at statements made by my previous employer, as he looked at the performance record they had faxed him. I was awarded twenty-six weeks of unemployment benefits. What a relief! I made it over that hurdle but had no idea what to expect next.

Having the comfort of money coming in gave me enough time to find a job. What I didn't realize is that the day I allowed that company to fire me, I sealed my own fate. No one in town would hire me for any bank position, though an ad did pop up in the Sunday paper several weeks later that gave me a glimmer of hope. A girl I had met at the very first savings and loan I ever worked for was now the vice president of a local savings and loan in another county, and they were advertising for a manager's job. She knew me, my work history and ultimately, offered me a management position.

Because of what was going on in my life though, I knew I couldn't accept it. My history thus far had been turbulent, and I did not want to take the chance of letting her down. I ended up declining her offer for the position. My most important concern was my daughter, and I did not want to have to make a forty-five minute drive to get to her if she needed me. Maybe I was wrong, but I didn't have the advice of anyone I felt knew my life and situation. I felt alone and knew I only had myself to depend on.

I finally got a job with a health care agency. My income was nowhere close to what I made as a bank manager, but at least I had a job. I felt things with this new job were progressing nicely, but sixty days after being hired, I was fired. Computers were just coming into the marketplace, and I had a hard time understanding them. My heart just wasn't into working with computers, but everything else I was asked to do came naturally; I did it with ease. I had just started getting my feet wet and was learning a new field of business, thinking I was doing a good job, but the woman who hired me called me into her office one day and fired me. I couldn't really believe my ears. I was stunned and sat there in shock. She said I was hired on a trial basis and that it just wasn't working out. What a mess! I left there relieved that I wouldn't have to face that boss anymore, because for some reason, I irritated her. I began the process of looking for another job, but this time, I was not collecting any money from unemployment.

———

Due to all the hell that was coming at me from all sides, I had gotten heavy again. My husband thought that if I just had a professional dress, it would fix everything, so he took the liberty of going to buy me one. I had been out, and when I came back home, there he stood, half drunk, with the dress that was going to turn my whole life around. Of course, he had forgotten I had worn suits to work most of my life.

I was sick of him. I started to work out again in an attempt to lose some of the weight I had gained. My husband had the guts to tell me how his ex-girlfriend would work out all the time. One day while working out, I thought I was having a stroke, so I drove myself to the emergency room. I thought, *Well, finally, I am going to die.* I suffered from panic attacks, but this did not feel like that. There was something different happening——a heavy pressing on my chest that wouldn't go away.

The ER doctor was very kind and kept me overnight to make certain I was going to be okay. He ran some tests and said that he didn't think it was a stroke, but to make absolutely certain, he wanted to monitor me for twenty-four hours and would make a determination the following morning.

This incident was the final straw; this proved to be the beginning of the end of my marriage to this man. They found nothing wrong with me. It was all stress-related. My family knew, to some extent, what kind of animal he was, but I never told them any details. I kept hanging on because I didn't want to fail at another marriage. He had moved out once before, and I had let him come back because I just had to have a man, but this time, I just wanted to be rid of him forever. I came home, and he left the following weekend.

I was afraid that he was going to come back and try to kill me. I felt he wouldn't harm my daughter, but I knew he was capable of killing me. His sister called my house one day after he left. She said she had talked to her parents and they all wanted me to have him committed. All I knew was that I wanted nothing more to do with him or his family ever again. I wanted to erase all of them from my memory. Why were they calling me? His sister said that I was still legally married to him, and as his wife, I could have him locked away. I actually thought about it for a split second. Then I realized something. I knew that if he ever got out of wherever he was, he would come after me for doing such a thing.

He kept calling me, trying to weasel his way back into my life, but that was absolutely out of the question. It was over, red rover, and you aren't coming over. He got angry at one point, and I made the mistake of telling him that his parents wanted me to have him committed. Well, he got furious and hung up the phone. He called back several days later and told me he confronted them with this statement, and they denied ever having said such a thing. I do understand why now; they were just plain scared of him. I barely managed to keep up a façade for my daughter through it all. To this day, she calls him "black cloud." I just ask her not to even speak the name that makes me think of him—at all. We were legally divorced June 26, 1990.

I AM NOT A LIAR,
HONEST INJUN,
AND SUICIDE

How about an emergency room director's position? Now, that would lift me up out of my state of depression! I had no idea what particular skills or resources a person needed to have to qualify for this position, but I figured if I could run a branch office of a bank, that I could do this job. Think about all the doctors I would encounter! I was hungry again for something better and for something that would give me a renewed sense of self-worth. I called about the ad in the paper and went late one Friday afternoon for the interview.

I hit it off immediately with the woman who was in charge of hiring. She was excited about my professionalism and my working knowledge, and she hired me on the spot. The salary was excellent, and the job came with good benefits. I had lost weight, "black cloud" was gone, and it appeared that once again my life would turn around.

Monday came and I went for my employment physical. I gave my name to the receptionist, and she ushered me to the general manager's office. I wondered about this but thought that perhaps this was routine procedure after a new director had been hired. I walked in, sat down, and the woman who hired me appeared. The general manager proceeded to tell me that I had lied on my résumé; therefore, they were terminating my employment with them.

I replied, "I didn't lie." They looked at one another and then at me quizzically, as if in disbelief.

The woman who hired me the previous Friday had been to a party over the weekend. My old boss from the health care agency who had just fired me was in attendance. They started discussing the new emergency room director's position, and guess whose name came up in conversation? The prospective employer said that I had not even mentioned this previous job on my résumé.

I proceeded to explain to them why I hadn't listed the job. I had been advised by the unemployment office to leave the health care agency job off of my résumé since I had only worked there for sixty days. They said, "Everyone usually gives a ninety-day trial period, and since you only worked there for sixty days, it will make you appear as though you have been job-hopping."

I continued, "That is the only reason I left the job off the résumé." However, in my new employer's eyes, I had lied. I told them I felt uneasy when the agency advised me to do this, but what did I know? I had never been in a predicament like this, and they were supposed to be the employment professionals. I started to cry and couldn't seem to stop, and they got very quiet. I was not a liar and would never have done that unless advised to do so. I got up to leave; I was in a state of shock.

———

Dara was with her dad the following weekend. I purposefully bought a bottle of Jack Daniels Black——and I sat in the middle of my living room. I had a death wish. I tipped the bottle up to my lips and I drank until I couldn't drink anymore. Yes, I knew I was mixing liquor with my depression medication, but I didn't care. I drank in the past while taking them, but this time I was going to drink until my heart stopped and I died.

Speaking out loud into the atmosphere I cursed the day I was born. I cursed my very existence. I started to sob, and I drank and drank and drank until my lips and throat were so numb I couldn't feel them. Maybe my heart wouldn't stop. Maybe I would just choke to death instead. I didn't really care how it happened. David was dead. I was on my second divorce after having married the devil himself; he had taken me for everything I had. I already had five abortions, and I was hardly able to provide a good home for my only daughter. I wasn't a good mother and I was a whore on top of it all. I knew I was flawed but I couldn't seem to stop my behavior. I was going to have to file bankruptcy, sell my townhouse, and turn in my car. I couldn't get a decent job. I hated myself. Dara would be better off if I weren't alive. She would be better off without me in her life and her dad would support her beautifully. I drank until I passed out and woke up two hours later. I looked up to heaven and screamed where I thought God might be. I said, "Why do you keep letting me wake up?"

DR. JEKYLL AND MOLLY HYDE

I began to scour the papers for a job and answered an ad from a dental office in search of a manager. I made the call and much to my amazement, they were interested in meeting with me. I was hired on the spot with virtually no questions asked about my work history. I was ecstatic.

Yes, I had plumped up again, and my teeth also started aching and bothering me quite a lot. I had free dental care, so one afternoon I was given a free exam. The troubled areas were fixed, but the doctor—my boss—had to end up giving me Vicodin. I could work twice as hard, twice as long, and was able to go hours without eating. Another added "benefit" to this drug was that I could feel high without having a hangover. The feeling Vicodin gave me was euphoric but it didn't fix my life. I seemed to drift from one day to the next—collecting my paycheck—I was going through the motions of living, not feeling much of anything about life.

"Black cloud" found out where I worked. I was lonely and his voice was very enticing. I talked with him a couple of times but felt very strange inside after hanging up the phone, as if something was very wrong. I mulled him over in my mind for several weeks, talking with him three times and then thought to myself, "What are you doing?" This man literally destroyed your life. Are you going to let him creep back in again? The very next time he called, my heartfelt emotions about him finally came out and I blasted him with the truth of what he had done. Before I hung up, I made sure to tell him never to call me again. I knew he was sick and he was never coming near me or my daughter again. That was that.

I established a payment method in the dental office for patients to be able to pay on credit, and the dentist was very pleased. I started trying to collect unpaid, old debts he had, and I sent out letters notifying customers of due balances. I believed that was a part of managing the office efficiently.

He came into work several weeks later and said he wanted to see me after work. I went into his office and sat down. He said he had customers calling him at home complaining about the letter that I had sent them. He said I was ruining his business, so he handed me a check for two weeks' salary and let me go. I had been there about five months, and frankly, I was relieved. For some reason, I had dreaded going to work there every day. I felt lost, scared, and lonely, and I wondered what I was going to do next.

I had become friends with a patient from the dental office who worked for a huge insurance company. She had been tugging at me for weeks to come and interview where she worked, so I called her up. I was given an interview and hired the very same day.

Health care insurance—now that was something different. I settled in quickly to my new job. I had my own cubicle which was situated in front of my friend. My duties included answering anywhere from sixty to one hundred phone calls a day, helping customers resolve medical claims, and answering any questions they had. I liked helping people, and since this only involved phone work, it gave me an opportunity not to have to confront people face-to-face. I felt I always had to be "on." Doing this gave me a break in order to regroup mentally. Occasionally, a customer would come in requesting to meet me for being so kind and professional to them on the phone. My reviews were good, and my employers liked me. I was able to go in and do my work without anyone bothering me. I felt like a wounded puppy that needed to be soothed. I managed to keep my exterior façade, but a façade was exactly what I was putting up ... How had I gone from managing a 53 million dollar bank to doing clerical work, barely able to survive?

My friend and I were able to converse anytime during the day, and we became rather close. She was lonely and wanted to have a man to love. We decided one day that the next time Dara was with her dad, we would go out on the town dancing. Besides, where else do you find a man? What harm could one night possibly do? Time to lose some weight!

The Mr. Hyde in me couldn't just settle for one night—oh, no. I started going out every weekend Dara was with her dad. I never drank at home, but when I went out—that was a different story. I would get fixed up to the nines and hit the bar. I drank until I couldn't speak, and my friend always made sure I got home safely. Most of the time, I would argue with her that I was perfectly fine to drive, so she would reluctantly hand me my keys and watch me drive off into the sunset. I would drive home with one eye closed to resolve the double vision I had, and somehow, I would make it home unscathed.

We were at work one day after having a wild Saturday night. She looked at me intently, telling me first that she was my friend, and then she said, "I have something to tell you that you might not like."

I took a deep breath, sighed, and said, "Go ahead." I couldn't imagine what she had to say. What had I done now?

She said, "You are a sloppy drunk, and I am not going to go out with you again until you stop."

Well, I thought, *the nerve of her!* Who did she think she was anyway?

I was finally being called on the carpet for my behavior. It was as if someone had taken an ice-cold bucket of water and dumped it on my perfect façade, my perfect figure—I had gotten small again—my perfect hair, perfect makeup, and my perfect little imagination. I stopped drinking, almost cold turkey. We went out a couple more times together, and when we did, I really didn't drink a lot. I was amazed at how different everything appeared when I was sober.

TEN BEAUTIFUL NAILS, FINALLY!

I stood outside one day after work and looked up into the beautiful, blue sky, where I thought God might be, and asked out loud, "What do you want me to do? My life is a mess."

In the course of one week, people from three different places told me how pretty my nails were. They would ask, "Where do you get your nails done? They are so pretty."

My reply was always the same: "Phar-Mor, for about $2.36." I had to stop having my nails done professionally because I couldn't afford it. I was looking in the nail department there and a thought came to me. *I bet I can glue some fake ones on—reshape and polish them. No one would be the wiser.*

I took those remarks from complete strangers as a sign from heaven that I needed to obtain my nail license. I made a call to the local cosmetology school and found out that it would cost me $1,200 to attend. The only problem was that I didn't have the money to pay it. I hesitantly called my dad; his answer was no. Due to having filed bankruptcy, I wasn't able to get a loan. I had no credit any longer or any credit cards. I had nothing.

By this time, I had already been under the care of two different psychologists and two different psychiatrists. Was I destined to be a phone operator the rest of my life? I felt the tug to go to nail school but couldn't because of my lack of finances. I got severely depressed. I knew I had to do something, so I made a call and started going back to the original psychiatrist—my savior.

Dara and I had to move into a cheaper apartment because that is all my salary would afford. I had gotten to the point where I was sick and tired of being sick and tired. I was tired of changing all the time. This job, while stress free, was making me feel less than adequate. There was something in me that couldn't seem to settle for a nine-to-five existence. I felt like I was supposed to do something more with my life. I kept wishing I had gone to college and become something. I would see people who seemed happy, so I knew happiness was possible, but then I thought, *Could they be faking it too?*

I had been seeing my old psychiatrist for several months, and he suggested shock treatments. Thoughts of my aunt and my grandparents came flooding back to my mind. I guessed I was crazy after all. I came home early one day, stood in the middle of our apartment, picked up the phone, and made the call. I told him I wanted the treatments and to check me into the hospital.

I called my family and told them what I was going to do. I made all the arrangements with work, packed my bag, and drove myself to the hospital. Dara stayed with my sister and family for three weeks. We decided to tell everyone that I had to go in for an emergency female operation.

Yes, I was scared, but I was more scared of living the way I had been and thinking the thoughts I had been thinking than of having shock treatments. I had heard horror stories about what shock treatments did to people. My aunt said that she had forgotten how to play the piano; I never knew she even played! I saw horrible things on TV and in the movies about them as well, but something in this life of mine was going to have to change. The deep pain, hurt, and regret were too much for me to bear any longer. I was more scared of living the same merry-go-round of life than of having shock treatments. I had a daughter to think about, and she needed a fit mother.

The doctor assured me that shock treatments today were more refined than they had been years earlier. He explained each detail to me step by step, as if talking to a child. He told me he would give me a sedative that would knock me out before the treatment was given, so I wouldn't even know they were taking place. Electrodes would then be placed on my head.

He said, "I am going to actually go in and change the brain wave patterns, shocking them back into working properly."

My dad had remarried and showed up at the hospital with his new wife the night before I was due to begin treatments. Evidently someone in my family told Dad the truth of what was going on. They both begged me not to go through with the treatments. My dad said, "If you will not have shock treatments, I will give you the money to go to nail school."

I said, "No."

I wasn't like him, my aunt, or my grandparents, and I was going to have whatever was in me shocked out. My life wasn't supposed to end up like this. For once, I really didn't care what he thought. If I had a choice whether to listen to him or depend on what I thought I should do based on the advice of my psychiatrist who I had grown to trust, then I was going to follow what my doctor said. Why would I listen to my dad now? Twelve hundred dollars wasn't going to fix what was going on inside of me. Money hadn't fixed me before, and it wasn't going to fix me now.

I was in the hospital for three weeks and given multiple shock treatments. The doctor stood at the end of my bed with one of the biggest machines I had ever seen. The electrodes were attached to my head, I was given a sedative, and I had no clue what happened from that moment on. I awoke each time to a nurse sitting beside me, reading a magazine.

Dara knew nothing of what was taking place. I was able to talk to her on the phone but was not allowed visitors for the first week. I assured her that everything was fine and that I would see her soon. She was having fun staying with my sister and her family, so that removed a burden of guilt from my heart. I knew this alternative was the last option for me, and it had to work—it just had to. I felt this was the last straw for me. I had to help myself so I could help her.

A daily devotional arrived for me one day, sent by my brother and his wife. Once again, I wondered, *What is it that makes people want to shove God down your throat when you are down and out?*

I let it sit on the table beside me for a day or two and then picked it up because I didn't have any other reading material. I slowly began to thumb through it, and I was moved by the real-life stories it contained. I had never read anything quite like it before, and it captured my heart from the first few pages.

That one little devotional opened my eyes to God and brought him down to my level. There were stories entwined with scriptures that made perfect sense to me. I would read each one, stop, and then meditate on what I had read. It was as if my eyes had been opened, and I had been given understanding of things I had never been able to grasp before. This book became a lifeline to me, and I came out of the hospital carrying it every-where I went.

I went back to work the following month with a sense of renewed hope. My mind was sharp, and I hadn't forgotten much of anything, but I now knew that I had to do something with my life and not waste the second chance I felt I had been given by God. I knew I was headed for nail school, so I drove there one day to inquire about the financial part of it. I was told that if I could put $400 down, that monthly payments could be made for the remainder. Mom said she would give me the down payment if I would continue to work. She also said she would help with groceries and anything Dara needed since I was going to make the effort to help myself.

I worked full-time by day and went to nail school at night and on weekends; I was able to make my monthly tuition payments. I believed that I was on the right track—not just *some* track. I had an inner peace I had never felt before. I was working full-time and going to school to learn something I loved. I discovered the true grit that existed within me.

The manager of the cosmetology school called me to his office one day and said, "If you will come to work here as an instructor, I will give you your instructor's license and pay you to teach classes." That little gift would have saved me $1,500 plus multiple hours in class time. I firmly told him no. The school wasn't in a good area, and I really couldn't picture myself working there. I wanted to work in an upper-class salon, making a lot of money. I couldn't afford to start at the bottom and work my way up. I shut that door immediately.

A good nail tech could make anywhere from $25,000 up. I thought that amount of income, coupled with Dara's child support, would be enough to take care of us beautifully. I didn't even consider bars, drinking, or men any longer. I threw myself into this new direction with every breath I took.

I discovered a job opening in a hair salon where I had gotten my hair done from time to time. I was still working at the insurance company but believed that this was what I had been looking for, so I resigned my insurance job, which had benefits, to begin my new life in the beauty industry. I wasn't fired that time!

I soon discovered the owner of the salon was controlling. However, I loved what I did for the first time in my life so I tried to ignore her and just do my job. I had worked there for several months when she asked me to come into the back. She was in the bathroom fiddling with something, turned around, and asked me to help her with her bra. She proceeded to move forward as if to kiss me on the lips, and I quickly ducked my head. It was sickening. I made some lame excuse and said I had to go wait on a customer. She proceeded to keep her thumb on me so tightly that I could hardly breathe. I had gone to lunch one day and when I returned, she got furious with me, wanting to know where I had been.

I wanted to get away from that situation, so I went to the biggest nail salon in town to check them out. I met with the owner over lunch, and she hired me but told me (I was soon to find out) some of the biggest BS I had ever heard. Clients followed me, but when they saw the way other clients were yelled at and treated, they asked, "What are you doing here?"

In addition to doing nails, the owner wanted employees to sell the clothes and jewelry she peddled. She would sell people anything to make a buck. When she tried her tactics on a few of my customers, they rolled their eyes at me and once again, I knew I had evidently made a big mistake by coming to work for her.

As I walked around, I noticed how they maintained their equipment. Implements were not properly sterilized, and my conscience would not allow me to be a part of this operation, no matter what the money, so we parted ways. I was sitting at home, and a bright idea came to me about operating a finger-nail business out of my apartment. I remembered a time when I had my nails done by someone who worked out of her home. I did nails quite well by this time and thought I had gained enough customers to make it work.

I was impulsive and I didn't stop to consider the conse-quences of anything. Customers knew of my desire to work and at the same time, be at home with my daughter, so they agreed to come to the apartment to get their nails done. Every once in a while someone would help me out financially. On one occasion, I bartered rent for manicuring fingernails until the balance was paid. I was doing what I loved to do for a living, but the money situation was dreadful. I got very antsy and had no clue what to do next. I wondered if I had made another mistake.

———————

I sat on my couch one night watching the Psychic Network. I had a customer—a proclaimed Christian and research chemist—who told me of a woman who came to town every several months who could predict futures. She was said to be right on the money with her fortune-telling skills, even taping the dialog between her and "the spirits," for the low, low price of seventy-five dollars an hour. I wanted desperately to talk to someone who had other world powers and could tell me what to do. I also thought, *Maybe she knows where Amelia Earhart is.* Alas, I never had the money to go to her, but I could charge this call on my phone bill and make payments every month.

The draw to make this phone call to the Psychic Network became strong. I thought if someone could give me some answers so I could get on the right path, the call would be worth every cent. I went back and forth over this issue for about thirty minutes. Finally, I picked up the phone and made the call. I ended up counseling the so-called counselor, and I had to pay her seventy-five dollars to do it! She commented that I would be great in her line of work and said I ought to consider it. I hung up the phone and thought, *You dummy.* What a waste of time and money.

I kept searching for answers. I had a customer finally fess up and tell me she was a good witch. She said she could help me with some of the answers I desperately sought and invited me to her home to read tarot cards for me; she did it for free. Her home was beautiful and situated in a very exclusive neighborhood. I was enthralled with her.

Later, she came to my apartment and read cards for Dara and myself. I began to notice and feel something odd about her. I ended our friendship because it was one thing for me to listen to her; I didn't want my daughter taking to heart anything she said. I discovered a couple of years later that she had a bizarre and untimely death in the hospital while having a very simple female procedure. The last thing she told me was that I was related to Paul Newman—right!

PART THREE

GET NAILED

My feelings of not knowing what to do next came to a halt one day as I was talking to one of my customers. She had been searching for a business opportunity to invest in. She said she had $3,000, and my first thought was, *How about a fingernail business?* Feeling it was time to give the biggest nail salon in town some honest competition, I proposed a nail shop. I knew I was good at nails and knew people liked me. I had a little bit of faith—based on what I knew faith was. I had a daily devotional and $3,000; what more could I possibly ask for? Consequences? What were those? This was the open door I was looking for, and I was not about to let it pass me by.

I leased a location in a small shopping center, had flyers printed up, paid the first month's rent, and I was in business. I had not even bothered to think far enough ahead to concern myself about the following month's rent. Wasn't that what faith was for—what I read about in my daily devotional? The nail tables were designed from cinder blocks that were spray painted a cream color, then stenciled in purple, and finished with specially ordered glass tops. In addition, my sister stenciled around the inside of the shop with purple, aqua, and cream so that everything coordinated. I had a sign printed up in the same colors and was able to rent purple chairs and reception furniture. By the time I opened the front door, I only had $88.29 left, which I kept in a gray metal box that functioned as my cash register. I had no credit cards or any other safety net to fall back on if needed, but I was determined to make it work.

I wanted to do something for God because I believed he brought me through shock treatments with flying colors, giving me a second chance at life. I had started believing, through the daily devotional I carried, he was a somewhat touchable God and was intervening in my life. I wanted to believe in him so badly, so I just chose to believe he was real and that he was guiding me. There wasn't a Magic Eight Ball, a Ouija board, or even a Psychic Network involved in the decision for this business. I called the shop Get Nailed. Jesus got nailed on the cross. I couldn't call it Got Nailed, because that didn't make any sense, so Get Nailed was born. I heard varying comments—from, "Great, neat name!" to snickers about sexual innuendo, but everyone loved it. For me, it became an automatic witness of God.

Each day I began to take note of others' reactions to God. I didn't know how far I would step out for Jesus yet, knowing that I could be labeled a Jesus freak. I also felt my family would laugh at me for loving God so much, but in my heart, I knew he was more than I had ever known. I didn't know what it was all about yet, but I knew I was going to try to do things God's way.

In this shop was the first time I said the name of Jesus out loud without being in a church. I mean, this was the public, not a sanctuary. You know—the separation of church, state, and definitely business! I recall looking sheepishly around to see people's reactions one day when I said his name out loud. I didn't know what would happen. Maybe they would come after me—send a lynch mob and burn me at the stake. I was always so concerned about what others thought of me and was relieved when no one got a torch.

I had to work long hours, and my family suggested I move in with them until the first year was up so I could see where the business was going. I followed their advice, and Dara and I both moved again, only this time, we didn't move together.

There was no extra room for Dara at my sister's house, so she moved in with her grandparents. I hated it for her, but I felt that if I could just get this business up and running, I could provide for her properly and get us settled for good. I told her that this business was for us and that it would be better in the long run if I could devote all of my time there for right now. I knew she would be well taken care of at her grandparents' house, and I made her a solemn promise that by Christmas, which was five months away, we would be together again.

I knew I was going to conduct business with the utmost integrity, believing God was watching. I used the Cadillac of nail products, the best sanitation available, and had prices everyone could afford. I was all about giving people the best I had to offer and treated everyone exactly the same—rich or poor. I had learned as a child the scripture, "Do unto others as you would have them do unto you," and it would always flood back into my mind.

I worked ten to eleven hours a day, six days a week. Get Nailed taught me many things, but one of the biggest things I learned along the way was what I was truly made of. I had always told people I was just as tough as any two men put together, and now I was able to prove it to myself. I was not lazy and walked uprightly in my business dealings. For the first time, I was proud of myself for the effort. I slept better than I had in years, knowing that every day I put in a full day's work and strived for something better for Dara and me, but was it God's will that I wasn't spending any time with her?

I was constantly listening to what was going on in customers' lives, which included knowing every problem they had. I began counseling—the student has become the teacher!—people in all aspects of their lives. I would talk to them about their marriages, female problems, children, money, investments, medication, depression, and everything else.

Occasionally there would be as many as four or five women sitting around in a circle while I manicured someone's nails. I also became a great entertainer, and we decided that this needed to be a TV show. We would laugh and laugh. It made the hours not seem so long, and we solved many personal and a few world issues at Get Nailed.

I was going to keep my promise to Dara if it killed me, so I moved us into another apartment by Christmas. Having us back together again made us both feel better, even though I was never at home.

My brother had moved up from Florida just in time to help me when the shop first opened and was kind enough to help take care of Dara after I had moved us into another apartment. I worked long hours and supported us all, but the business didn't seem to be going anywhere. I was literally killing myself by working as long and hard as I could.

There was another drawback to having the shop. No one wanted anybody but me to do their nails. I had a couple of girls come in and try to work there, but honestly, the customers just preferred me. Here I was in a storefront building with a lease, and it was up to me to make it a success. Failure was not an option. I recall someone wanting to come in for a nail appointment at 10:00 p.m. one night because that was the only time I had open. I never dreamed anyone would actually come that hour of the night to have fingernails done, but she did. My mother called that evening to check on me and said, "Molly, please tell me you still aren't there."

Then a light bulb went off in my head. I had become friends with a customer who wanted to be part owner in a business. She stated she would even like to quit her job and come and help me do nails for a living. *Why not this one?* I had confided in her the ongoing problem I was facing with the original investor I had who had become such an annoyance that I had to stop answering her calls. From the beginning, I had sent her monthly checks to pay back what I owed her, but she didn't seem to understand she wasn't going to get it all back at once and in the timeframe she wanted.

I continued to confide in her that I faced the decision of closing the shop or keeping it open for another year to see what would take place. I had always heard it takes at least a year, if not two, to determine if a business was going to succeed or not. What if I closed it too early? If I decided to take on this new partner, I could pay the original one back her full investment. I believed the new investor was going to work with me as well, so that gave me hope that Get Nailed could actually succeed. I liked her, she seemed trustworthy, and she loved God, so I took the money she offered and signed the lease for one more year.

Then several months into the new lease, I realized that the new partner would not be coming to work with me. My dreams were dashed, and once again, I was left to run the business alone. I became very down in my heart and needed something or someone to tell me what to do. Was I always going to need major help? I was around other people who didn't seem to be so needy. I thought God wanted me to do this, but at the same time, I started having doubts.

It was late one night, and I was sitting at home on my couch, which also doubled as my bed. (My brother had a bedroom, and my daughter had a bedroom in the apartment where we lived.) I grabbed the only Bible I had, that had been given to me by The First Presbyterian Church of St. Albans, West Virginia. It had hardly been used through the years, but that night I opened it up. I was working hard, long hours and seemed to be going nowhere. I turned to the part in this old Bible where it talked about Jesus and his crucifixion. I looked up to heaven and said, "I really don't get all the 'thees' and 'thous.' I would like to, but I just don't get it." Tears were streaming down my face. I continued, "I need your help."

Three nights later, my older brother walked in and said, "God told me to buy you this book." It was a student NIV Bible. The way it was written was simple and clear, just like my daily devotional was. I actually started to understand the words on the pages which had seemed so foreign to me. I didn't know there was such a simple Bible. That gesture was really nice, but how was that going to help me out of the situation I was in?

MY LITTLE SANCTUARY

In the midst of Get Nailed, my eldest brother, who ran a regional office for Primerica Financial Services, suggested I obtain my Series 6 license, which would enable me to sell life insurance and various financial products, coupled with doing fingernails. He said, "Just come over to the office, and let me show you what it's all about, and you can make your own decision." Once he showed me the figures in black and white, I was infuriated at how insurance companies finagle people. That fact alone was enough to make me want to get my Series 6 license.

Facts and figures don't lie, and the honest Abe in me wanted justice for others who get conned. I could tell my customers about insurance while doing their nails. There was no BS, lying, or conning involved, so I was in. I went to school on the weekends while still working and running Get Nailed. I was feeling very run-down, yet satisfied in my heart that I was trying to do everything I knew how to help myself so I could make a better life for Dara. For once, I could look in the mirror and be proud of who I saw looking back. I didn't gripe, I didn't complain, and I started talking to God out loud about me, my life, and Dara. I felt as if someone were guiding me, even though I couldn't see them. The feeling was truly unbelievable but in a good way.

I loved the nail shop and the people, but I couldn't run it alone any longer. I actually thought of just shutting it down and trying to find a way to pay off the lease. I then thought better of it, knowing I had to honor the commitment I had made. I had filed bankruptcy once, so that wasn't an option again. The pattern in my life had always been, "If it gets too tough, just quit." Also, the part of me that had wanted to do something for God for pulling me through those shock treatments, was not going to run. I knew I had made my bed, and now I would have to lie in it until it was over, no matter what happened. I just knew I had to keep getting up and facing what was in front of me.

I finished my classes with Primerica and passed the exam. I also concluded that something was going to have to change. I had been having severe chest pains for months by this time—pains that lasted for thirty to forty-five minutes at a time. I started just calling them "attacks." I had no clue what they were but since I had not died, I figured I hadn't had a heart attack. More than once, the attacks caused me to break out in cold sweats and double over in pain. After they would subside, I was left feeling very weak but would push myself to be at work. I asked a couple of the nurses who were nail customers what they thought it could be. They both said it sounded like my gallbladder. They said that many people suffered with gallbladder problems for years and never had to have an operation. They told me to eat light foods only, so when I ate at all, I did as they suggested.

I never took a lunch hour, but due to the way I was feeling, I had to start putting a sign up on the door from 1:00 to 2:00 every day and go to the back to rest so I could muster enough strength for the remainder of the day. I was determined not to quit.

I had a customer who was a proclaimed born-again Christian, and she told me to start quoting the scripture, "By his stripes, I am healed." She explained the thirty-nine stripes Jesus bore on his back before going to the cross would actually heal my sickness today. What did I have to lose? I was going to try anything at this point that would help me overcome whatever was happening inside of me. I didn't have any insurance and had no doctor. I had no clue how I would even pay for an operation if it came to that. Quoting scripture was my only hope, and I believed this woman. I had been quoting the scripture for several months by then, and when an exceptionally bad attack would hit me, I would quote it twice as much and twice as loud until the pain would subside. I had no other choice.

The lease was due to be renewed again, and I finally cried uncle and closed the shop. I knew positively and unquestionably that I had tried my hardest and had given everything I had to give until there was nothing left. I knew women loved to come there, and I felt I had done something good for a change by listening to them, helping them, and even praying occasionally for them. I had wanted to do something for God, but I was worn out physically. Of course, the customers balked and wanted me to stay open. I made a joke of it and said, "If you want to get together and pay me a salary, I will be more than happy to keep the shop open for you." They just laughed, but to me, it really wasn't funny. I had become the neighborhood counselor and friend, and my shop was the gathering place. I would miss them as much as they said they would miss me, but something was wrong. I was ill, and I was missing Dara's life.

I had believed this shop was going to be the answer for my career and life and the way of providing support for Dara and me, but it had to be shut down. I felt like I was a failure. My sister and brother-in-law came to me out of the blue before I closed it and said they had a proposition for me. I took the time to listen before saying no right off the bat. Dara and I could come and live with them while I took the time to figure out what I was going to do. They said they had it all planned out. My daughter would share a room with her cousin, and I could use their garage as a place to manicure nails by day, letting it serve as my bedroom at night. It was closed off from the rest of the house, so it could be my own little haven.

I felt my family thought I would start selling insurance full-time with my older brother, but I didn't feel any inclination to make that my full-time occupation. I believed there was something more in life for me, but I didn't know how to tap into it. Dara was excited at the proposition, and if she was happy, then I was happy.

I always thought that as long as she was happy—the exact phrase my dad used—then I could pick up, dust myself off, and keep going. At any rate, I was given an answer to my plight, and I was relieved. But this time, I was able to pay them rent so I didn't feel guilty about moving back in with them. Wanting to make sure all was legal, I checked with the county regarding codes and regulations before opening my business in my sister's residence.

Most of the women who had been customers at the shop followed me there. The garage served beautifully as a nail shop by day and a place of refuge by night. I felt temporarily settled *again.*

Within two weeks of closing the shop, I had to have emergency gallbladder surgery. I will never forget the doctor coming into the hospital room after surgery and standing over my bed. His glasses were tilted on his nose, and he was scribbling something on the clipboard he held. He said, "I don't know what you have been doing, but your gallbladder was so gangrenous, I had to pick it out in pieces." He was very put out with me.

The most mind-boggling thing of all was what he said next. "Something formed all the way around your gallbladder, keeping it from poisoning you to death."

The exact—and I mean exact—moment he made that statement, I knew what had happened. He was considered one of the top surgeons in his field, and he had no idea what had formed around my gallbladder protecting me from dying, but I did. It all came flooding back.

The scripture I had learned to speak out loud while working at the shop kept me protected. I would speak that scripture aloud and then just shut up, not speaking anything negative into the atmosphere about how I felt. I didn't tell anyone how rotten I was feeling. Whatever had formed around that sick part of my body protected me from being poisoned to death. I knew it was from heaven; I just knew it. From that moment on, I wondered how much healing power I had available to me that I did not know about. What else could have possibly kept me from dying?

I had surgery on a Thursday. I was given pain medication and sent home to recuperate. I was back working in my new nail shop the following Tuesday. I had proven to myself that I was not a quitter. I had worked harder than I ever had in my entire life, and I was going to continue to do so.

Learning I had been supernaturally protected in my body by merely speaking a scripture aloud drove me to God. I purposed to go after the God who had been knocking on the door of my heart for years now. I didn't know if he was real or not, but something had saved me from being poisoned to death. I made a decision to go after him the way I had gone after men. If he could do this, then what else could he do?

I would tuck my daughter in bed at night, making certain she was happy. I would hear her prayers and sit on the side of her bed, rubbing her head until she fell off to sleep. I would watch her sleeping and know that she trusted me, even though I felt I had let her down. I had made so many promises to her that I never kept. I loved her more than I loved myself.

I would wait until she was sound asleep and then go downstairs into my nail shop for the evening. My custom was to pull out a TV tray, set my Bible on it, and start reading. I had no clue where or what to read, but I was now on a quest for the God who had healed me.

One evening I was led by something deep inside of me to sit on the floor of the garage. I took the NIV Bible my brother bought me in my left hand, and I raised my right arm to heaven. Then I pointed my finger at God and said, as if talking directly to God, "If you are really real, you are going to have to help me 'cause I don't want to live down here like this anymore. I would rather that you bring me home now." I continued, "I will be dammed to hell if my daughter's life is going to end up like mine. Give me a hunger and thirst for your Word that I can't satiate with anything else but you."

From that moment on, my life started to change. If I could have the same grit and staying power of learning about God that I had in working the last several years, I could find out just who he was once and for all. *Could he help someone like me get on a solid path? I would settle forever the question in my heart about him: Was he really real?* He had been trying to get to me for years now, always sending someone to me with a Bible in tow to reach me, but I didn't want to listen. Things were different this time. I thought God was a God in outer space somewhere, who I would have to deal with in the "sweet by and by," but him saving me from being poisoned to death did something to me I wasn't expecting. Moreover, who in the world was the Holy Spirit I kept hearing about, and how did three people get into one body anyway?

I didn't know these answers, but nothing or no one was going to stop me, especially anyone I was around who was experiencing defeat in their own lives. I was going to shut my ears to people whose advice I had listened to for years. They didn't appear to have any answers, so why would I continue to listen if I wanted things in my life to be different? I didn't tell anyone what I had purposed in my heart. It was none of their business as long as I kept up my end of the bargain to pay rent.

THE WILD STALLION
GETS ROPED

The few people I had been around who were walking with the Lord seemed to have twenty-four-hour smiles slapped on their faces. I used to have a twenty-four-hour smile too, but it was a fake smile most of the time.

My fake smile was finally taken from me at the nail shop. I bit into rice and my second-to-the-front tooth broke off. Who breaks a tooth on rice? I couldn't afford to have it fixed, so when I smiled, it was a lip smile only—no teeth showed. I was humiliated. That really knocked me down a couple of pride rungs on the ladder of life. After several months, I was able to get a replacement, which gave me a newfound appreciation of the smile I had always griped about.

The smile I wanted now came with a new way of life, and I wanted that. I also wanted again the material things I once had that had been stripped from me, little by little, until I had almost nothing left. I would have given anything for a good job with benefits. *I want. I want. I want.* Did God have any of these things for me?

I discovered that the same man who wrote the daily devotional I had been given in the hospital when I had shock treatments had a TV program. What he said and how he said it was unlike anything I had ever heard before from anyone, in church or out of church. He touched something deep inside of me that I knew, that I knew, that I knew was coming from a supernatural source. I thought I had felt every type of emotion that a human could feel, but the feelings I was now having were deeper, containing a hope that there was something yet to be discovered in this life. I heard that I could be forgiven for all of my sins, even five abortions.

The preacher would say, "You can be made new." That triggered the picture my ex-brother-in-law painted for me years earlier right after my first husband left that said, "If any man be in Christ, he is a new creation" (2 Corinthians 5:17). My brother-in-law had tried so hard to convince me years earlier that Jesus was the only answer for me, as he would calmly stare into my eyes. As each day would pass, turning into the next without my husband returning home, at my deepest times of despair, I would hear a knock at my back door. There my brother-in-law would stand ready to tell me about a new life.

Now the time had come and I wanted to be new, and I wanted a new life. Dara needed me to be her parent, and clearly, I wasn't doing a good job of it, but I was trying. What I thought was going to be the answer—the nail shop—wasn't.

I figured that, while I had the time, I would use it to my advantage. At night, when everyone was settled in bed, I could study the Word and not have to be concerned about anything but soaking up God. This time became my refuge.

The days passed, and I was beginning to feel that this was going to be my last chance. I knew I had better buck up, get my crap together, and do this—find out what God had just for me—so I wouldn't be a living, breathing failure for the rest of my natural-born days. I could almost imagine myself standing in a corner, smoking cigarettes, pointing my finger at others and blaming them for my lot in life. I knew I had a choice to make, and it seemed as though God was trying to get something to me. This time no one had to make me go after God.

Every single night, I would race to my sanctuary to be alone with God. I would pull out my TV tray, open my NIV Bible, have pencil and paper ready, and get right into the Word. The feelings I had were overwhelming, and I was determined not to quit. Through the guidance of the man who wrote the daily devotional I had carried now every day for several years, I began in the New Testament. I would read and talk to God out loud. I pretended as though I was speaking right to him and that he was listening to every word I said. I was talking, but then I also got still and listened. Listening was a major change for me; I was always so busy talking that others could hardly get a word in.

I was thrilled. Something started to change inside my heart. I felt like God was on the throne 24/7, and his ears and his eyes were attentive only to me. I felt as though he gave me his undivided attention. He never one time said, "Time's up. Give me a hundred dollars, and I'll see you next week." It was glorious and I didn't have to have insurance to do it.

From youth I had been concerned with the way I looked and how others perceived me. I spent time posing my legs and shoes just right, admiring the way I looked while people would sit in front of me talking. Was my look okay? I would always be thinking, *Yeah, whatever, just hurry up so I can speak.* I would even be going over different things in my mind that I had ready to say, waiting for my open door. However, when I was overweight, all the "self care maintenance" I was concerned with when I was thin was abandoned. I withdrew into a cocoon I felt was my safe place that sheltered me from the hurt and pain I suffered deep inside my heart. Being heavy took my eyes off myself during those times. I wanted to break the cycle of instability in all areas of my life once and for all.

I had never done this Jesus thing before, but this time I believed that there were going to be permanent and drastic changes coming in several areas of my life. I believed I would become different, but I was not sure just how it was going to take place. Was God going to zap me? The answer was unclear at this point. I did know, however, that if I put my heart into it, I was going to find out. I had lived the "me" life all of my life, but I was now willing to put God first above *my* wants.

There was so much in the Bible that it was overwhelming to me. So, I decided to close my Bible and then flip it open, hoping the words I would read would speak to me in some way, much like the old Eight Ball I had as a child—except I wasn't looking for a yes or no answer this time.

As I was kind of flipping through the Bible one night, I repeatedly came across the word "fear." I looked up to heaven and said, "What is this word "fear" I keep coming across? Do you want me to be afraid of you or something?"

All of a sudden, a very clear voice stated, "Molly, I want you to have a healthy enough fear of me. It is going to help keep you in line."

Fear God? I thought God was a God of love. What was this I had just heard?

For some reason, I just looked up in the air and in my mind, I could see a big, black, wild stallion bucking and fighting against the rope that was around his neck. I spoke out to God, "I feel like a wild stallion that you are just going to have to break."

I started laughing. I thought it was funny. Then a voice sternly said, "How hard you fight against me is going to determine how easy or hard your ride with me is going to be."

Well, *that* wasn't very funny. That night has since become known as the "wild stallion night."

I didn't like what I was hearing. Fear had stopped me from everything in my life, and now I was going to have more of it? My heart sank. I then came upon the scripture in Matthew 7:13–14, which says that the way to life is through a narrow gate, and that wide is the road to destruction.

All I could picture was being a horse with blinders on. I had to keep them on either side of my face, keeping my eyes straight ahead, not looking to the right or left in order to stay on my path. I had always paid too much attention to what others were doing instead of what I should be doing. I would always look all around, even when I was driving, to see who I could spot as my next quest.

Suddenly, I knew all of that was going to have to be over. I was going to have to straighten up and do this God's way, but I needed to know what this fear was I was now encountering. I thought God was only a God of love, and I was getting an ache in my stomach again; I didn't like it. *On second thought, I could just stop doing this Jesus stuff.*

That very night when I went to sleep, I was just plain scared. The hour was late, and I was the last one awake in the house. I was so scared inside I could almost feel myself shaking.

Fear was looming all around me. I knew I was becoming afraid of God. What would he do to me? Would he hurt me? Would he destroy me? Would he rain down fire on me? Would I be awakened drowning in water, as in the days of Noah? I didn't know, but I wasn't sure that night when I went to bed if I wanted to go on with this. I thought I had wanted to go after God, but I couldn't bear the thought of him hurting me. I turned my face to the back of the couch, which was unusual for me. I always slept facing forward so I could see anything that might try to harm me; I *never* turned my face to the wall to sleep.

I cried out, "I am scared, God. I don't know why I am scared, but I am. I am scared of you." I almost didn't utter those words. Then I trailed off to sleep.

For the first time since his initial appearance in the dream years earlier, David appeared to me again in a dream. I couldn't tell where he was, but it seemed as though it was green, like a grassy area. He was sitting with his hands folded around his legs. He said, "Molly, I am happy, and there is nothing to be scared of." I woke up the next morning mulling over the dream for a while before it started to make sense.

Seeing him as clearly as I could anyone else on the planet somehow assured me in my childlike heart that everything was going to be all right. In one fell swoop, it settled the fear in my heart. I knew he must be in heaven, and if he wasn't scared, then I wasn't going to be scared either. I knew he was with God, and God loved me enough to send someone I had loved to tell me there was nothing to be afraid of. God talked to me through David, but I didn't tell anyone. What was going on in my little sanctuary was between God and me. No one else needed to know except Dara. I pressed into God and kept doing what I knew to do. Days later the actual fear of God started to disapate.

Unexpectedly, my life became rooted in something supernatural; it was giving me strength from within. This was the greatest Sherlock Holmes mystery of all. I could picture me with a magnifying glass, looking in every place for the answer, and now I was being given bits and pieces of answers. I was being driven forward by something I felt but couldn't see, and I knew it was going to be up to me to get what God had waiting. I searched it out, guided by an unseen hand. The answers for my life this time couldn't be obtained by calling a stranger on the Psychic Network, obtained by having someone look into a crystal ball, going to a bar picking up a man, or by being drug-addled. This time, I couldn't suck people dry for what I needed.

I was learning that I was not going to be able to go and grab what I wanted from God—or what I thought I needed—and go back to doing life my way. If anyone could have stood on a stage in front of millions of people singing the song, "My Way" it was me, but now things had changed. I asked God to show me he was real, and by God, he was doing it.

I tried to keep a low profile and not beat people over the head with Jesus, yet at the same time, I was becoming very curious, picking the brains of my customers about what their knowledge of God was. I took the information I learned from them to the Word to see what it said about their interpretation of it, and I wondered why their thinking was twisted at times. Who was right?

———

I would get up in the middle of the night after working all day, sit down, and talk in to the blackness of night for several hours about my life—what I had heard from others and any concerns I had. Then I sat and listened for God to talk to me. Many times, something would come into my heart that I had been through in my life, and I would begin crying and asking God to forgive me. When I would get it all out of my system, I would tell God how much I loved him and then I would fall into an exhausted but sweet sleep.

I started asking God to give me back the time I had spent with him so I wouldn't be tired the next day, and that is exactly what happened. It was like dope to me, only it was better than any drink or drug I ever took. I talked to him about my hopes, my dreams—what I wanted to do. Some nights, I would get up, hold the Bible in my hands, walk back and forth in my little sanctuary, and talk to crowds of people on the wall. (Of course, the people were there only in my mind's eye.) I would be like a full balloon, then after a couple of hours, I would be all out of air. I emerged from these times with a feeling of great release—a feeling I had not felt before. It was as though I was being set free from prison bars within myself that couldn't come off any other way. It was supernatural.

There is a scripture in the Bible that says, "Whom the Son sets free is free indeed" (John 8:36). My steps were becoming lighter as the days went by, and I felt freer than I ever thought I would.

The more I got into the Word, the more I was changing. There were deep-seated things inside of me that I wasn't able to deal with, except with God. God knew how much I could take, as far as coming to grips with the things that were in me, and he was bringing up what needed to be healed with his hands one piece at a time.

One night something happened that sealed my fate and belief in God forever. I had seen David twice now through dreams, but this was something entirely different. After this experience, I was never the same.

Dara was all tucked in; I had studied in the Word as I always did—had one of my marathon nights with God—then went peacefully to sleep on my couch. As I lay there dozing off, my last thoughts were, *The peace I feel is amazing, and my mind doesn't reel on and on like it used to.*

All of a sudden, something like a mighty force I had never felt before propped me up. I had no choice; I was going to sit up! The first thing I saw was the brightest white light I have ever seen. It was blinding. Immediately, I knew who it was; there was no mistaking it.

I felt a foreboding—that I must be in trouble. My head was bowed, and I did not look up. I thought, *You cannot look upon the face of God and live, so keep your eyes from his gaze. No one looks God in the face and lives except Moses or Abraham—not Molly Painter from St. Albans, West Virginia.*

I fumbled and reached out my hand to feel the person who was sitting on the end of my couch. Why was this happening to me? Naturally all I could think of was, *This is not good.*

I slowly started to look up somewhat—curiosity getting the better of me—and all I could see was about four inches of brown hair laying on a white robe. My eyes then slowly began to look all the way down his knees, and I glimpsed brown sandals. Then my eyes slowly moved up his figure, and I saw his hands, which were crossed on his lap. They were the most beautiful hands and feet I had ever seen on any man. Then my eyes rested upon scars in his wrists.

All I could seem to think was, *Why are you here? Why had he appeared to me?* As usual, I started blabbing my big mouth before he could say anything. I said, "I promise I'll do better. I promise. I promise."

In the most beautiful, manly voice I have ever heard, he said, "You are not being obedient."

Again, I replied, "I know. I'll try harder. I promise. I promise."

I woke up the next morning not remembering any of this, but as I gradually woke up, thoughts of what had taken place started flooding back into my memory. I was in shock—in awe—and wondered why Jesus had appeared to me.

I didn't dare tell anyone in my family for fear of what they would say, but I told Dara and swore her to secrecy. Several days later, I became a little more brazen and told two people I thought I could trust. They listened but had quizzical looks on their faces as if in disbelief, so I stopped telling others anything about what I was experiencing. I mulled the word "obedient" over and over in my mind. What was he saying to me? Evidently God was not happy with me, and I was doing something wrong. I had always been a people pleaser, and I thought I was doing better, but I guess I was wrong. A recurrent voice in my head had told me to stop smoking. Was that it? I didn't know, but I had given up most everything else. Did I have to give up cigarettes too? Everybody has vices. Couldn't I have at least one? After all, I didn't smoke while I was praying or talking to God. I mean, come on. Was that it?

I held my Bible now as not just another study book, but as the living, breathing words of God Almighty—period. It was settled in my heart; no one could tell me differently. I knew who I had seen. Death, eternity, and every question I had ever had about life hereafter were answered, but I had no clue what my future held or what to expect.

I was feeling the need to worship the God that I now knew was real, so one evening, I went down into my sanctuary, looked at my couch, and thought, *Well, I'll just spread out my Bible on my couch in front of me. I will sit in front of the couch, face the wall and sing.*

I was a little shy and embarrassed, but there was no one watching me but God. I didn't know what worship songs were so I just started to sing. I sang, "Jesus loves me! This I know, For the Bible tells me so." Then I sang, "O Holy Night." I sang any song I had learned in Vacation Bible School as a child that directly related to Jesus. I didn't have anybody telling me what to do or how to do it. It was simple, yet I loved Jesus and wanted him to know.

Then I stood up and started thanking him for loving me and helping me. I went on and on from the bottom of my heart and kept singing out loud to Jesus. I had my eyes closed and my hands raised, and all of a sudden, I could almost feel Jesus standing in front of me. I got scared, and it startled me, so I stopped. Things were beginning to happen to me that started to blow my mind.

Any devotion to God had been in the form of going to church. I vividly recall when I was young, sitting in the pew right beside Mom falling asleep on her shoulder during the service. A collection plate would be passed around. The pastor would preach about seventeen minutes, and then we would hurry home to eat, and don't forget the afternoon nap! I would always feel better about myself having gone, but I didn't even know why. However, several months into my new life, I was feeling a draw to go again to church. I knew I was going to be obedient, so I attended a church my younger brother suggested. Most of my life I had been with someone else wherever I went, never wanting to go anywhere alone. I did this for a couple of reasons: sometimes because of fear of panic attacks, and sometimes I was afraid of what others would think of me as a single woman alone. Now I didn't feel alone anymore, and a new feeling of self-confidence was arising within me, so I tried still another church all by myself. The more time I spent with God, the more self-confident I became. The feeling I started to have was empowering yet in a humble way. The fears I had lived with for years were beginning to subside, and it was truly liberating.

Christmas Eve was upon us and Dara was going to be with her dad. I ate our traditional, huge dinner with my family and then announced I was going to church. When I felt convicted about doing something, I knew I had better follow through so I wouldn't get in trouble with heaven. I attended a church I had just been to the previous Sunday but on this particular Christmas Eve, I felt like I was intruding on a close-knit family. I felt very unwelcomed, and I never went back to that church. I knew that if God wanted me in a church, regardless of location or the denomination or how I was feeling about it, he would somehow tell me. But for the moment, I would worship him in my little sanctuary staying focused on saturating myself in the Word.

WOULD YOU
DIE FOR ME?

One Sunday my younger brother went to his church with my mother. Around twelve thirty, the door to my sanctuary opened, and he said, "You are way out there. Something is not right with you. You are in that Bible way too much." He was furious at me. I was stunned. What had I done? I picked up the Bible he had been told by God to buy me and replied, "Tell me where it says in this Word that you can have too much of Jesus!" That was the beginning of me taking a stand for what I believed in, even if that meant standing against everyone— even my family.

As I would get into my Bible, there would be times that I would feel all hot and flushed when I would read a particular scripture. I began to understand that this meant Jesus was talking to me. One scripture that really got to me was: "Let the little children come to Me, and do not forbid them; for of such is the kingdom of heaven" (Matthew 19:14).

Slowly, I sat and meditated on the two words "of such." I kept rolling them over in my heart. I knew deep inside that Jesus was telling me I could enter into the kingdom of heaven while I lived here *if* I just believed and accepted it as a little child would.

In the eighties, I was an avid watcher of *Beauty and the Beast,* starring Ron Perlman and Linda Hamilton. Now I was careful not to watch a lot of anything that I thought was not appropriate for me. Not wanting to offend the Lord, I thought, *Well, if Jesus won't sit beside me and watch something, then I really shouldn't be watching it either.* Reruns of this show were on, and I thought they were harmless. Anyway, what caught my attention was how Vincent would be sitting at a table writing in a log of some kind as the show ended.

For days, I couldn't seem to get the picture of Vincent and his writing out of my mind. I was compelled to buy a little book at the Dollar Tree and begin writing my own thoughts on paper. I felt like I was doing something I was supposed to do.

I heard Ruth Graham (Billy Graham's wife) say she kept a journal of all of the prayers she prayed. She said when God was slow in answering some prayers, she would look back in her journal and see prayers he had answered. This gave her the encouragement she needed in times of impatience. This reinforced the knowledge that an answer was on the way. Well, if it was good enough for Vincent and for Ruth Graham, it was good enough for Molly.

I was sitting on my couch journaling, and a poem started coming on my heart, so I just penned it down. When I was done, what I saw was positively amazing. It was a complete poem! The only thing I ever used to like to write was my name as I was signing for my prescriptions. It had come out so fast that I really didn't comprehend the meaning, so I stopped and methodically read every line, and when I got to the end, I gasped as I read the words I had written down:
"Would you have died for me?"

I felt as if a knife cut through my heart, and blood was pouring out all over me. I believed Jesus was asking me unequivo-
cally, through that poem, if I would die for him. I sat still for a
moment and pondered the question. I mean, come on—if God
asked you to do something and you knew he was real, what
would you do? Unwaveringly, my answer to him was, "Yes."
What else was down inside of me besides that poem? I quickly
filled up my first journal and then headed for the Dollar Tree
to buy another one.

———

I had been diligent about studying, praying, seeking, and listening. I would sit all evening and memorize scriptures, depos-
iting them in my spirit man. One evening something touched
my heart to stop doing what I was engaged in at the time,
and I was led to just sit still and recount my life from the very
first memory I could ever remember. The process took what
seemed to have been several hours, and when I had finished, I
said to Jesus, "No one would ever believe this."

I was open and truthful with myself for the very first time
in my life, leaving no holds barred. I thought I had always
been an honest woman, but this was something different. I
realized I had been a big, loud-mouthed woman who sang, "I
Am Woman, Hear Me Roar."

Something had started to change in me over the last several years. I didn't always have to have the first word, the final
word, and every word in-between. A transformation was taking place inside of me that was not of my doing but was definitely of my liking. Peace replaced torment. I was sleeping
better than I had in years without being comatose. I started
feeling happier even though I was living with my relatives and
had no clue what was in my future. I knew I had something to
say, but to whom would I say it, and how would I say it? I had

always said a lot that meant nothing, but I was now feeling I had something more to say to others. I also felt that what I had to say would be life-changing for others, enabling them to overcome pain, hurt, angst and undo suffering.

Several days later, I received a package in the mail from Kenneth Copeland Ministries. Contained within were two tapes. I did not—I repeat, did not—order those tapes. I wondered how in the world I received them. I assumed I was supposed to have them, so I put on my headphones and went walking. I was hearing things I had never heard before in my life. He kept repeating something about powers, principalities, rulers of darkness, and evil and wicked spirits in the heavenly realms (Ephesians 6:12).

I stopped the tape. I rewound it. I listened again. I did that several times, and yes, he was definitely saying what I thought he was, but I had no idea what it meant, and I couldn't wait to get back to the house to look it up. To my amazement, I found the exact scripture in the Bible referred to on the tape. I sat and thought a moment or two about it and realized I was being told about the devil. What now—is he real too?

It was late one evening days later, and I stood in the middle of my room and pointed my finger into the air at where I thought Satan might be. If Jesus was out there, then maybe Satan was too. I talked to him like I talked to Jesus, except I was fuming mad at him. No one was home, and I shouted at him, daring him to come and get me. I continued on my rampage, telling him I hated him for what he had done to me.

"You stole my life!" I went on, "Come and get me, and give me all you've got. With all the might in me, I yelled, "I hate you for what you did to Jesus! Bring it on." I was firm and authoritative, and from that moment on, all hell was unleashed on me.

I snuggled up on my couch after my little tirade and dozed right off to sleep. I had been asleep for what seemed to be several hours when, all of a sudden, I was hovering in the back of the room at the top of the dividing wall that separated my nail shop from the work area. It was pitch dark all around except for a little light in the corner. I could think, and I knew exactly who I was, but I became aware that I was not in my body. I vividly thought, *What is going on? Where am I? Am I at the top of this partition? How did I get here? What is my family going to think? Am I dead? Dara! She will be so upset over my death and won't be able to go on. She doesn't need this.*

Then in an instant I was sailing through space. Stars were sailing past me at the speed of light as I was being hurled faster and faster forward, heading for an unknown destination. Was I in my body? I realized I wasn't. Something was dreadfully wrong. Then a thought popped into my head: *Yell for archangel Michael.* "archangel Michael—Michael, please help me!"

Simultaneously, I heard and felt a loud swish, and then I was kneeling before a giant angel. At once I felt safe. There was a blinding light all around, and all I could make out was this humongous angel. I uttered with very short breaths, "Thank you. I just praise you; thank you for saving me."

He said, "Do not worship me. I am a servant of the Lord also. The next time you are in trouble, call for Jesus." His voice was commanding, firm and unwavering in its deliverance and clearly, I was being called onto the carpet.

I said, "I'm sorry. I will. I will. I promise."

I felt a loud thump, and I awoke the next morning not fully comprehending what had happened. I felt weak and was not able to get motivated. I started to move around so I could go get a cup of coffee. I knew what had happened the night before was real, but I also knew I dare not tell anyone.

The fingernail customer of mine who was a research chemist sat before me the next day, and I felt led to tell her what had happened the night before. She said, "Well, Molly, don't you know what happened?"

I replied, "No."

She said, "The hard thump was you reentering your body."

She stood at the back door of the shop as she was leaving and said, "You need to put your spiritual ears on."

Well, what on earth were those? Where do you buy them? All I could imagine was that she was standing there with great big ears on. What was she telling me? What were spiritual ears? You mean that angels are really real too? The angel I saw did not look like any angel I had seen on greeting cards or as a figurine—you know, cute, fluffy babies with little wings. This angel was huge, had blonde hair, a big belt around his waist, and had a blue outfit on. Why was he stern with me? I mean, come on—I didn't know I was going to be flying in the air, scared to death and in trouble. The reason I called for archangel Michael was because it was the first thing that popped into my head. I didn't want to bother Jesus; I thought Jesus was too busy for stuff like that anyway. After all, in my mind, he had already done the big thing by dying for me. What did I know about calling on Jesus when I was in trouble? I hadn't expected to leave my body!

This situation opened up a whole new realm to me I didn't even know existed. I hadn't really even stopped to consider a spiritual realm before. First, the healing takes place in my body by my quoting scriptures; then, my high school sweetheart appears to me again. Then Jesus appears to me, and if that alone weren't enough, archangel Michael appears to me! What was going to happen next?

The supernatural things that were happening to me were astounding and drove me even closer to Jesus. I continued getting up in the middle of the night as I was led, to sit, pray, and talk to God about my life, my family, and my regrets about things I had done, what I hadn't done, and what I could have done—the list goes on. Sometimes I would spend several hours talking, crying, and repenting. I would cry so hard at times I didn't think I was going to stop. His Word promised he would wash my sins away as far as the east is from the west, so I was going to make certain that I repented for them all. I also did not want to kneel before the Lord, who I knew now was real, look him in the eyes, and have to go through the horrible crimes I had committed again. I really didn't think I could bear the disappointment I would see. If archangel Michael was real, then I knew Satan was real and there was undeniable spiritual warfare I was going to have to deal with. Satan was not going to have Dara and try to destroy her life the way he had tried to destroy mine. I would fight him to the death over her and defend Jesus, even if it meant my own demise.

I learned on those tapes to take authority over the devil. Every morning, I would get up around 5:15 a.m. to begin my day. First, I would hit the floor and start praying before drinking any coffee, knowing this was more serious than before. I would plead the blood of Christ over my family, my daughter, and myself. Then I would take authority over every demon in every realm. Satan was going to have a fight on his hands with me and was not going to destroy my life anymore, and he wasn't going to get Dara.

Every single day, this went on along with everything else I was learning. I was beginning to feel I was becoming equipped to fight something I couldn't see that had been coming at me all of my life. I had already begun to teach Dara what I was learning. I hadn't known anything growing up about what it meant to follow Christ; that was not going to happen to Dara. I did not care what it took, and I did not care how tired she might have gotten of hearing me always talk about God. I simply did not care. I knew what I had been through; I knew what life without him had cost me, and it wasn't going to be like that for her.

TWO OR MORE

The Bible teaches that where two or more are gathered in Jesus' name, agreeing upon touching anything, it will be done for them (Matthew 18:19). Dara and I had been living with my family now for well over a year, and things were fine, but I couldn't see any end to our living with them and us moving into a place of our own. I wanted more than to live with my family, and I thought that maybe I just had to ask Jesus for it.

A thought rose upon my heart and thinking it was from heaven, Dara and I came into agreement for a home of our own. We knelt down in my little sanctuary before the Lord, I took all the cash I had at the time—$9.97—and we made an offering to him into the ministry that taught me about tithing. We signed and dated the agreement paper which detailed what we were asking for, got up, and did not say a word to anyone about what we had done.

One of the key factors I learned in receiving from heaven is that "if you believe, you will receive" (Mark 11:24). We believed and didn't waver. We did not even speak to each other about what we had done. Every time she would start to ask me about what we prayed for, I would tell her that God heard us, and he would move on our behalf. She believed and trusted me just the way I trusted God. If he had placed this on my heart, I knew it would happen. This prayer took place in October 1997. That following spring, we were living in a four-bedroom, two-and-a-half bath home with a garage and were not paying one thin dime to live there.

We moved our things out of storage, but we didn't have a washer, dryer, or refrigerator, and I had no money to buy them. I did have a small refrigerator with a freezer that came from my old nail shop. It would have to do until I could figure something else out.

I had learned to tithe when I had moved into my sister's house. At the end of every week, I would go before the Lord, show him what I had earned, and show him what I was sending off to the ministry he placed upon my heart. I learned to honor God first with what he gave me. I had been going to the launderette with our clothes, when out of the blue, Dara's grandfather called stating he needed to do something with a refrigerator and a washer and a dyer that one of his renters had left behind when they moved out. He asked if we would be interested in storing them for him adding, "You are welcome to use them until I find somewhere else to situate them." I accepted, feeling great relief for Dara, and much to my astonishment, they were the exact color we wanted.

Without even knowing it, I was living on sheer, raw faith. Every time we needed something, it would supernaturally be given to us. There was not a lot of extra money ever, but we were together, we were happy, and we had what we needed. I continued doing fingernails, with my income supplemented by child support. I was able to be at home for Dara, and that meant the world to me. There were several times when I really felt I should go and get a part-time job in addition so we could have plenty of money, but my pride and hard head kept me from it.

I was standing at the kitchen sink one day, and a very clear, stern voice said, "You had better enjoy this time with your daughter because this will be the last time you will live together." I was doing something I had never known, and I wasn't around anyone who had ever done what I was doing. I would watch *The 700 Club* and listen to people who were living on faith. I had gone to a huge church several years earlier to consult a pastor about the things I was feeling. All he said to me, as I gave him twenty-five dollars for his time, was, "You sound like you are charismatic." I was not crazy in regard to what I was seeing and doing, but he made me feel that way, and I didn't like it. From then on, I just talked to God, stood blindly on my faith, and kept doing what I knew to do.

I felt, though, that even with as much as I had witnessed, I still didn't know enough to understand fully when I was making a mess of things. But, there was no one in the flesh I could talk to about what was happening with me. No one who knew what I was doing was able to understand how we were able to live in that home freely, with no strings attached. But I knew God had answered our agreement prayer.

Shortly thereafter I was in a deep sleep one night and was taken by the Spirit of the Lord right into the middle of the sky. I looked all around and saw beautiful stars as we hung there, and then a movie screen was pulled down to reveal the most horrific individual I had ever seen. I knew in my spirit that it was Satan. He was sitting at a table cursing me and telling me how he abhorred the sight of me. I was in a major battle for my destiny, and Satan wanted to stop me. The tapes I had received months earlier made me aware of demonic powers, and I had been praying against them ever since, but seeing Satan was something different. I knew Satan was at my every turn trying to stop me. After this dream, I knew I had to buck up and be even stronger for Dara and me. No matter what, I would *never* give up. Never give up.

God promises in his Word, "If you delight yourself in him, he will give you the desires of your heart" (Psalm 37:4). You cannot—I repeat, cannot—just name and claim anything you want. I was led by the Holy Spirit to believe for this house. I delighted myself in the Lord, so he did give me a desire of my heart, which was a home for Dara and me. However, it came with a price, and I wasn't certain I could pay.

The thought occurred to me, *If I just had one million dollars, all would be well.* I was realizing we needed more income. I couldn't even afford trash pickup, so I would keep the trash outside neatly arranged, and then every month, I would borrow a friend's old truck and take the trash to the dump.

We had believed for a house and gotten it, so now I stood in my little sanctuary and claimed one million dollars. I thought, "If I just had one million dollars, I could help different ministries, people, and my family while getting Dara and I settled for good."

God had let me have this house to live in, but after hearing the voice at the kitchen sink, I knew it wasn't permanent, and that kept me very unsettled. This was not exactly the way I wanted it. I was trying to keep a stiff upper lip for Dara's sake, but I began seriously to wonder if I was doing the right thing.

My family had moved to North Carolina the year before and was concerned about what was going on with us. Mom had come up to Richmond for the weekend to see what in the world I was doing. No one in our family had ever done anything like this before, and they all thought I was crazy. They even sent my nephew by to scope out my situation and living arrangement. I knew deep in my heart they were worried, but I also knew God had ordained this, and I was not in the mood to fight them over the issue of my sanity or God's sovereignty; I had already done that.

Dara confessed to me one day that my family had written a letter to her trying to convince her I was crazy. The old ache in my stomach started to come back, and I felt just overwhelmed about the whole situation. Something just didn't seem right, and I was tired of barely being able to eke out a living. I really didn't know what in the world to do.

Would it be better for the sake of Dara if we moved near my family? We had visited there previously one weekend, and they wanted us to move to North Carolina permanently and live with them. Dara seemed to light up at the prospect; she'd met some new friends while on that visit. Could I move in with them again? I was supposed to be the parent, but I once again questioned if I was failing at that too. Had the woman psychologist been right all those years before? Was I not fit to be a mother? I thought all of my indecisive behavior and decision making would be rectified when I turned to God. Why was this happening to me?

I had well-educated customers sit right in front of me and tell me that God was with me. They, through me, were experiencing a move of God right under their noses and would help cheer me on from time to time by telling me, "Well, Molly, who else could be doing this?" The comments comforted me momentarily but I pondered if I could continue to stand the heat.

By this time, I had sent poems to many different publishing companies, had written a TV sitcom and was trying to sell it. Time and time again, I tried to make something—anything—happen, but nothing but poetry was ever published. Over and over and over I did what I thought I was supposed to be doing. I knew I had a new life in Christ, but there was something else I was trying to reach for. I just didn't know how to get to it. It seemed like I was being stopped at every turn.

I was in my little sanctuary reading my Bible and I came across the scripture in Genesis 12:1–3. God told Abraham to leave his country and go to a place he did not know. I felt a rush of heat all over me, from the top of my head to the soles of my feet. That is all the confirmation about God's will that I needed for Dara and me. We had been living in this free house for a year by now. Dara was co-captain of the flag team at school, and her leader was a customer of mine. She was devastated upon hearing Dara wouldn't be back for her senior year. Dara's dad and grandparents weren't happy about her moving, but I had sole custody and believed this was God's will, and I was willing to stand against anyone to accomplish it. Dara seemed to be excited, and we talked extensively about its prospects. We decided she could finish high school in North Carolina. We packed up our belongings, I took all the money I had—$550— and we moved.

Somewhere in the back of my mind, I knew that God had something that was going to help support Dara and me. I believed that by moving to North Carolina, things would open up, come together, and eventually we could move into a home that I would buy for us. We were leaving a four-bedroom house, a city where Dara was born, a town that I had lived in since moving there with my family, and relocating all the way to North Carolina. I wondered what would take the place of what we were leaving behind.

I hadn't seen my dad in several years, so leaving him behind was nothing for me. I had sent him a copy of the first poem I had ever written which is as follows,

He said, "Turn to Me ... I'll set you free
from the bondage you feel inside.
I promised you I'd give you peace, abounding love and happiness.
I'll fill the void of emptiness.
I'll give you joy unendless.
My grace is yours.
Just believe in Me and you will live for eternity."
Jesus said, "I died for you to give you
grace ... would you have died for Me?"

The poem was sent back to me with a note that said, "Your father just wants some peace." I never heard from him again. I also never got a million dollars ...

"LET GO"

Two days after we moved to North Carolina, I got word that my dad had died. Unbeknownst to me, he had been in hospice care for about three months. I was shocked that my dad was gone. The last time we had seen each other was four years earlier, when he had disowned me. Remorse set in; I knew I would never get to hold his hand and tell him that I loved him. I wished for one more chance to tell him I knew he had done the best he could by me and that I should have done better as his daughter. I wanted to turn the clock back so I could have nursed him. Many regrets started to set in.

I didn't attend the funeral. I knew that once your soul leaves your body, you are either in heaven or in hell—period. He wasn't in a casket waiting for me to come and see him.

The previous summer, I had been led through prayer to stop praying to Jesus and pray to the Father through Jesus, his Son. After I got the revelation of God being my Father, it changed in my heart the whole dynamic about the Trinity. God actually began to rise up to me as my true Father, and I began to respect God in a way I never had before. Without my consent, the Holy Spirit was constantly working on me for God's grand design. This didn't make me love my dad any less, but my perspective had shifted, and I was able to see my dad as one of God's children, which in turn caused me to be able to pray more effectively for him.

In one of my middle-of-the-night sessions with God, I began to recount my dad's life to him. I began with my earliest childhood memory, telling God everything I knew about the man I called Dad. I told him what he had gone through as a child, detailing the abuse he suffered and the reasons I believed he committed adultery while married to my mother. I recounted the people I knew he had helped in one way or another. I pleaded with God on behalf of my dad, explaining why he deserved to be in heaven for eternity. In doing this, I also started to forgive him. Great comfort and healing took place inside of me. When I heard of his death, I began to wonder if he actually did make it to heaven.

I stood on the front porch of my sister's house in North Carolina crying out to my Father God. I looked up into the sky, sobbed, and I told God how much I missed my dad. I told God I didn't even know if Dad had made it to heaven. There was no closure for me, and it rocked my insides. It was odd realizing that there was no longer a Walter Painter on earth, and in that moment, I felt as though my life had come to a standstill.

I went to sleep that night beside Dara on the pullout futon that was now in the room we occupied. I was taken by the Spirit into a kitchen somewhere. We—the Spirit and I—were positioned in the left corner of the room, and I felt like I was spying on a scene from a movie. There were people sitting all around a table laughing, which reminded me of how people always gathered in our kitchen when I was young. I recognized my mother's aunt, and then all of a sudden, a man turned around—it was my dad! I couldn't believe it.

He appeared to be in his mid-thirties, was very handsome, and had the biggest grin on his face I had ever seen, which displayed his beautiful teeth. I had always loved to look at his teeth, but I think I noticed each and every one of them that night. He seemed so happy to see me and said, "The joy," very slowly as he smiled. I knew he was finally happy, content, and with people he loved—his family. I knew that even though Satan had tormented his whole life, in the end, God had won. I was now able to rest in the satisfaction of knowing that my dad was in heaven for eternity. I felt as though I somehow had helped plead his case before God so he could go home and be with Jesus, where Jesus promised he would wipe away every tear.

My brothers attended my dad's funeral, and upon coming back, one stated that my dad's favorite preacher was John Hagee. I wanted to see firsthand the man who got to my dad, who I once heard say, "If Jesus Christ were to walk down that road," as he pointed to his driveway, "I would ask him, "What can I do for you?"

I discovered Christian television was available twenty-four hours a day in North Carolina, and I was thrilled. There were so many people, preachers, and stories that it was truly overwhelming. I had no clue who to watch, but now I knew I was going to start with John Hagee. I was feeding on Christian TV twenty-four hours a day.

I felt that Dara and I needed to find a church somewhere and associate with other Christians. I knew she wouldn't receive much of anything from me since my family had tried to poison her mind in regard to my sanity, but she couldn't deny a pastor or other fellow brothers and sisters in the faith.

We started attending a small church on a six-by-three-mile island where the pastor played the guitar and sang throughout his sermons. I had visited there on a previous trip to my sister's, and since my family had been attending there, it was a natural move for me. The way he talked, I believed he must know God as I did, and I wanted so desperately to talk to him about what I was hearing, seeing, and dreaming. I thought what was happening to me was unusual, and I needed divine perspective from a godly man. He would stand at the end of every service and ask people to join the church and bring whatever gifts and talents they possessed. I started looking for the answer there. After all, there was a big cross on the top of the building.

A month or two went by, and nothing had happened in terms of me receiving any revelation about why I had been called to North Carolina. I tried to open up to the pastor there, but he would be silent as I tried to talk to him about some of the things I had seen. That hurt my feelings and caused me to clam up. I felt lost and a sense of dread began to return. Had I erred in making the move there?

I would sit on the steps of the front porch and look for a sign from Jesus. Why was I here? How was he going to use me? I had not thought about securing employment, and my family was pressuring me to do something. With no money except child support coming in, I couldn't afford to pay my car payment, and eventually my car was repossessed. I was in trouble, and therefore, claimed a new car. I said, "Well, if God took that one, he must want me to have a better one." But day after day went by and no car came.

So I ended up working at a little clothing store on the beach that paid me minimum wage. Every day someone in my family would have to drive me to work and pick me up, but at least I was working. I was humiliated and felt I was somehow in trouble with the Lord.

In the meantime, Dara had begun school. Her cousin had taken over $300 and bought Dara new school clothes so she would feel better about her new environment. Dara said when she walked up the steps to the school the first day, she was so scared that she almost turned around. She said, "I took a deep breath and knew if I went in, it would be okay." Moving to a new town had been too much for her.

I continued to work at the beach shop for about a month, and then due to slow business, they had to let me go. My bubble was really burst one evening when my brother came into the room that was now my new little sanctuary and said, "If you don't help your sister clean houses or go get another job, we are going to have you locked up."

I couldn't believe the gall. I screamed at him and ran outside of the house. Who did they think they were?

Dara was anxious, and I knew she was watching me to see if I was going to buckle under pressure or pick myself up and get moving. I knew what my family was telling her, and the last thing in the world I wanted my daughter to believe about me was that I was crazy; I didn't want her to see me locked up. I had no choice, so I began cleaning houses with my sister, and then remembered I had a nail license.

My sister mentioned that perhaps her hairdresser, who owned a salon in town, could use a nail tech, so I called her, made an appointment, and got a job doing fingernails again. I carried my Bible with me every day. I hadn't been in the regular workforce day after day for several years by then, and I knew that if I just had the Bible with me, it would help keep me in line. I was timid about talking about Jesus, but I knew he was real, so I just picked the times carefully. I didn't want to have anyone think I was crazy.

Each day, a family member took me to work; I would place a call in the afternoon, and someone would come to pick me up. This wasn't what I had thought it was going to be, but I had no choice but to keep going. One thing I had learned early on with Jesus was, "I can do all things through Christ who strengthens me."

I sat there one afternoon looking out the front door of the salon with a blank stare on my face. I knew I had made a mistake moving to North Carolina, but there was nothing to be done about it now.

The owner of the salon had agreed to charge me no rent for a month so that I could build up my clientele, but after several months, I was making hardly any money after booth rent was paid. I knew I couldn't survive this way of life if I wanted to provide for Dara and me.

One of my sister's neighbors suggested that I go to his hairdresser and inquire whether he needed a nail tech. There was no booth rent, and I could work strictly on commission. Being there was much better monetarily, and I met several women who became good friends.

I continued to feed on Christian television every moment I could. I knew that only God could help me out of the mess I found myself in if I would pursue him. I learned to fast in offering to the Lord, which was completely new for me. I thought fasting was rather weird, but something in me was being convicted that it really wasn't, so I took my questions to the Lord, got in the Word, and discovered that it wasn't something bogus.

Upon visiting North Carolina the previous year, Dara and her cousin had gone out bowling, and Dara had met a boy who stole her heart. I was thrilled because I had never been happy about the boy she was dating. I saw him lose his temper with her one evening and shove her up against the wall, and I knew the only way he was going to marry Dara was over my dead body. This new boy had given her the courage to leave her old boyfriend and move with me to North Carolina, but I soon discovered that this new fellow was not whom he said he was. I became hell-bent on my daughter not ending up with him.

Marriage had already been proposed, an engagement ring had been given, and they were going to move in together. I had never fasted or offered up money the way I was being led to do now, but I was willing to try anything to stop their union. I went before the Lord one day with communion, proclaiming a three-day fast. I made an offering into the ministry where I was led and offered everything I had, which was $224, to break this demonic hold off her life.

I learned that once I prayed a prayer or proclaimed a fast for any reason, I was to get up off my knees, shut up, and wait for God to move. I got up that day after prayer, and I knew in my heart that things between Dara and that boy were over. My family said, "Well, Dara has just gone to see the apartment she is moving into with her boyfriend."

I said, "We'll see about that."

They laughed at me as I walked out of the kitchen to go back down into my little hole, and I was furious. I shouldn't have been there, and I knew it. I hated being there. I came home from work three days later and guess what? Dara had gone to her new apartment and discovered her fiancé in bed with another girl. Everyone was shocked but I knew God had moved in this situation revealing the truth.

This one instance taught me that I was going to have to war for Dara and myself in way I never had to before. I was constantly praying, interceding, and going to church every time the door was open. As long as she was okay, then I could face my meager existence. I felt caught in a trap that I wasn't able to get out of, and I just was not able to understand what was happening to me, but I wasn't going to quit.

One day, my brother-in-law and I were outside smoking—no, I hadn't quit yet. He was a very close-mouthed individual who never said much of anything, but I felt led to tell him of the vision of Jesus. After I told him, all he could say was, "Really?"

I knew he didn't believe me, and I wished I had kept my big mouth shut; evidently it was not God leading me to tell him anything. His reaction made me keep quiet around the whole family from that moment on when it came to God. I only told Dara about things I had seen. They were telling her

I was crazy, and I was telling her visions I had seen. What a tangled web she was in. Who would she end up following?

I was standing at the kitchen sink one evening when no one was around. I looked up to heaven right into where I thought God's face would be and said, "Teach me to hear your voice so I will know clearly what to do."

I longed for a job with a steady paycheck and benefits. I had been talking about my employment status to the manager of the storage facility where I had stored our few belongings and he said his wife managed a temp agency. He said, "Why don't you give her a call to see if she can help you find a job?"

I called, made an appointment, and was offered a job at a medical facility, processing medical papers. I used a computer—by this time, I was pretty proficient with one—and sat in a little cubicle typing in information from several hundred medical sheets a day. As with most jobs, this job included a ninety-day probationary period, and after the ninety days, I was hired as a full-time employee with benefits and given a company car. Dara and my family were happy about it all. My new job entailed driving around town, picking up lab work, and bringing it back to the main facility for further processing.

I had to go through a two-week training period with a seasoned driver. My new life was starting, and I was scared but still excited about what lay ahead for me. My trainer and I started our route one morning, and the first stop we made was to a women's medical facility where outpatient surgery was performed. As I walked in and signed the log to pick up the order, I got closer to the counter, and my heart started to race. Lined up against the wall were what looked like big cold cream jars that contained something I could not readily identify, but I already knew in my heart what they were. I asked the attendant with me what was in the containers. The staff was sitting in the kitchen area at a table having lunch, laughing and having what seemed to be a high time.

She replied, "You know what they are."

Upon closer examination, I looked and could see dead fetuses floating in a gel-like substance, which confirmed my suspicions. My heart sank to the floor. I was extremely distraught inside as I walked out the door. With each step I took as I walked to the car, I felt like I was picking up lead. The voice I heard said, "You have a choice to make." I already knew what the choice was. I had to make a choice of whether to keep the job for the sake of a paycheck or to take a stand and do what I knew was morally right.

I went to the manager of the corporation, who really liked me, and explained my stance. I asked her if this particular stop could be taken off my route, if I could trade it for another. I made it clear I would do any other stop, no matter where it was, even if it meant the stop was two or three hours away. She said she would do everything she could to change it, stating this had never come up before. She said she would have to call corporate headquarters to get a decision, which might take up to two weeks.

Those were the two longest weeks I had ever spent, but I was determined not to back down because I needed a paycheck. I was kept busy around the facility while I awaited my fate. The two weeks passed, and she called me into her office and gave me the news. The run would stay the way it was and could not be altered.

All I wanted to do on this green earth was work for God. How did I find myself in this situation? Someone had already been hired for my old position, so it was this job or no job at all, and I knew I couldn't make that stop, even in lieu of the fact I had had five abortions myself. I had to resign.

They allowed me to work out two more weeks doing deskwork, and the manager sat there that day and told me how much she admired me for standing up for what I believed in. She said that I had made an impact on her life and that she would miss me. The last day I was there, I stopped by her office and gave her a few of the poems I had written. I wanted her to know this was a sort of thank-you for her being so kind to me.

When I came home that day, my younger brother—the one who was going to have me locked up—said that God would reward me one day for standing up for what was right. That was nice to know, but what about in the time being? Once again I found myself out of work and in search of employment. I called the temp agency, but they had nothing available, so I started looking in the paper again and sending out résumés to everyone who wanted anyone to do anything.

I felt that if I could just get back into banking, it would give me a good salary and benefits, and in turn, Dara and I could move out from beneath my family's thumb. I would borrow a car sometimes and go out driving around, looking at houses and dreaming of having a house for Dara and me. Yes, maybe banking was the answer.

I knew I needed to proclaim a fast for the situation. I knew that fasting was like taking a radio station that had a lot of static on it and tuning it in so you could hear clearly from heaven. By doing this, you could put a noose around Satan's neck so he couldn't get to you and stop you from receiving a clear answer—a fast it was!

I applied for a branch manager's job. I went before the Lord and explained to him all the reasons why I needed the job. I begged him to let me have it, knowing that if he could move so mightily in exposing Dara's boyfriend for who he really was, he could move on my behalf to get me a job. I went before the Lord, proclaimed a three-day fast, took communion, and made a fifty-dollar offering to the Lord so I could be a branch manager again.

Sunday evening came, and I decided not to attend regular service at church, opting instead for my futon and a blanket in front of the TV. The first preacher on was Jentzen Franklin. He stepped up to the podium and said he had been fasting all week long, and he had a message to deliver that he really did not want to deliver. He continued to say that he had a knot in his stomach because he really didn't want to have to come and bring this word, but he knew he had to be obedient.

He said, "I don't know who I have come here for tonight, but God told me to tell you, "No." I was sitting, and a heat rush went all over my body. Instantly, I knew the Spirit of the Lord was using him to talk directly to me, but I tried to shove it out of my heart. Wouldn't God want me to have this good job and benefits? Yes, I was certain he would, and I would let the phone call to the office determine my fate—not Jentzen Franklin.

The next day, I called and learned I was not selected for the position. I believed I lost about three inches in dignity when I hung up the phone. My spirit was crushed, and I went down into my room, fell across the bed, and sobbed. During the next several days, I realized that God was speaking to me in a new way and that I couldn't jerk his chain for anything I wanted. What was I going to do for work?

Right after that, I got up in the middle of the night as I had done in the past and sat before God. Dara was sound asleep, and I began whispering to God. I told him I didn't think I was a very good mother. I continued to whisper, explaining I wasn't able to provide for her in a solid way. The tears started to flow, and I cried and cried and asked God to forgive me. I repented until I thought I couldn't utter any more words, and I grabbed the front of my shirt and tore it open because I was so angry with myself. I was a failure. Something was still not right inside of me. Dara never woke up.

From that night forward, I started to realize I was still lost. I had no idea what to do except to keep going and to keep working. How could God actually love a person like me? I knew I deserved everything I was getting and felt broken inside. Dara really didn't confide in me at all anymore. It was as if a wall had been placed between us. She came home one afternoon and announced she was moving out. The time had come to pass—the time the voice had spoken of when he told me to enjoy our time in Richmond together. I had continued to make promises to her of a home and us being together but had not been able to produce one. She said she was fed up with the way we lived.

She stated, "I am going to go to college now, and I am working."

The dreams were over. The confirmation about me became a reality. I felt I had failed as a mother and as a person. My self-worth and self-esteem were shot. As she packed her belongings to leave, I cried and cried. She started to cry. I was distraught.

"Please don't go," I cried. "Please don't leave me."

She had met another boy and was going to move in with him. She said, "Mom, you promise all these things, and nothing ever happens."

I knew it, and it cut my heart. What could I do about it? The voice came to me and said firmly, "Let go."

I heard this phrase repeatedly as I sobbed. I was sick inside. I hated my life. I hated myself. I was praying for her and everyone in my family to help them. How could God let this happen? Didn't he see she would be better off with me?

That night as I trailed off to sleep exhausted, I had another vision, and in it I was driving in a car, and there was a voice behind my right shoulder that said, "Let go." This time the voice was a calm and reassuring voice, and again uttered, "Let go."

My hands were gripped so tightly on the wheel that my knuckles turned white. We were driving through the air much like the *Jetsons* did in the cartoon show. Lights and traffic were all around. Up ahead, I saw a mountain that seemed to come out of nowhere. The voice again said, "Let go."

I cried, "I can't!"

Again, I heard, "Let go."

All of a sudden, I just knew that if I didn't let go of the wheel, I was going to crash into that mountain. All at once I was thinking, *I am going to crash and die if I don't let go.* Then I thought, *I am going to die anyway, so I might as well let go.*

I released my hands from the steering wheel, and the car started to plummet. As if by some unseen force, the car started to glide through the air. I awoke the next morning, and slowly the revelation of this dream came to me. I was trying to control everything, and I needed to let God take the controls or I was going to die. I needed to let go. I needed to trust God.

"MY PEOPLE ARE STARVING"

Dara was gone. Then due to lack of money, I finally had to let go of the storage unit that held all the worldly possessions I had, which by that time, weren't many. I either gave or trashed anything that was in there. Little by little and bit by bit, everything was being taken away from me. I was becoming numb to life, all the while pretending that it didn't matter, but deep inside, it mattered a great deal to me. I knew if I stopped and didn't get out of bed that life as I had ever known it would be over, and my family would see to it that I was locked up, no matter what I tried to tell them. I had no dignity left.

Had I known God at all? I thought I had learned about God in a way that most people didn't—by way of dreams, visions, and having the Lord appear to me—but I had missed it. I still wanted to do great things for God but realized I was around people who didn't believe like I did. Dara's presence kept me able to live with my family, but after she moved out, I knew they were just putting up with me, and I didn't know how long it would last.

All I did was soak myself in Christian TV for an answer. I was a complete failure, but something in me wouldn't let me quit. I saw people in churches on TV who were changed, set free, and delivered. I heard testimonies of extreme situations that were turned around. Why was this happening to me?

The body of believers I was around would refer to some of the same preachers on TV I was watching, but I didn't see things happening in the church I attended—nothing like what I heard the folks on TV talk about. I wanted to know why; I just could not understand it. If I was hearing about how God was moving in just a few people's lives, I might have understood, but many people were having life-changing moments. Who was right, and who was wrong? I was going to church and seeing people who seemed to love the Lord but at the same time, were defeated in their everyday lives. Why was this? Was I one of them?

An announcement was made at church that testimonies would start to be heard on Wednesday nights. Well, maybe this was my chance. Maybe something would open up for me by giving mine, so I told the pastor one Sunday after service what I wanted to do. A time slot was given to me for the following Wednesday. I borrowed my brother's word processor and typed out a testimony. I went to Walmart and bought new pants and a shirt just for the occasion.

As I drove to the church on the big night, I took an extra dose of Buspar, which had replaced the Ativan I had always taken, to calm my nerves. As I swallowed them, I promised God I would stop taking medication when he actually started using me in public. My family came out of curiosity that night. After being given a microphone for the big event, I arose and went to the podium; I felt this is where I belonged.

I began speaking, and the people in the pews just looked at me as if they were dead. The more I talked, the worse it got, and I became very nervous. No one moved as I finished and took my place in the front pew.

The man in charge got up, tied up the few things I had said with a neat little ribbon, we sang a hymn, and the service was over. Only two or three people came up to me afterward to offer remarks about how courageous I was. Nothing was said about how God did what he did through me. No one wanted to talk about what had happened in my life, and I felt as though I had a scarlet letter on my forehead once again.

From that moment forward, I stopped talking about the things I had been through and the miracles that had taken place in my life. Being the people pleaser that I still was, it was easy for me to fit myself into their way of doing God. No one wanted to hear about my deliverance, so I just pushed it down inside of me and tried to do church the way the people there did. I was quiet around my family, and now I was going to be quiet around the church congregation because no one wanted to hear it. I left that night feeling that I was wrong after all and had no call on my life by God.

I took a shower one Saturday evening, laid down on the futon, and started to doze off. All of a sudden, a voice passed over my face and said, "My people are starving for lack of food and Word." It startled me so much that I jumped up. The words "food" and "word" were said simultaneously, but the strange part was that it was my dad's voice I was hearing. His voice and breath were so near that I thought he was right in the room with me. I pondered over that for days until it hit me; people don't really know what is in the Word of God (Hosea 4:6).

I met a couple of elderly women at one of the salons where I had done fingernails, and we had become friends. They had asked me go with them to their church, so I did. This was a huge Presbyterian church, and I went to a couple of healing services and laid hands on the sick and afflicted. My church didn't talk about how Jesus healed, even though we all had the same Bible, and I thought to myself how odd it was. These two churches were about five miles apart, yet worlds apart in their beliefs.

I had begun to overeat again, and my hair started to fall out right where my part was. I looked up to heaven and told God, "I can do just about anything you want me to, but I cannot take having my hair fall out."

The next evening, I tuned into Trinity Broadcasting Network for the evening. There sat a panel of eight doctors who were educated, authored, and—on top of all of that—Christians. They had come on the channel to teach people how to take care of their bodies. Jan Crouch (co-owner of the network) had awakened with her eye full of blood one morning, which prompted her to ask a panel of doctors to come on the show and teach others about the only temple we have.

All of a sudden, a woman doctor said, "And by the way, if your hair is falling out, take Omega-3s!" The show was three hours long, and I sat on my futon and took several pages of notes to use as a guide for my health. This show made me aware that even though God had done miracles in my body, I needed to do my part. I went the following day to Walmart and loaded up on Omega-3s.

I felt so alone with Dara gone—as if my very breath had been taken from me. I stayed in my room when I wasn't working, trying to stay close to God. I had been ignoring the Holy Spirit telling me to quit smoking for too long now. The voice had been so loud and clear; it would utter, "Stop smoking! Stop smoking!"

I loved to smoke—absolutely loved it. I had tried to stop while living in Richmond but never could seem to get the monkey off my back. The local pharmacist who doled out my prescription pills had become my friend. She and I had coffee several times, and she would bring me boxes of Nicorette Gum her husband didn't use. I tried to quit by chewing this gum, but all I ended up doing was smoking and chewing gum due to my constant uncertainty. Cigarettes and medications were the only crutches I had, and I felt I needed them all.

One Friday evening it all came to a head. I was watching TBN and Carman, a Christian singer, was leading worship. He stopped right in the middle of the song and said, as he pointed his finger into the camera, "By the Spirit of the Lord, there is someone who needs to stop smoking and taking medications." I got a heat rush all over my body and knew God was speaking to me through him, telling me to stop smoking and taking my medications; I just knew it. It was the same feeling I had when Jentzen delivered the word "No," so I knew once again God was trying to tell me something. Hadn't I asked him to speak to me clearly? Hadn't I asked him to teach me to hear his voice? But this time I received the word given without question.

Dad had died with terminal cancer that had eaten him up from his brains to his toes, and I was not going to have the same thing happen to me. What had begun as a high with my mother years earlier was going to kill me if I didn't stop. I was still taking my antidepressants, a female hormone, and Synthroid as well, but that Friday night, I laid them all down. I stopped smoking and quit taking all of my meds, not knowing how I was going to make it through life without any of them. The word was given, and I was going to be obedient.

Knowing the power that I possessed by quoting scripture, I started quoting it when I started to crave nicotine, which was only twice after I stopped smoking. I would quote, "Greater is he that is within me than he that is within the world." I would continue, "I take authority over this craving in the name of Jesus, and command you leave this body. Get out of here, Satan, in Jesus' name." The craving would subside, leaving no further desire for nicotine. I was amazed at what speaking scriptures aloud would do when I backed them up with my faith.

I no longer took the medications I had taken for panic attacks, and I did not suffer from any recurring episodes. If one would try to creep up on me, I just took authority over it in the name of Jesus.

I also knew if I didn't stop smoking, I was going to contract cancer; I just knew it deep inside. I was given a choice that night to stop smoking or suffer the consequences. Remember the show *Truth or Consequences?* That's how it was for me. I always had to have the cold, hard truth put in my face before I would wake up and take action or I could suffer the consequences.

I really separated myself from others when I was at home but continued going to the same church my family attended. I had never had a vision or seen anything in that church until one Sunday. There was a woman in my mind's eye, walking back and forth on the stage where the pulpit was. Prison bars were all around her. Behind those bars, she could walk, talk, eat, go to the bathroom, and sleep. She could visit with friends as they came up. She didn't realize she was behind those bars. Then as if by some unseen hand—quite dramatically—the bars were raised. She was truly set free for the first time in her life and realized she had been stuck in her own personal prison. Who was the vision for?

I stopped trying to make my life happen. I just got up every day and did what I knew how to do. My family was pressuring me to get a job again, so I borrowed a family car and headed for Food Lion one Saturday afternoon. I had never worked in a grocery store, but I needed money, and claiming it wasn't going to cut the mustard with God. I was hired on the spot and started there a few days later. Every two weeks, I was handed a paycheck, and I would come home and hand it to my family for my rent there. Memories of *should have* gone Food Lion in Richmond flooded my mind.

My younger brother had become friends with someone who ran a coffee shop in the heart of Wilmington. He said, "Maybe she will let you go down there and read some of your poetry." *Poetry?* I thought. *Ha!* Then I thought, *I am called to preach the gospel, but I could use the poetry to get my foot in the door and then give my testimony. Now that's an idea!*

I was friends with several girls in Wilmington who seemed stable—they had homes, husbands, and children and attended church; they wanted the more of God as I did. They came the night I was to give my testimony to give me support. I fasted that day, dressed up in a suit, and headed to give my testimony in a public setting.

There were about twenty-five people there as I stepped up to the open mic to speak. The earth didn't quake, and people didn't fall out on the floor under the anointing of Christ. No one screamed for more as I spoke. I stepped down from the little riser and walked quietly and slowly to the bathroom. The voice I had come to know said, "Do not forsake the days of small beginnings."

I looked at myself in the mirror and thought, *I know I did what God wanted me to do tonight.* I walked out of the restroom feeling very sullen, wondering what had just happened. I thought, *Well, maybe this is the start of what I am supposed to be doing for God, and there will be an offer to go speak somewhere else.*

I was walking back to my group, and two strangers who were sitting in the bar area stopped me. They stared at me oddly and said, "We were at home praying, and God told us to stop and come down here."

My eyes became huge as saucers. They continued, "We are to lay hands on you and call you forth."

All of a sudden, they started to pray over me. One laid her hands on my stomach and the other on my shoulders. They started speaking in a way that I had only heard of—in tongues. When they stopped, I was amazed at how I felt. I started to walk away, and one of them said, "You need to write *the* book."

It wasn't *a* book; it was *the* book. I said, "I know. I will."

The word delivered to me that night gave me hope to keep going a little bit longer and try harder knowing God was, in fact, still with me. It helped me to know not all was lost, as I had come to believe.

I wanted to move out on my own, but I had no means with which to do it. I held onto the belief and hope that if I was obedient, worked hard, and kept going, somehow God would give me a place of my own, even though I didn't know how. I had come to discover that the house my daughter and I had lived in rent-free was still empty and remained that way through the time my daughter would have graduated from high school. God had made a way for us both to live there until she finished school, but I had goofed by moving us a year too soon.

There I was at Food Lion, standing at my checkout register one evening, and a voice said, "How do like your job here? How do you like standing on your feet all day? You have been very blessed in your life, haven't you?"

I almost hung my head in shame and wept on the spot. It was one of my cold-water-in-the-face moments. I knew I had been very blessed in my life, and I had taken it all for granted and destroyed it all. The lesson had been learned; I got it. He had me there to teach me a lesson I hadn't gotten previously.

I would go to work, come home, ice down my back, and not move so that I could make it to the next shift. I knew I was working an honest job and doing the best I knew how, but wasn't there something more for me? As I was standing at the register one day, I bent down and said under my breath, "Jesus, save me."

I stood up, and the next man in line said, "Do you get forty hours a week here?"

I said, "No."

He said his mother had a little health store and asked if I'd come by to fill out an application. I couldn't believe it. "Yes!" I said with glee. It was time for me to move again.

I went to the interview several weeks later, and the owner said the hair on the back of her neck stood up as I stood there. She said she had never hired anyone on the spot before, but she offered me a job with the understanding that it was only temporary.

I resigned my job at Food Lion and gave two weeks' notice. My supervisor told me that anytime I needed a job, all I had to do was ask. After all the jobs I had had, job stability wasn't even something I thought of anymore. I just needed to work, make an honest living, and just keep going. I was on a course set by God, and I might as well buck up and accept it. I didn't tell anyone in my family about my continuing, developing relationship with the Lord. I just kept working, praying, and interceding for others, all the while trying to get to where God wanted me to go.

Dara received a newer car from her dad as a high school graduation present. She asked him what he wanted to do with the old car he had bought her when we moved here, and he said, "Whatever you want to do." Well, she gave it to me. I had a car! I felt like a million dollars. Evidently I was doing something right.

With this new job, I embarked on a completely new career that involved things I knew nothing about. This business's purpose was providing and teaching people ways to live and eat healthily. They carried an array of vitamins, and the reading material showed people how to promote and maintain a fit body using natural methods. I was clueless about all of this but thought it might be a very interesting undertaking for me. To top it off, I was working forty hours a week.

While I was there, I started upon a health quest for myself. I stood in the aisle and looked at 2,700 different vitamins one day; it was overwhelming. I didn't know there were so many different kinds of vitamins. Little by little, I was led to take this or that and obeyed those leadings. I knew from watching the show on TBN with the panel of doctors that there was more I needed to know about how to take better care of myself.

I knew that I had to be accountable for the one body I was going to have while I was here on earth. I hadn't run to the doctor for years with my ailments because I didn't have the money or insurance to seek medical advice. Instead, I used scriptures to keep myself going, but I now felt led to learn and help myself by taking vitamins.

In the midst of all of the upheaval in my life, my family decided to move. Up until the last minute, I had no idea if I would be allowed to go with them. They had not mentioned or asked me to go, and I didn't know what I was going to do. My sister told me that I could get a room at the YWCA. I thought that if I ended up there, I would be so depressed I wouldn't be able to get up out of bed. I went to God lamenting more than once, not knowing what to do, but only heard a dead, deafening silence. My mother also lived with my sister and family, and

I asked her if I could just go live with them for a while and sleep on the floor of her bedroom. No one ever said I could or couldn't, and since I had nowhere else to go, I moved with them.

I didn't have any worldly possessions but a few clothes, shoes, and toiletries by then, but I needed somewhere to lay my head. I didn't consider myself anything but a burden; I knew my mere presence irritated them. I slept on the floor of my mother's room on an inflatable mattress, and believe me, it was not a good one. It would deflate in the night, and I would have to blow it back up the following evening. Still, I was safe and secure, and I knew no one could hurt me. I was with family, even though I never said much around them. I continued to pray, fast, and tithe to the Lord. I got up extra early to have prayer time with the Lord. I couldn't stop now.

I didn't tell anyone I worked with, went to church with, or any of my friends where I slept or what was going on; I was humiliated enough. God knew my situation, and no one else needed to know. I held my head high through Christ and just kept working, believing God would make a way for me out of no way at all.

A popular book began to circulate around the group of people with whom I was associating. The friends I had were of several different denominations, so I was able to hear what they were experiencing. What they all said was not very different, but one thing was clear—the people I was around all wanted a move of God in their churches. We wanted what we were seeing on TV, but we weren't getting it.

The book was called *The Prayer of Jabez,* and we were all hot to get it. I never seemed to have any extra money to buy anything, but God always saw that I had what I needed and what he wanted me to have. One of my friends called me one day at the store and said, "I called around and found the last copy in town. I won't be able to read it for a couple of days, so I will bring it to you." She promptly drove to the health store and delivered the book. I couldn't wait to get home and read it.

I rushed home, up the stairs and into my room with a cup of coffee, and I settled in to read. When I finished that night, I almost fell off the air mattress. God was trying to get something more to me about him being my Father, but I didn't understand it all yet, so I prayed and asked him, "What is it I am to receive from all of this?" I shut up and just waited for the Holy Spirit to reveal to me the answer.

The author of this book prayed the short little prayer found in Chronicles 4:10 each day, and then God would bring strangers to him to minister to. What did I have to lose? I added this prayer to my morning prayers. After the very first day, I went home that evening to reflect on what had happened, and God had indeed sent strangers for me to help.

There was a woman at the health store I really liked. She worked during the week, and her daughter worked there on the weekends, so I got to know them fairly well as a family. Her husband was getting ready to retire from the city police department. He would stop in from time to time on his breaks. My custom was to carry my Bible with me everywhere I went; just having it near helped me stay focused. As time passed, we started talking about Jesus. I also explained Satan to her. I had learned to plead the blood of Christ over everyone in my family and felt she needed to know how to do this in order to protect her family as well.

We weren't busy one afternoon, and we found ourselves in a deep conversation about the blood Christ shed for us at

Calvary. I told her to go home and try to plead the blood of Christ over her home and family. I wrote down exactly what to say. I said, "I know it sounds weird, but just try it, and let me know what you discover."

She walked into work the next morning hardly able to contain herself. We were busy the first part of the morning, but when we had the first free moment, she started to recount what she had done the night before. She said she quoted out loud, word for word, what I had written down on that piece of paper. She told me she felt as if she could almost see Satan walking back and forth on her front lawn, snarling, huffing, and puffing out smoke. She said it was if he was like a beast that was standing up on his hind legs, furious about what she was doing.

I knew the power of the blood was real; we both knew. Together, we wrote on slips of paper exactly how to plead the blood of Christ over yourself, your family, your homes, etc., and we handed out copies we made to customers as we were led. We didn't have the permission of the owner to do this, but we did it nonetheless.

Usually people just took them with them without even bothering to look at them as they left, but one day, I handed one to a black man, and he stopped to read it. He turned around and started walking toward me. All I could think of was I was going to be in big trouble. He asked, "Who taught you to do this?"

I responded, "The Holy Spirit."

He said, "Keep up the good work." I later discovered he was a prominent pastor of a large church in town.

A very big man—tall in stature walked up to the check out counter one day. I rung up his order, he pulled out his wallet to pay but then he began to stare at me with a glazed look in his eyes. He began to step backward in slow motion. There was no one else around, which was unusual. He started telling me that

God had called me to the nations. I immediately asked him to wait before he continued any further. I wanted a witness. I quickly grabbed my friend by the arm so she could listen in case I forgot anything he said. He continued, "God has had his hand on your life since"—his hand started at about where five feet would be, and he kept moving it down until it was about two feet from the floor—"you were a child. God said you were to write a book." I stood there stunned for a moment, and so did my friend.

This was the second confirmation I had received of what the Holy Spirit had put on my heart years earlier—how I had been saved by grace, and how I needed to write a book. Receiving that prophecy kept me going a little longer. I explained to the Lord one time, "Even a rabbit needs a carrot to go a little bit further, and I could sure use a carrot." He always gave me one just at the right time, when I thought I couldn't go on any further.

I fell into bed one evening after work and quickly dozed off, feeling as though I were actually slipping away from my body. I was worn out. Someone appeared over me, saying, "Fight back. Fight back." The voice that I had come to know well by this time was telling me I needed to fight for myself. I never felt worthy enough to fight for myself due to the guilt of my horrific life and sin. I didn't have any self-worth or self-esteem, and I still used a façade to mask my hurt. I could fight for others all day long, but not for myself.

I knew that if I didn't do something, I would continue to slip away. I was conscious enough to utter—it had become second nature to me by then—the only words I knew that would help. I said, "I plead the blood of Christ over myself. I take authority over every principality, every power, every ruler of darkness, and every evil and wicked spirit in the heavenly realms. I command you get away from me, Satan, in Jesus' name."

I didn't cry out for help. I didn't yell for anyone to come. I didn't scream out in fear. I spoke the only words I knew that would help me and then drifted off to a sweet slumber, realizing once again that Satan was out to destroy me but the blood of Christ had saved me.

————————

My friend stated she thought she had been hired to help close out the books in order to shut the health store down because business had been so slow, but a once-dying business now started to flourish. However, the resurgence that was taking place was truly unexplainable. We would gather every morning in the back and start praying over the shop. We would plead the blood of Christ over the building and started calling people there from the north, south, east, and the west, and I would end with Jabez's prayer. Somehow, the tide started to change. It was amazing. One day, a woman said she had come specifically because God told her to get up, take the bus, and go to the health store.

I had learned quickly that there were items that I, in all good conscience, was not going to sell to anyone. Some of the things in the store were questionable to one's well-being, and I wasn't going to push something like Ephedra on others, knowing it could cause them to have a stroke. I had asked a long time co-worker and friend of the owner one afternoon to show me a couple of items that wouldn't be detrimental to an individual. I started to tell people about items I knew would help and not harm them. There were medical journals and written materials by doctors on the benefits of vitamins, minerals, and other health-related substances that we gave out to customers. I enjoyed learning things about the body God had given to me. I had depended on doctors all of my life to tell me what to do, but being exposed to the information firsthand caused my thinking to broaden. I talked to others, taking it all in. I would go home, pray, and talk to God about things I was learning. I would then be directed by the Holy Spirit what to take.

I went home one evening and crashed on my mother's bed. She had gone back to visit relatives in our hometown, so I had her bedroom all to myself, and her bed felt like heaven to me. This particular evening, I was feeling overly exhausted. I had been interceding for strangers at work. I was always striking up conversations with anyone. If they had something that needed praying about, I would, or my friend and I would, come into agreement about it with them. I didn't realize how much energy was being sucked from my body.

Then upon falling asleep, I had a vision. I was standing in a long line, and there were several other people ahead of me. There were also two or three figures I couldn't make out. They would both take an arm of an individual, and the person being held would be hit with something. Their knees would buckle beneath them, causing them to crumple on the ground, and then the two figures would raise them up and send them out into a sea of people. I don't know who the individuals were, but they were in control.

It was my turn, and I stood there waiting as they each grabbed an arm, knowing I had no other choice. I told them, "I am scared." They assured me there was nothing to fear. I knew I had to buck up and take whatever was being dished out. All of a sudden, they touched me with something. I felt as though I was being knocked down with a stun gun. My whole body went limp. I was awakened from this vision just enough to be able to really feel what I was experiencing. I was tingling all over and feeling as though I was being washed in love, cream, and everything good. The feeling was so comforting that I did not want to be fully awakened. I wanted to stay in that state of being forever. What did it mean?

Once again, I shared what had happened with my friend at the health store. No one could explain to me what was going on, so I stopped sharing the things that I was experiencing, and life at the health store continued.

Stranger things began to happen. I was talking to a male customer one day about vitamins, and then, naturally, the conversation turned to Jesus. He stated, "You are a warrior."

A what? Yes, I had warred for people on my knees. I would pray for people, and tangible things would happen, but what was the designation he was giving me by calling me a warrior?

Then there was the day I had a woman come up and growl at me. I was straightening the vitamins on the shelves and heard a growling sound over my right shoulder. I stopped, as calmly as one could when being growled at by a person, and called my friend over. I told her what had just occurred. I couldn't believe my ears. My friend and I stood there as this woman walked slowly away. She stopped then turned around, pointed at me with a great big grin and said, "I'll see you later." She smirked and went off. Again I knew I was being shown more things in the spiritual realm I would have to deal with. Seeing, hearing, and watching tangible things happen kept me in the Word. The only TV I watched was TBN when I got an opportunity. I had no TV in my room and no one in my family wanted a steady diet of Christian TV, so the opportunities were few and far between for television any more.

Due to all that I had been through and was experiencing in the spiritual realm, I wondered what else was available for use on earth to those who followed Jesus. My health store friend and I came into agreement for a customer who was to have quadruple bypass surgery. We stood and called his heart back into alignment in the name of Jesus. We commanded every artery be opened as well. Several weeks later, the man and his wife came into the store. They said they could hardly wait to get there to tell us the news. He only had to have two stints put in, as opposed to having to undergo major surgery. They were thrilled. We were excited that we had been able to help him by doing the bidding of the Lord.

After a Wednesday evening service at church, I was asked by the person who led the youth if I would be interested in directing the children's Christmas play. Well, this offer surprised me, and I was a little rocked but listened to what he had to say. I wanted to work for God, but with children? I stood there a moment and then gave my usual, hearty, "Yes."

At first, I didn't know what I could do, but I wasn't preaching or teaching the gospel, so I had the time. Besides, the youth guide was neat—even though he was married—and I thought it might be fun.

The more I got involved in writing and directing the Christmas play, the more my feelings started to change toward the youth guide I was working with. This man was married but had experienced a troubled marriage from the get-go, and everyone knew it. I knew what the Word of God said about adultery, and I was not going to go there, but surely working together for the good of the children couldn't hurt, could it?

Then, weeks later, one of my friends called me to tell me of a dream she had about me. In this dream, she and I were sitting beside each other in Sunday school. She had a chart in her hands. She said on this chart there was a scripture followed by the word "test." Then there was another scripture, and then the word "test" again. This went on and on, as she read the chart. It was as if I was being tested, and then if I passed, I would be tested again.

Men had always been my downfall. I always had to have a man. This time was somehow different, wasn't it? He loved Jesus, I loved Jesus, and yes, he was unhappy at home, and I was the shoulder he was leaning on. Was that a bad thing?

JESUS FIRST,
OTHERS SECOND ...

My family bought a new home and prepared to move again. I had no idea if I was going to be allowed to move with them or not. Nothing was said one way or another, so I assumed I would be allowed to move with them once again, since I had no other viable options. I didn't make enough money to support myself, even though I was working full-time. I was still working hard at the health store and now involved heavily at church.

I began to feel for the very first time my steps were actually being ordered by the Lord, and I had no say in the matter. I realized that I needed to shut up, just keep getting up every day and continue to do what I knew to do. If and when God determined it was time for me to live on my own, he would make a way.

I continually warred for Dara, even though she wasn't physically present with me, because I knew her only hope was going to be in Christ. I learned tangibly that there was no distance or time in prayer, and you didn't have to be physically present to help someone receive from heaven. Not having her with me was still unsettling, yet I knew that the blood of Christ, backed up by my belief in the power of my words when applied over her by faith, kept her safe from Satan. She knew

I did not care for the young man she was living with, but neither she nor my family ever discussed her living arrangements when I was present. I didn't feel led in any way to go to battle about this relationship by fasting and offering as I had before. This time, I had to wait on God.

The unofficial youth guide at our church started a contemporary service and asked Dara to be a part of a three-person singing group, which thrilled me to death. I was better able to keep close tabs on her, and I felt just being in a church setting would help her. She had a beautiful voice, and I prayed that this was how God would use her. I joined the team in the capacity of chaperone, lighting director, and gofer, all the while being a secret warrior for everyone. The extra work involved many hours of planning, discussion, and practice.

I felt I was warring not only for strangers at work but now also for my church body. It was more than I ever imagined in terms of exhaustion. I realized there was more going on in the spiritual realm that affected us here on earth than most of us were aware of. No one was teaching others that demonic powers had to be dealt with. At times, I felt like a one-woman crusade, and I carried a heavy burden about it all.

I was also feeling that God wanted me to learn to come up under the authority of the pastor he had placed there. I did what I believed I was being told to do every step of the way and stopped trying to be in control. I learned that silence is golden. Had I not learned to be a better listener, I would have missed hearing things from others that helped me pray for them more effectively, accomplishing the bidding of the Lord.

Inside of me were strong feelings of righteousness, truth and justice. I couldn't understand why others couldn't just stand up for what was right in regard to reaching out and helping the truly needy and the poor in spirit. I wanted to turn the world upside down for Jesus and it seemed like I was being held back. And no matter what happened to me, honest Abe was always in there ready to help, even if I had to do it alone. I also felt a growing sense of having a little Joan of Arc inside, who wanted to lead God's children to the death in the cause of Christ, but I kept hitting a wall with religious traditions. Because others wanted to sweep my past under the rug, no one at church really understood the real me. They wanted me to do church their way, so that is what I did. I did nothing that wasn't approved by the church members and the pastor, and I felt boxed in, pretending again as I had always done. I encountered more demonic forces within the boundaries of those four walls than even I could believe. Martin Luther King, Jr. was quoted as saying, "I saw Satan fall like lightening from the sky, and he dropped into my choir."

I didn't understand that statement until I got involved in this body of believers. I came to know there are just as many demons in a church as there are followers of Christ, and you had to fight in order to further the kingdom of God. I had always thought if you bothered to go to church, it was because you were there to work together for the common good of the Lord, but the arguing, backbiting, and gossiping from members hurt my heart. I confided in my friend at the health store about the demonic activity that was occurring at my church. One Friday evening, we felt convicted to fast, go there, and physically walk the grounds, pleading the blood of Christ over it. I discovered I could be Joan of Arc after all, warring on behalf of heaven, and no one needed to know but my Father who had ordained it. A great peace started to fall over me, and I knew I was doing God's bidding in a way that fulfilled me.

It was Christmas 2001, I was sitting in church, minding my own business and looking at all of the boxes at the front that had been filled to send to Samaritan's Purse. Samaritan's Purse provides Christmas boxes to boys and girls worldwide who may not otherwise receive anything. The Holy Spirit spoke to me and said, "Why are you sending those halfway around the world when there are children right here who need your help?"

I flicked the area around my ear as if I didn't hear anything; I pushed the voice away. As I drove home from the service that night, however, I had the sinking feeling that there were children right in front of my face and the church's face who would not be having any Christmas.

The following year, I was not going to be allowed to get by without doing something about it. I decided that if I was going to birth a mission outreach helping needy children, I wanted to make certain God was telling me to do it. I especially knew that with this body of believers, I would have a fight on my hands to accomplish such a task. It took me a while, but I finally discovered what the Lord wanted me to do. I sought opinions from within the church setting as well as from others I worked with.

The response was always the same: "Why wouldn't you help needy children?" This was usually followed by, "Let me know if you need any help."

I made the mistake of telling my family what I was going to attempt. A family member made the comment, "You ought to be good at this since you're homeless too."

Joy of a Child Mission Outreach was birthed through my local church in 2002, but it was not accomplished without tremendous battling in the spiritual realm. There were those who couldn't understand why Joy of a Child was needed. I had seen firsthand, by working with the children and seeing the needy parents, just how much of a need there was for this outreach program; it was staring me—actually all of us—right in the face. I was aware of every little detail. Sometimes, the children would come to children's church appearing hungry, so we started giving them something to eat on Sunday mornings.

Secretly I had already helped one family within the walls of the church. I told a wealthy customer about this family, and they, in turn, bought the child, mother, and grandmother new clothes, along with some food. I discreetly took them and dropped them at the church office to be delivered by the missions committee. I knew there were people right in front of our faces who needed help, and more importantly, so did God. I was going to do the outreach come hell or high water, and I couldn't understand why people did not see the same need. It infuriated me.

Even though the pastor had approved the project, I had to go through the red tape of getting the outreach approved from the missions committee and then if approved at that level, I would have to bring it to the church for a final vote. A female friend by the name of Wendy volunteered to help me with the outreach, as did a customer of mine, named Linda, who attended a nearby church.

We all attended the initial meeting, but I was the spokesperson. Sitting beside me in the meeting were a couple I will never forget. Bill and Sherry Setzer spoke up and agreed that something needed to be done for the people locally instead of concentrating our efforts in some faraway land. What a relief that was! They let me know through their encouragement and vocal support that they wanted the same things I did.

If I could just get all the churches to come together, we could make certain that year that no one on the island would go without Christmas. *Wouldn't it be wonderful?* I thought. I was determined that we would leave no stone unturned in the effort to seek out every needy child.

We were beginning from the ground up, depending solely on prayer and faith to see us through. We had no money to begin this outreach, but I knew if God ordained it, the money was out there; I just had to go and get it. The three of us met, prayed, and asked God for guidance. We each had God-given gifts, and he was the only one who really knew how he wanted them utilized. We felt we needed to get in touch with every church on the island and talk to the pastors, so I made the calls. I actually had one pastor yell at me, telling me I was trying to steal from Samaritan's Purse. I could not believe my ears! His comment stung. He didn't even know me.

We decided to start our efforts by calling Social Services, explaining what we were endeavoring to do. It was suggested that we begin by going to the one elementary school on the island and discussing our idea with the counselor. I made the initial contact with Amy. She was thrilled at the proposition and even came up with the original idea of how to get the names of the children without hurting anyone's feelings. She knew each family's circumstances intimately. She ended our conversation by asking how many children we wanted, and I piped up and said, "All of them." I had the faith to know God was big enough to handle whatever he gave us.

Through prayer and fasting, it was determined we would not only target the children whose names we were given, but would also help any siblings and parents in the home as well. We wrapped donation boxes like presents and placed them in businesses all over the island. We also placed ads in the local paper and on the radio to try to garner support. What I discovered was that people genuinely wanted to help the needy within their own communities. I also heard, as I walked about, that people were disheartened by church. When I was asked where I attended church, I would stop and take the time to tell them about my church, Jesus, and God. One of the other women in our group had the time to contact each family, asking them if they wanted or needed help. The ones who accepted were given time to inquire what their children would like, and then it was up to the family to call us back with the wants and needs of each child in the home. The system worked beautifully.

While in prayer one morning, my mind's eye saw a great big present with names all over it. I knew what I was being told, so I wrapped a huge box. I fashioned it to look like a present, and the following Sunday, the pastor's face lit up as I walked up the church steps into the vestibule. He commented heartily on what a wonderful idea it was. It was placed in the front of the church on a stand with the names of the children on index cards, containing each wish they had for Christmas. In this way, others could select what they wanted to buy, from socks to bikes.

That first year we raised a little over $1,700 from area businesses. It had been made clear previously through prayer that the Holy Spirit wanted us to use all the money; the money was not to be saved for another year and not to be used by the church for any other reason. In addition, we were to *first* tithe from the money raised before using it.

Along with spearheading this outreach, I was also directing the children's Christmas play. We came up with the bright idea one day in practice to have any presents the congregation members purchased for the outreach, to be brought up at the end of the play and laid at the feet of baby Jesus as an offering. The night of the play came, and there seemed to be something in the air that was just pure magic. The play was performed, and the youth guide stood up and made the announcement for the gifts to be brought forward. I then stood in front of the church and led the cast of the play in a verse of "Silent Night."

I asked the people in the pews to join in, and the gifts started coming up the aisles. We sang and sang. I had to fight back the tears. Bikes, clothes, toys, and toiletries were brought; I didn't think it was going to end.

It was a miracle and a true gift to be able to witness the outpouring of love offered for families who truly needed help. Everyone got exactly what they asked for, down to the smallest item. I had truly received a word from God, and it was glorious, to say the least, to see it manifest right before my very eyes. Seventeen families with a total of forty-two children were blessed that year by one act of obedience, and three out of eleven churches on this island participated.

I seemed to be on hold, waiting for further instruction from God about what he was calling me to do next. As I was waiting, I learned that I had to keep living, working, and doing the things that were right before me. I learned I still needed healing from deep-seated wounds. Helping the children as much as I did helped penetrate the wall I had built around myself due to the abortions I had. I reached out every Sunday and hugged them as they left children's church. I needed it more than they did. I went overboard, trying to work my way into the graces of God through church work, the children, and the outreaches.

Originally, I had been hired on a temporary basis at the health store; however, the owner wanted to offer me a full-time job. They said they had had Christians work for them before, but not one was like me. While working there, I learned to go in each day and perform my duties as though Jesus Christ was in the back managing the place. I thought to myself, *If he were really sitting back there, I would do my job differently. I would do my job better.*

I pretended Jesus was watching me 24/7 in every aspect of my life. I started actually enjoying going to work every day and putting in a good day's work because I knew it pleased the Holy Spirit. The lesson had been learned: Stop, take it slower and easier, and do it the right way.

Instead of wiping around the dirt, I would take everything off the shelves to clean them. I always made certain, even if I did not feel like it, to do the job that I felt was up to his code. This helped change the way I approached my life in other areas too. I was being broken by the Holy Spirit to live my life a new way. In addition, my flesh was calming down so I could take a deep breath and do things the right way instead of trying to hurry and get it all done now. Most of my life, I did just what I had to do to get by, but that had changed. I wanted all God had for me while I was here on earth. I started becoming more careful in the way I handled my life, believing it would affect what I would be doing in eternity. I wanted to make him proud of me.

My friend came to me one day stating she thought God wanted her to open her own store. She wanted to carry a variety of vitamins, Christian books, jewelry, and reading material so people could learn how to take care of the body they had God's way. She and her husband wanted me to come and work with them, but I wasn't sure how I felt about it. I hadn't prayed or fasted about it. I had no clear answer from heaven what course to take, and the ache in my stomach started coming back. I liked her and her husband and felt she and I had bonded together while doing some exceptional things for God. I couldn't understand why she was so antsy to leave, but she was hell-bent on it. Recognizing her mind was made up and that she would never listen to what I had to say, I kept my mouth shut. I was very unsure of what it all meant, and I didn't know what to do. The owner of the store and her son said that others had come there, learned about the business, and left to open their own stores, and they hoped we would never do such a thing. I shuddered inside, knowing the plan. I would never hurt anyone intentionally, but they had hit the nail on the head.

I was currently selling so many products that my friend and her husband thought they needed me. I let them goad me into going with them, and I reluctantly gave a two-week notice to go to yet another job. Was this was an open door I needed to take? I had no clue.

My friends' store was opened right in the heart of the city. The first time I went there, I gasped when I went in. One wall, which ran across the back of the store, mirrored the Wailing Wall of Jerusalem. The Wailing Wall of Jerusalem dates back to the Second Temple period and considered a sacred place. People from all over the world go there to pray. They place prayers in cracks and crevasses, believing God will hear and answer them. I immediately said, "We can have people place prayers in the wall, and we can pray over them every evening before leaving."

The place was readied, and we opened. One morning several days later, my friend came to me and told me that they didn't have enough money to pay for the shipment of vitamins that were due to be there within three days. She was frantic. My first thought was, *Didn't you know what this was going to cost you?*

I said, "Bring the bill"—which was a little over $3,000— "and we will come into agreement that God will move financially for you." We knelt before the Lord, signed the bill in agreement, prayed, then got up from the floor, shut up, and believed God would move.

My friend's husband retired from the police force two days later and received his retirement check. He had calculated beforehand how much his retirement check should be to the penny. However, upon receiving his check, he discovered it was for $12,000 more than he had originally come up with. They went straight from the retirement function to the accounting personnel for the city. He showed the clerk his calculations and she said, "There is no mistake in the amount." The figures were checked and double checked for accuracy. My friend came in the next day stunned, recounting to me what had happened, and I knew God had moved in this situation.

The car Dara had given me was on its last legs, and I had been quoting the scripture from Philippians 4:19: "And my God shall supply all your needs according to His riches in glory by Christ Jesus."

Because of my repossessions, my credit was shot, and I was unable to purchase a car, much less anything else. My brother, who worked for a dealership, encouraged me to try to get a car anyway. He kept saying, "You have nothing to lose." I reluctantly filled out an application for a car. He called me back two days later and said, "Come and get your new car." I was shocked. I discovered later that the manager of the dealership told the financing company "just do the loan."

The patrons were very receptive to the prayer wall. They would write their prayers on pieces of paper and place them ever so carefully in the Wailing Wall. We never looked at anyone's prayer, and we were faithful to pray over each individual one as we had told God we would do.

The owner decided we needed to expand and set up a service where people could go online and buy vitamins, books, etc., from us. I was feeling that God wanted to do something more as well, in the form of a ministry. I had been going around teaching others about the Lord for several years by this time, and they listened, taking heed to what I would tell them. I had an idea about instructing people on the store's site through written teaching letters.

The Web site needed to be designed, and I enlisted the help of one of the best designers and technical people I knew.

He asked us to put some ideas together and come up with a concept that would capture the essence of what we were trying to accomplish there. One evening, as I was propped up on my bed, I sketched a drawing for the site. Through our brainstorming, we came up with a business name, which was The Olive Tree. The day arrived for the meeting with our designer, and he brought three designs with him. I saw one and gasped.

He said, "What's wrong?" I carefully flipped open the notebook I was using and showed him my drawing for the Web site. It exactly matched one of the ones he had done. That sealed it. We knew the sketch was from heaven, and it was the one we chose.

I, in the meantime, had begun to write letters about what the Holy Spirit was speaking to my heart. We published a new one every week on the site. Much to my amazement, people were hitting the pages where the letters were posted. We also opened up the opportunity for others to come and pray in a concentrated manner every Friday morning for an hour before opening for business. Many tangible answers to prayers came from heaven through those Friday morning prayer times.

We were selling enough in the beginning to keep abreast of the bills, and the owners had seen the power of God manifest itself in ways that blessed the store. I will never forget the day a girl arrived with a brand new printer in tow, stating God had told her to go buy it and bring it to us. The owners were always so surprised when good things happened, but on a day-to-day basis, the bottom line was about money, and the time came when she said she could no longer afford to pay me. I was stunned. She gave me two weeks' pay, and just like that, I was left without a job.

With the family's latest move, I was still rooming with my mother, but I had moved up in the world as far as my sleeping arrangements were concerned. My mom and sister had gone to the Goodwill and purchased a box spring and mattress for me for ten dollars. I had my very own bed for the first time in years. And instead of getting up early and having to go pray in the bathroom before anyone got up, I now used my mom's walk-in closet as my private sanctuary.

I was out and about one day and happened to run into the owner of the previous hair salon where I had worked. He asked me where I was working. Without going into too much detail, I stated that I needed a job, and he said, "Why don't you come back and do nails for me?" That was the opening I needed. I enthusiastically said yes. For some reason, I thought maybe working there this time would be different.

I was in prayer one morning (in my prayer closet), kneeling on the floor as I always did, and I told the Lord that I had had enough. I said, "I can't go on any further." I slowly continued, "I can't fight for people any longer." I couldn't pray anymore. I couldn't believe anymore. I said, "I would rather you just take me home." I needed more than a carrot this time.

I had moved and moved and moved. I had stood on faith and given my tithes, my time, my talents, and my intercession to others as I walked through my life after turning to Christ. I couldn't give to anyone anymore. I had helped and helped until I couldn't help anymore. I didn't feel settled, and I longed so to be settled in my life. I just felt so distressed in my heart that day that I really didn't care what happened to me anymore. I didn't pray for anyone that morning. I barely eked out the words, "I plead the blood of Christ over Dara. I take authority over you, Satan. Get your hands off of her, in Jesus' name."

That was it. I thought to myself upon arising, *As long as she will be all right, I don't care anymore.* I walked out of the closet, and the voice I had come to listen for said, "A little while longer."

Okay, but what was going to happen in "a little while longer"? I didn't know, but I knew that as long as God was going to let me keep waking up, I couldn't stop going and doing. If I stopped, Satan would win, and my family would lock me up and throw away the key. I had learned over the years that if I gave up and quit, I would be defeated. Through the hard knocks I took in life, I had learned to fight the good fight of faith. But how much could one human possibly take? I also knew that if I received a word from God, then that settled it— no matter what. That word alone that morning was enough to give me hope that God was still listening and that someday I might be settled. Getting up from my knees to leave the closet that morning, I knew deep within my spirit I would continue on my journey with Jesus, not knowing what lay ahead.

STAND DOWN

I had been back in the fingernail business for several months and was making less than minimum wage. The owner said, "How much do you need? Aren't you living with your family?"

A couple of the girls working there doing hair started confiding in me about what they knew about his finances and how he would pay them every week. There was never any paycheck stub or records issued. There would be a wad of cash given, and everyone started to smell a rat. They became very concerned that the IRS would find out and that they would get into trouble; they felt they were being involved in some underhanded business tactics. I hated anyone who was unjust.

The owner started telling me things he had done in business dealings that he shouldn't have done, and finally everything came to a head. For some reason, I confided in my family—which was rare for me—about what was happening there.

Divine intervention took over, and through a series of phone calls, I discovered that my nephew had a friend who owned a huge hair salon. I decided to share with the man what was going on with my current employer, and after a lengthy conversation, he said, "Why don't you just quit there and come to work for me? I would love to have you."

I knew in my heart that it was the right move for me, even though I felt apprehensive. This exclusive hair salon catered to some of the most elite clients in town, and if I was going to keep doing nails for a living, then I needed some clients and some money. I believed this was an open door I was going to have to walk through.

I knew I had to confront my current employer, who had hired me for the second time, by resigning, and I dreaded it. Through much prayer, I had been given a word by God to deliver to this man. I went to an early morning meeting with him and reluctantly told him what God had said. I walked away that day knowing that if he didn't seek Christ, the outcome of his life would not be good, and I knew the purpose for my being there the second time was completed.

Certain people knew that Dara was living with someone without the benefit of marriage, and it was alluded to that this was a sticky point, as she was a worship leader at church. I was so proud of what she was accomplishing, yet I knew that God didn't like the fact she was living with this boy. God had begun to deal with me regarding this situation. I was faithful to tell her the truth of what God was laying on my heart, even though I knew it would hurt her. If there was anyone who wanted the best for Dara, it was I, and she had to know that God didn't accept just any kind of behavior. Shortly thereafter, she was confronted and told by the youth guide who had begun this contemporary service that she could no longer sing in church due to her infidelity. Of course, she cried, and I cried.

Dara sang like an angel and was always there for practice, giving 110 percent. Several times, I overheard others talk about how beautiful her voice was, but that still didn't excuse her sin and the fact that God was not going to allow anyone to lead souls to heaven when they were blatantly sinning right in front of his face. I understood God's will in this matter, but still, being her mother, I felt a deep hurt knowing that others at this church were sinning too, but she was the one who was used as the scapegoat.

I had been working at the new shop for some time and while doing nails for a friend, I started talking to her about Dara. I had learned to develop a personal, close relationship with Christ by not telling everyone everything, but this day, I felt led to open up. I explained to her that Dara was living with a boy, and I didn't like it. I shared with her that I thought some kind of spiritual warfare was needed to break this situation.

Dara had continued to go to school while working full-time, and I had been faithful to intercede on her behalf every day, sometimes more than once a day, as the Spirit of the Lord would lead me. Dara was coming to see me at the new shop, and I was around her enough to know what was going on in her life, but we had no further discussion about her living situation; she knew I didn't approve.

After a few moments, the customer, who had been a teacher of Dara's at school said, "I am feeling that you need to unbind the hands of God in her situation and let him move."

As soon as she made this statement, I knew what I had to do. I had to stand down—stop praying and pleading the blood of Christ over her. God was not able to move through this situation spiritually because of all I was doing for her, and he confirmed to me that I was tying his hands from him being able to help her.

The following morning, I had a sinking feeling in the pit of my stomach as I went into Mom's closet to pray. For the first time after all of the years I had prayed, fasted, and offered money—unbeknownst to Dara—to get her on a stable path, keeping Satan's grasp on her at bay, I was going to totally give her to God for protection. I couldn't figure out why he was asking me to "stand down." She was my only living child, and I adored her. How could I let her be open to Satan and his wily ways? I had been given a word however, and I was going to be obedient and follow through with the instructions I knew had come from heaven.

The very first thing I told the Lord as I opened my prayers that next morning was, "I don't want to stand down for Dara. You gave her to me when I was in the labor room, and I promised you I would do better if you would let me have her." I continued, "The cord was wrapped around her neck, her heartbeat went down to twenty-three beats a minute, and still she lived. I know I have not been a good mother and I repent for that, but you are asking me to stand down for her. How could you want me to do that knowing that Satan is real?" I hung my head low and just sat there feeling forlorn. But I knew in my heart God had delivered a word to me through Dara's teacher and I would *have* to be obedient. I didn't want to, though. I ended my time with God saying, "Nevertheless, (pausing) I will give her to you." I got up after I finished but was not wholly certain what would happen. I walked out of my closet feeling very down again and wondered what was coming for my one and only child.

Exactly seven days later, Dara and a friend had gone out for New Year's Eve, and Dara met a guy with whom she fell head over heels in love. Shortly thereafter, she moved out of her two-bedroom apartment where she had been living with her boyfriend and moved into a studio apartment by herself. *Pleading the blood of Christ over her bound God's hands?* I was really going to have to meditate on that one. I knew I had learned yet another way to war for my daughter.

Several weeks later, a girl who was a trusted friend and prayer partner, by the name of Lynn Thompson, came to me. She had just received a large inheritance and she believed that God wanted her to help me move away from my family into my own apartment. I was excited at the prospect, yet still I felt funny about having someone help me with money. She told me to pray about it and to let her know what I wanted to do. I didn't take the money at first because I felt weird about it, as much as I wanted to live on my own.

I would literally go to work, come home, go to my room, and stay there the rest of the night. Yes, I would leave my room to go run, work out, or go to church, but I wouldn't socialize, watch TV, or do much of anything else. I knew that my family loved me, in some odd sense, but they didn't like what I did most of the time or how I believed, even though we all went to the same church and all of us were proclaimed Christians. They thought I was way out in my beliefs, and nothing I was going to do, no matter how successful I was, would ever change their opinion of me.

Possibly my friend's offering was God's answer to me when I told him I could not go on any longer the way I was living. Maybe this was what he meant when I heard the voice say, "A little while longer." Perhaps this was the open door I was being given that would allow me to move from under my family's roof. Open door or not, I had to try this and thought of it as the opportunity I needed to take, not knowing what would happen to me. I had no clue where consistent rent money would be coming from, but I took a step of faith and guided by the Holy Spirit, filled out an application at the apartment complex where Dara lived. I got a part-time job at a chocolate business to meet the financial criteria. The combined income from both jobs satisfied the requirement, and despite my past credit history, my application was approved. I couldn't believe it. I called Lynn to tell her that I would accept her offer. She asked me how much I needed. Without giving it much thought, I said, "I think $600.00 will take care of it." We came together and she used her monetary gift as an offering to the Lord and the wheels were set in motion. My mother was visiting relatives when all of this transpired, which was a relief to me. There was no fanfare as I told my family I was moving. Many emotions ran through my heart as I drove off that day, but one thing was clear to me: I knew I *had* to go to move forward in my life.

Once again, I had stepped out in faith to do what I believed God was telling me. No, I did not hear an audible voice say, "Go rent an apartment," but I had walked closely enough with God that I was beginning, with more certainty, to be able to discern when he was telling me to do something. I moved into my new apartment with only a box spring and mattress from Goodwill. I had no bedding or silverware; I had nothing. Then another friend, by the name of Jewel, who I had met early in my arrival to North Carolina, called me out of the blue and asked me to come by and see her. She ended up giving me an offering of one hundred dollars, and with it, I bought a TV.

The story would always be the same: "God told me to give this to you." Then unbeknownst to me, Lynn had gone to Walmart and bought me a futon. She also went to the Dollar Tree—my favorite place—and bought me every household item you could imagine.

I scarcely had any money, but I had gone to the store and bought some eggs, bread, oatmeal, and bacon to get by. I was scared, but it was a good kind of scared. I went to church that first Sunday morning, came home, and fixed breakfast. After praying and eating, I started talking to God. I ended up telling him I didn't mean to be ungrateful but that it sure would be a nice convenience to have a microwave oven. I made it clear though, that if he decided I didn't need one, that would be fine with me as well. Later that next week, a family member called and said they had an extra microwave and offered it for my use.

I didn't have a vacuum cleaner so I would use a broom to sweep out the apartment. Every two weeks or so, I would walk around the corner to my daughter's and she would allow me to use her vacuum. I went to the apartment facility to wash clothes a couple of times. I realized that I was able to take a bubble bath for the first time in years—in my own tub—without having to be concerned that I was using too much hot water or someone else's bathroom time. I felt oddly funny about the whole thing, but I felt good, believing that I had been rewarded for my obedience. Of course, when I watched TV, I watched the Christian network, except for the few times I allowed myself to watch the last few episodes of American Idol and the sing off between Clay Aiken and Reuben Stoddard. I didn't have anyone telling me I couldn't. I didn't have to answer to anyone but God for what I did.

Living right around the corner from Dara meant the world to me. Mother's Day rolled around, and it was the same weekend she was graduating from college with a two-year degree. She called me and said, "Mom, I bought you something for Mother's Day, and I need to come over so I can give it to you."

I really didn't feel worthy to receive anything from her, but I opened the box she put in my hands and started to cry. Inside was a birthstone ring of sapphires and diamonds. After all we had been through, her loving me was—well—the icing on the cake. I knew she must not think I was crazy after all.

My work area at the nail shop was up front beside the reception desk, and I really wanted to be in a different area. I was informed there was an empty space in the back corner across from the bathroom if I wanted it. I had been using a small nail table, and out of the blue, an old friend called and told me to come over—that she had something for me. She had tried the nail business but had not succeeded and asked if I wanted her table and supplies. Without hesitating, I heartily accepted the offer, knowing that God was giving unto my bosom from other people.

I had seen so much in the spiritual realm by this time and was living solely on faith, having others sow into my life so much so that I wouldn't stop talking about God. I can tell you that many at the salon did not like it, but since we were considered independent contractors, they couldn't stop me. It wasn't that I was obnoxious and loud about it, but if you were going to sit at my table, we were going to end up talking about Jesus.

Several months passed, and then money started becoming tight for the owner of the salon. I was told one day that another hairdresser had been hired, and she was going to need my space to work. I was told my new work area was going to be a tiny closet area with a curtain hanging over the doorframe that separated it from the rest of the salon. I didn't know what to make of all of this at the time. Regardless, I kept my chin up, moved into the little closet, and worked as if nothing happened. I felt that I had been downsized though, and my stomach began the familiar ache again. Money had also started to become very tight, but I stayed true to what I knew, and at the end of every week, I would go before the Lord with my tithes.

A thought came to me, and I went to the owner and offered to clean the shop as a part of my rent payment. I charged seventy-five dollars to clean a huge shop, which employed nine operators and two nail techs. In addition, I paid him another fifty a week to complete the amount owed. I held my head high, put a smile on my face, and kept working. Small closet or not, I served my clients with professionalism and style. Just because I had a change in work area, that did not keep my clients away. They kept right on making appointments with me, and they would comment that the room always seemed much bigger than it was.

One particular week, I had not fared well monetarily and needed $400 to make my car and insurance payments. I knew what I had to do. I had to make a monetary offering to the Lord. That night, I went home, took communion, and offered up my last forty-five dollars to heaven. I sowed it where the Holy Spirit led me, and the next morning upon my arrival at work, a woman came up to me. She said, "Someone stopped me in the parking lot this morning, placed this envelope in my hands, and asked me to give it to you." She handed me an unmarked envelope, and I went into my closet area. I laid my things down and looked inside—there were four one-hundred-dollar bills!

Tithing always kept the windows of heaven opened over my life, and I wasn't about to stop no matter how much I didn't have. I didn't have the luxury of a cell phone, but one day, a customer came in, sat down, and asked me if I had one. I said, "No."

She said, "I just got a new one, and I have one that is paid up for six months, and if you don't take it, it will go to waste." I reluctantly took the phone, even though I knew it was God's will. Little by little, material wealth was being given to me as I continued to be obedient and I was going to have to accept the fact it was from heaven. Stubborn pride? No longer an issue.

THE WILLOW TREE FIGURINE

It was time for Joy of a Child Mission Outreach again. I went to my employer and received permission to put a box at the front of his shop for donations. Much to my surprise, other contractors wanted to be involved. Some of the hairdressers put jars at their stations so people could make donations. Everyone was excited with helping out, and there seemed to be magic in the air because of it.

I was working in a very upscale salon where some of the oldest and wealthiest families from Wilmington came. A few of the customers brought in used items, and my spirit was immediately turned off. I went to the Lord about it, feeling I might be wrong, and then took what I was feeling to the core members of the Joy group. The answer came down from heaven that needy people had been given sloppy seconds most of their lives, and only new items were to be accepted.

In addition this year, the Lord had made it clear that we should add a benefit concert to raise money for Joy. The Holy Spirit had been telling me that the traditional service in my church needed a new form of worship. I was told to call forth a praise choir and introduce them at the concert, and I was obedient to follow through. Through prayer, I was given the outline of what was to happen with this concert. I was amazed that twenty-six people volunteered to sing for the cause of needy families. I got in touch with a local sorority house, and they were going to use Joy as their annual mission outreach. I brought the praise choir and the house band together, and lastly, I was to emcee the whole thing, giving a brief testimony in the very church that hadn't wanted to hear what I had to say about my life several years earlier.

I proclaimed a three-day fast before the event and that night I drove to the church about three hours before the concert to make certain I had enough quiet time with the Lord. As I was driving across the bridge to the island, the Holy Spirit spoke to me and said, "Your soul has been atoned for." This revelation stunned me, and I felt as though I was driving on autopilot. The work I had been doing for the Lord—the toiling and all the repenting—flooded back to my mind in an instant. I knew God had forgiven me for the destructive and apathetic lifestyle I once lived.

The pastor showed up and told me to "get the show on the road." I looked inside the church where there were people sprinkled all around. Where was everyone? I went downstairs to the bathroom to muster my courage for what was to come. I was scared, yet told myself, "This is God's concert that you are bringing forth, so whatever happens in regard to attendance or comments, just know it is God's will."

I walked back up the steps, which took—it seemed—an eternity. I was responsible for this concert all by myself. I had usually done everything in church with the youth guide, but not this time. I got to the top of the stairs. I turned my head and gazed into the sanctuary, and there were people every-where. They were being directed upstairs to the balcony, and the side room overflowed. It was glorious. I walked to the front, took my seat, and nodded for the intro music to begin.

My heart raced. I knew the time was coming for me to give my testimony to the crowd who had shoved it under the rug as though my sin didn't exist. This time though, the church was stuffed with people who didn't attend there on a regular basis, and that gave me a sense of courage I hadn't felt before, as I stood drug-free to give my testimony. The air was so thick with the Spirit you could have cut it with a knife, and I could see people were moved.

As we were packing up to leave that night, the head of the missions committee came up to me and made a single comment: "May I make a suggestion to you? Since so many people have to go to work the next day, please consider having this at 6:00 p.m. next year." Others came to me giving glory to God for what he had done. We hurriedly tallied the money before handing it to the church secretary. That night, we raised $700 for needy families, and I was thrilled. The concert was a huge success. This was in addition to the money we raised in the boxes we had spread all over the island which totaled a little over $2100.

After all of the hoopla of Christmas was behind us, several weeks later, I sat on the front pew of the church after the Sunday morning service exhausted hardly able to think. The previous day, I had been sitting at my nail table and started to cry from sheer weariness. I had not only put on the benefit concert for Joy but did all of what was necessary to see that numerous families were brought Christmas that year. I had directed the Christmas play again, and when I say I directed the play, I mean I went all out. Nothing was done halfway. That year, we added hair and makeup, which Dara agreed to do in addition to the costumes, lighting, and music. I placed hay anywhere there was an empty spot up front. That night, I wanted to transport everyone to the little town of Bethlehem in their hearts. I even had a real live infant, by the name of Samuel, who represented our Lord and Savior.

With each passing year the play became more real. It had become one of the highlights of the year at our church. When

I did anything for God, I did it with all the gifts and strength I had. To top it all off, I was teaching the Sunday school class called "The Mixed-Up Adults."

But that Sunday morning, I began to cry in front of the man who had always been the other half of what I did at church—the married youth guide. I told him that I felt called to preach the gospel, not all of this other work I had so arduously been doing for the past several years. His response was, "Then why don't you do it?"

I thought, *Well, no one will give me a chance, that's why!* All I had done was work myself to death trying to please everyone while thinking it was God's will. Christmas had indeed been a huge success, and I was left worn out. I could hardly drive home quickly enough that day because all I wanted to do was fall into bed. Was I to be so exhausted that I couldn't function from doing the will of God?

I had been nominated shortly thereafter to be a deacon, and someone ended up telling me that I had missed being elected by one vote. The Sunday school director asked me if I was disappointed, and I told him I wasn't, but really I kind of was. I reflected a moment and then added, if God had wanted me to be a deacon, I would have been made one; I then came to know in my heart I didn't need a title to do the will of God. I believed I had already been doing that.

———

Something had to give for me. Finally, I made the decision to stop teaching class on Sundays and I felt a great relief over it. I then ultimately came to realize that it could not be God's will for me to work so hard that I got physically sick. I started getting up and praying in my apartment instead of attending Sunday school. I felt like I needed rest more at this moment than anything else. It occurred to me, "What good would I be to anyone dead?" Several people didn't like it but I proceeded to tell them that I was just as effective on my knees as I was sitting in a church pew for social hour.

Then as I was going through my routine of attending church several months later, I heard the voice say, "It is time to move on." I kept hearing the voice telling me this, but I couldn't seem to bring myself to the point of completely cutting ties with this church.

One day after contemporary service rehearsals, something happened that I knew was not right. This incident helped me to come to terms with the fact I needed to be obedient. I was vacuuming the sanctuary in preparation for the nightly service and I was still very tired. I would only have several hours in which to go home, rest, and then return. The youth guide made the comment that I could come to his new apartment— since he had just split from his wife—and rest on his bed.

I had worked so long with him week after week over the past couple of years, and I thought I had fallen in love with him. He had already made the comment to me several weeks earlier, while his back was turned to me, that he was available. Here was the opening I thought I had longed for. I hadn't uttered a word in response the day he remarked he was available, and this day when he offered his bed to me at his apartment, I said, "No, thank you."

Even though he was separated from his wife, he was still married, and I would not allow myself to fall prey to temptation. From that moment, something in me started to change in terms of the way I was feeling about him and our working together at church. He was such a depressed person, and I just couldn't let him drag me into his mess. I had worked too hard to overcome my own circumstances; I couldn't take on his. I had already been married to Satan incarnate.

I went home after the service that evening, knelt down in front of the place I had designated as my altar before the Lord, and took it all to the only one who could help me sort out my feelings. Through intense prayer and great repentance, I came to my senses. It was what I have come to fondly call one of my "ice-cold bucket of water in the face moments." I knew that if I embarked upon this relationship, God's call, that I felt I had on my life, would be taken from me. Yes, it would be a perfect situation to have a man who loved God and to be able to work along side of him for the cause of Christ, but this wasn't the man and I knew it. I settled in my heart with God the situation that had plagued me for too long now. I knew I had been wrong. I had committed adultery in my heart with this youth guide against heaven.

I listened to the voice that had been prompting me to move on and started attending another church. I didn't know why I was to go there, but I knew the Holy Spirit was guiding me to yet another place of worship. I had a friend who was facilitating a class there, and she thought it would be a good idea to let me teach one Sunday. Well, as it always seemed to be, I was too "in your face" with the truth of what I had learned through the Holy Spirit. One couple did in fact come up and thank me after class that day.

Through continued prayer, I was told to intercede over the next several weeks for the pastor and congregants in this church as service was being held. With the pastor's permission, I would arrive early, go into a separate room, and pray scriptures the Holy Spirit had previously given to me. I would plead the blood of Christ over the church and pastor, taking authority over every principality in the heavenly realms. I felt useful in a way I hadn't before and was introduced to several nice pastors.

Then several months later, I was led back to the church where I had labored so long for God. My mother liked attending this particular church, and the instruction had come down from heaven and was crystal clear that I was to make certain she got there on Sundays. The first Sunday I took Mom back to this church, church members, feeling like I had been a traitor to them, were not particularly ready to receive me back with open arms. My heart ached. I knew I was being obedient to the Lord. My mother was the most important issue, not them, and if she liked going there, then I was going to take her, no matter what anyone said.

———

I was still cleaning the shop each Saturday to make up for my weekly booth rent. I will never forget this one Saturday after a long week, I was crying out to God, as was my custom when I was tired. I had at my disposal a little electric broom that I had been using to vacuum the hair up that had fallen in every crack and crevice of this massive hair salon. I remember sobbing and telling God, "At least if I have to continue to clean this shop, could I please have a better vacuum?"

The owner peeked in my little closet Tuesday morning and said, "Guess what I bought you this weekend?"

I said, "What?"

He said, "A Shop-Vac!"

I said, "Thank you," as I smiled broadly. Then I thought, *Oh, goody,* as he turned and walked away. Sitting there I then knew it must be the will of God that I continue cleaning the shop, which was disheartening. I sat there so down in my spirit at that moment. All I had wanted to do since turning to Christ was to go give my testimony and preach the gospel. I believed for so long that I had a call of God on my life, but I felt I could never get to it. *Why? What was I doing wrong?* It seemed that I had such a magnificent story, yet people didn't or couldn't acknowledge what God had done through my life. *Why wouldn't they listen? Why didn't anyone want me to come and tell what God had done in my life?* I became so sullen in my heart that I wondered if I was falling apart again.

Shortly after that incident, the owner appeared in the doorway of my little nail room. He stated, "I have someone else coming in to clean the shop." He continued to explain that the other nail tech was leaving and that I could move to the nice big area in the shop she had been using. Then he asked if he could talk with me outside. I was sort of in a daze as I rose to follow him. I heard the words he spoke, and yet the only thing going through my mind was, "Now what?" I knew most of the people in the shop really didn't like me, and I would have to work right in the midst of them. Quite frankly, I didn't know if I was up to the task. I also knew that I was barely able to eek by a living and couldn't afford the higher rent I was going to have to pay. I wondered what was going to happen to me. The dreaded ache reappeared as we walked outside; he lit up a cig, and continued: "She's leaving, and she would like to give you her clients, but you have to stop talking about Jesus."

Prior to this confrontation, the other nail tech, who had been only cordial to me, popped her head in my room and inquired if I would be interested in buying her clients. I let her know I was not interested in her proposition. The owner continued, "You can have her space in the shop, but your rent will be one-fifty a week, beginning in two weeks. I will give you two weeks' rent free."

First, a Christian was telling me that I had to stop talking about Jesus in order to get additional clients! Second, I could stay in my little closet or have the big nice area with its own private room for pedicures, but my rent, regardless, was going to be $150! I had been barely able to clean the shop and pay the additional fifty-dollar rent. I went home that evening and went before the Lord explaining to him in detail what was now happening at the salon. I was told by the Holy Spirit not to run, but to stay the ground. When I got up from prayer I knew I would accept the proposition of the bigger area, but my stomach ached over it. I was quite aware that most everyone in that shop thought I was a Jesus freak and would have loved to see me leave.

I went there the next day to prepare. I was coming out of the closet, literally! The following weekend, I went in, cleaned, and took over the new space I would be working in. I was given a vision of the pedicure room in a dream. What I saw was an individual pointing to a tree on the wall with names on the branches. In the next few weeks, things started to come into focus. As I studied the wall in the pedicure room, I could see a tree, which I had painted. Contained on the branches were salon services I offered. I went to work, decorated the wall, and received wonderful feedback on what I had done. I kept my area clean and pleasing, and I was nice and cordial to everyone, even though I knew they didn't care for me. Gradually, things began to change, and they all saw what a good worker I was. Little by little, they all started to come around and attitudes started to soften. Several had listened to others talk about me and had formed their original impressions based on secondhand talk. Now they were being less biased and they warmed up to me. I managed to pay my first week's rent of $150 and never missed from that moment on. The owner was shocked. I came to know that God would always provide for me as long as I would do my part by getting up and being faithful. Also, I didn't have to clean the shop any longer, and that was definitely a blessing. If I had quit and given up and run, it would have been all over for me as far as the path God wanted me to walk.

Christmas 2004 was upon us. Willow Tree figurines were becoming quite popular, and one of my customers gave me one as a gift. When I opened the box, I was a little stunned but thanked her nonetheless. This particular figurine was of a girl holding a cat. I had grown up with dogs all my life and I hated cats. Who would give someone anything with a cat on it without knowing if that person even liked cats? I didn't have much in the way of knick-knacks, so I accepted it with thanks and placed it on the ledge that separated my kitchen from my dining area.

Dara and I weren't living together, but having her right around the corner from me was the next best thing. She stopped by one afternoon to get her nails done and all of a sudden, I heard her gasp. I said, "What's wrong?"

She said, "It's a sign!" as she pointed to the figurine.

I thought, *What sign?*

She said, "Mom, that figurine is a sign that you need to bring the cat that has been hanging around the apartment inside. I remarked, "It is not a sign. If God had wanted me to bring that cat in, he would have told me. It is not a sign."

There was a cat in the neighborhood that had been coming to my front door for several months. It seemed to appear out of nowhere and would come and stare at my front door. She would curl up on the porch chair at night and go to sleep. The neighbors all told me I should take her in, and I would think, *You have no idea who you are talking to. I have a call of God on my life; I do not have time to take care of a cat.* I hardly had enough money after paying my shop rent to feed myself, much less a cat. I certainly wouldn't be able to afford to take her to the vet. I emphatically said no to everyone around me who asked me to become this cat's owner.

One evening it was raining cats and dogs. The thunder and lightning were horrific. Usually when it would rain, the cat would come up on the porch and hover. I had made her a makeshift lean-to as a shelter, but this evening, she was not under there; I couldn't find her anywhere. I was very concerned about a cat I didn't even like!

Immediately, I came inside and knelt down on the floor at the altar. I began my explanation to the Almighty: "I repent to you, God, for not taking the cat in. If I was being disobedient by not taking this cat in, I repent. If you will just bring her here safe, I will take that as a sign you want me to keep her."

Exactly fifteen minutes later, I heard a knock at my front door. There stood my next-door neighbor with a soaking wet cat in her arms. I said in a somewhat shaky, deep laugh, "Welcome home. Come on in." God had spoken.

There was a girl who lived across the street in the upstairs apartment who I discovered worked for a vet. On an earlier occasion, she had taken the cat, had it spayed, and made certain she had all the necessary shots. She was even on flea treatments that were very expensive. On top of that, my neighbor brought over that same night a litter box, cat litter, and other necessities. I was all set; I was a cat owner, and it hadn't cost one thin dime. My daughter had been right, and the figurine was a sign after all.

A couple of months later, I received the lesson I was supposed to learn. My heart, over the years, had become hardened. This cat needed someone to love her, and I too needed someone to love me unconditionally—without any strings attached. I didn't love myself. The things I had done were so deep and sinful that I was never able to forgive myself. She helped soften my heart so I could truly be able to love fully and openly again. I was a nice person, I had done many good works in the name of the Lord, but I had built a wall of protection around my broken heart without even realizing it. I told my daughter the revelation I had received from the Holy Spirit, and she was in total agreement. Kit is the name I gave my cat. She is ten years old now and has been "Living the life of Riley" with me for six wonderful years. If anyone had told me I would someday be a cat owner, I would have called them crazy. The Lord does work in mysterious ways his wonders to perform ... Who would have guessed that God would have used a figurine to get me the truth? Of course, he spoke through a donkey once to accomplish his will, so who am I to argue?

CONTROL

No matter what was going on in my life, I always told Dara, "There are no ifs, ands, or buts about it—you are going to college." I had ingrained this in her from childhood. She had recently graduated from a two-year college with her associate's degree and was at a crossroads. She is multi-talented and had worked alongside an aunt who was a hairdresser one summer, learning to cut hair. She would try out her hairdressing skills from time to time on various family members as well as a few of my customers. She was feeling the tug to attend cosmetology school, but she also wanted her four-year college degree.

Dara was advised by a counselor to continue with school; the counselor told Dara that she too had wanted a degree in cosmetology, but her family had always wanted her to have her four-year degree. She told Dara she could always go back and get her cosmetology license, but more than likely, if she didn't continue on now, she would never go back to obtain her four-year degree.

Dara and I came into agreement that God would show us clearly what to do. I, in the meantime, fasted for her so that there would be no confusion from the enemy. I knew that only God's will for her life would be the best one for her—not the will an extended family member or I would have chosen for her.

Her grandparents had a successful real estate business in Richmond, and Dara decided that she would obtain her degree in business and then go on to get her real estate license so she could eventually work in the family business. I felt skeptical about the decision she made.

Dara's communication teacher from college was a good friend of mine as well as a nail customer, and I confided to her what was happening with Dara and asked her opinion. She said, "Molly, there was a day that Dara stood in my class giving a speech, and I could see her going into the communications field. It was clear to me."

I listened to what she said and took it to Dara. Dara listened but was determined to go into business and take all of the classes that she really didn't like. Then several weeks later, she came over with a friend to my apartment. We ended the close of the evening with prayer. We had several things we prayed about that evening, but I hadn't mentioned the communications field again because she became defensive when I did. However, knowing that only God knew what would be best for her, I added this at the end of our prayer: "Lord, would you please confirm to Dara what you would have her to do with her life and school?"

We all sat up and the friend stated, "Communications."

As far as the friend knew, Dara was going into business and had not known anything of our continued discussion of Dara's destiny. Dara and I looked at each other and both uttered, "Do, do, do, do." Dara did not waver, however, and stuck to her guns about making business her major. I continued to seek the Lord's will about the situation.

We went to orientation and I remained calm, quiet, and supportive throughout the day. We tried to get her signed up for the labs required for a business degree but had a hard time finding open slots. Her decision about school put a wedge between us, but school hadn't started yet, and I wasn't going to give up easily; I believed she was making a wrong decision.

Two weeks before school started, we drove to school to get her finances in order and pay the tuition. I proclaimed a fast that morning and on the way to school, I gave her the best advice I had. I said, "Dara, life is a long time. If you are not happy doing what you do day in and day out, week after week, and year after year, you will be miserable, and you will end up making everyone around you miserable. Let us come into agreement one more time for your path. We will pray that if God wants you to pursue communications, he will open up the way, and if not, he will shut that avenue down. In this way, I will be content with the path you have chosen. Is that agreeable to you?"

She reluctantly replied, "Yes, but Mom, I don't even know what communications is."

I said, "I know, Dara. I don't either, but if it's God's will, we'll find out."

That day we drove from the campus and Dara was enrolled in communications.

I continued working at the hair salon. "Coming out of the closet" was one of the best things that had happened to me. I knew the owner had expected me to fail, leave, and take Jesus with me, but God turned it around and showed them all he was with me.

Fall had come, and Dara was settled in school. She was happy, and I was pleased. She had continued to see the boy she had met the eventful New Year's Eve when I had unbound the hands of God. I constantly drilled into her the importance of finishing school before getting married. I wanted her life to be all it could be, and the words would roll over and over in my mind: *"I will be damned to hell if her life is going to end up like mine."*

Repeatedly, I checked her to make certain she was doing just what I told her. She called and told me Joey, her boyfriend, wanted to come by to see me. The dreaded ache came back in my stomach, and I knew what was going to happen before he even got there, even though I hoped I might be wrong.

The evening came for Joey to come over, and I could see that as soon as he walked in the door, he was nervous. Emotionally I had been like a mother and father to Dara, and I was not going to let anyone have my daughter without God's permission. He had never given me any reason to doubt his character, but I still didn't trust him. He sat down and said, "I would like to have your permission to marry Dara."

I remained fairly calm and said, "You and Dara promised me you would wait, for Dara's sake, until she finished college to get married."

I wasn't happy about any of this, but I knew there was nothing legally I could do. But if God didn't want it happening, then it wasn't going to happen. I told him reluctantly that I would agree to it, but I already knew what my recourse was going to be.

I immediately called the prayer partner I had at the time, recounting the situation. She piped up and said she would fast the next day, and I already knew I was going to. She said she would come directly over to the apartment after work so we could go to battle for Dara. We knelt before the altar, took communion, came into agreement, and prayed that God's will be done for Dara. We got up, shut up, and waited on God. Immediately, great relief flooded over me knowing the Father was in control.

It was revealed in the days following that, in fact, it was God's will Dara be married and that I was the one who would have to come up under the authority of heaven. I can tell you

I had a tough time with God's decision for the first few weeks, but I knew God's divine will had come down from heaven for my one and only daughter.

Until I could come to terms with it, I didn't say much of anything. I knew that I had to buck up and be her mother— love and support her—even though I had no idea what was up ahead and how we would pay for her wedding.

Dara wanted a Cinderella wedding. From her wedding gown down to the wedding and reception itself, I fasted, offered, and prayed until God's will was accomplished in every area for her sake—not my own. I knew as long as Satan was taken out of the equation, then I could accept the outcome as God's will.

Before the wedding, Dara came to me, and we had a heart-to-heart talk. The Holy Spirit had revealed to me that she had some deep-seated wounds left from her childhood and our life together. If these issues were not addressed, they would cause her to bleed her husband dry in her efforts to fill these hurts and pains that only Christ could fill. Even though I didn't want to hurt her, I knew that confronting these issues was the only thing that would truly set her free.

I explained to her that getting married was not an answer for what she lacked in life. I also said I knew I hadn't done my job as her mother but could not go back and fix what had happened. I let her know I could help her come to terms with particular issues, making certain to guide her so she could be whole going into her marriage with a greater sense of awareness of who she was.

I was very to-the-point and honest with Dara, as I had always been once I had fully turned to Christ. I didn't want her life turning out like mine. I went on to assure her that if she truly loved him, I would treat him no less than I treated her.

Meanwhile, the owner of the hair salon where I worked, went from person to person, giving each of us a two-week notice. He was closing up shop. I had been working there almost four years by then. I lived and worked solely by faith, having no money to fall back on.

I had no clue what was going to happen to me, but in the span of that first week, four different jobs surfaced. I had always been like hot grease on a griddle, but this time I was not budging without knowing for certain what God wanted me to do. I knew by now I was not to jump the gun and make any rash decisions. My life had been so full of rash choices and moves that I was not going to make anymore, even if it meant dragging my feet.

Two different hairdressers talked to me about the path they would take. Through prayer, God gave me a word to deliver to each, telling them where to go next. One followed the word of the Lord; the other did not. The one who followed my advice was advised that her income would double the following year, and that is exactly what happened. To this day, her income continues to increase, much to her amazement.

The last week at the salon arrived and I still had no idea what direction to head in. I hadn't gone to see about any other job, not having received clear instructions, so I wasn't jumping. I didn't have many appointments on my books for the week and was uneasy about what was coming, but all of a sudden, Monday morning, phone calls started to pour in for my services. At the end of the week, I had put in some very long hours, but had made close to $1200.00 and this was enough to pay most of my bills for the following month. I was exhausted. The Holy Spirit told me to take the next week off in order to listen, so I did.

The following Monday I was told to call all of my customers telling them I would be working out of my apartment for at least the next thirty days. I further explained I didn't know specifically where I would settle in, but I didn't want to make any impulsive moves. I was honest. I was not going to make another mistake. I wanted my life settled. It was April of 2005, and I had absolutely no idea what lie ahead.

JESUSWITHOUTTHEJUNK

I continued to work out of my apartment—and the Lord brought the customers. There was no blueprint to follow for what I was doing. I believed I had a call of God on my life, but I had no idea how he would manifest it. There were times I felt I was trying to maneuver through a thick, dark, ominous cloud that wouldn't go away. I would then began to speak scriptures over myself and the apartment, knowing it would be the only thing to stop these unsettling feelings. The oppression would eventually subside so I could continue my day. The ups and downs were unbearable at times and again, I began to wonder if I had made the right decision in regard to staying home to work. God was faithful though, and in times of my greatest outcries to heaven over what I was doing, he would always send a word by someone to let me know he was still with me ordaining my steps. One person in particular called me one day and said, "God told me to tell you that your highs will be really high and your lows will be really low." Then I was in the shower one cold morning in January 2006 and the Holy Spirit spoke clearly to me and said, "Teach my children what I have taught you in a simple and clear way." He continued, "I want you to meet once a week and charge $1.00 each time from those who attend." My first thought was, *I am okay with the meetings, I guess, but please don't make me charge others.* I really didn't want to start a Bible study. I had been in them and never had seen how they benefited the lives of others. They would end up being social get-together gripe sessions more than anything else and the thoughts of having that were not pleasant for me. People always asked me where I attended church. My reply was always the same. What I learned came from one-on-one time spent with the Holy Spirit, Jesus, and God. Then I thought, *Would others even receive what I had to say in a closed setting?* I stepped out of the shower with an unsettled feeling in my heart. Knowing God had spoken, I had no choice but to be obedient.

A friend called me on the phone later that day and said she had had a dream about me; time had proven that her dreams are always right on the money so I listened intently. She said she saw me in a classroom setting, standing at a blackboard, teaching people. In the dream, she also saw a box of money. Once again, there was no format for what I was doing and I had no clue where it would lead. I placed a box on a table for the dollar bills that were to be received and began. Eventually, the Lord had me anoint a specific table as "The Table of Witness." All offerings were placed there and accounted for on yearly income taxes.

Week after week, I taught others what he had taught me in a simple but clear way. I tried to bring God out of the heavens into their everyday lives so they could understand his ways. At one point, I only had two regular attendees. For one reason or another, people who had originally come, dropped out. Others would come from time to time, but I felt certain that two would always be there. I thought I would begin a Bible study and my apartment would be filled with people from all walks of life. Why else would God have told me to do this? I imagined I would start out just like Joyce Meyer did. God began to deal with me about my not being Joyce Meyer. At times, I got so discouraged I thought about just quitting. Then the Holy Spirit would speak to my spirit, "Don't forsake the days of small beginnings." But he also started making it clear to me that there is only one Molly Painter. Someone would always seem to remark how much it helped or thanked me for even being there and teaching. These carrots, as I had come to call them, encouraged me and were just enough to keep me going a little longer. I had to keep my promise to God to "go" or to teach for just the one. I knew I had no choice unless no one showed up. I dressed the part each week—as if I were teaching millions.

I had been working on *the* book on and off since being at home full-time. Eventually I finished working on an overview. I typed it up and sent it to a couple of publishers to see what would happen. After all, I thought that if two different strangers had prophesied over me in regard to this book, then there must be someone who will be interested in buying it. An individual agent emerged who seemed to feel he could sell the work, but then a hurricane hit his home and I never heard from him again. For years, I had written various things, mailing them out to different publishers all over the country, only to have them turned down over and over for publication. I felt so overwhelmingly discouraged that I just stopped trying to make the book or anything else happen, but I kept feeling that now the time had come for it to be birthed.

Then in the spring of 2006, as directed by the Holy Spirit, I was led to write a play. It was not like anything I had done up to this point. A very detailed play just came up and out of me as if it were being written by someone else. Guided by the Holy Spirit, I performed it in my apartment one afternoon for a friend of mine who is a college teacher. With her encouragement, I took it to another college professor she worked with for further critique. He said, "You have a voice that needs to be heard." Through prayer and much fasting, it was made clear that I was to take this play to the stage at Christmas and the offerings given would be used to benefit needy families. Knowing I had no money to accomplish this, I practically stayed on my knees. The Holy Spirit opened the exact path I needed to take every step of the way, including giving me the exact location it was to be performed in, down to the props I would use, in order to perform God's will. Money, time, and talents were donated for the endeavor and I was amazed at the outpouring. I learned once again many valuable lessons of faith, but what I came away with most after the performance that evening and the days that followed, was that I *still* had much to learn about the God whom I called my Father.

I continued to work in my apartment, not having been called to Broadway yet, doing fingernails, and still holding weekly Bible class. For some time now, there was more than just dollar bills that were being placed in the "money box" after class. In the beginning of my walk with Jesus, I would literally fall right on my knees upon awaking and begin to pray. I had learned over the years, through many mornings of being almost too tired to think upon arising, that I needed to be coherent before coming to the only one who could help me. Gradually, it became my custom to wake up, have coffee and *then* pray, feeling I was more effective to do the Lord's bidding if I was clear in my thoughts. When I learned that I could take communion by myself, I added that to my prayer time. Every time something new was placed in front of me, I would go to the Word and then go to God with it to make certain it was his will. I was not going to blaspheme God by doing something I shouldn't. In the spring of 2007, upon awakening, having my coffee and getting settled in to pray, I grabbed the box that held any offerings that might have been placed in it from weekly class. I knelt before the Lord, opened the box and discovered a monetary gift of $10,000. I was stunned. I didn't know what God was doing. I got up from my knees, knowing better than to do anything with it until I knew exactly what his will was. Over the next several weeks, I indicated to him that I knew what a major responsibility this was and asked him to give me clear instructions. I told him I would do whatever he said, no matter what. The Holy Spirit revealed it was time to begin a ministry. So, I gathered three individuals, formed a board, checked into tax regulations, and opened a business account in my name. I did not quit work as a nail tech though. I had learned by then not to be headstrong in anything I did. I kept working, doing what I called "making tents" (working everyday) just like the disciples. I believed that when it was time to quit doing fingernails, God would tell me. I let him direct each step I took.

God had one of the board members tell me it was time to pick a name for the ministry. I really didn't want to call it by my name; I didn't want to gloat about myself. I starting asking others what they thought a good name would be. One of the women who had come to Bible classes that first year told me she told her friends about the way that I taught. They asked her what was so special about the classes. She stated, "It's Jesus without all the junk." Her suggestion was to call the ministry Jesus without the Junk. The first time I heard the name, I was offended, but I let it settle in my heart and finally knew this was good, and it was different—just like I am.

I didn't slack off just because I now had a ministry name and bank account. I knew if I was not obedient, God could take all of this away from me. One wrong move on my part could cost my whole destiny I felt God was trying to accomplish through me for his glory. Fear of that fact alone kept me in line just like he said it would all those years before. I got up each day and kept my face focused on God. I kept the belief that he was with me and enjoyed a renewed sense of confidence in knowing that I really must be called by heaven.

I now had the ministry I wanted but was antsy to make something *big* happen. I had no clear idea which direction to go in. I fell asleep one night weary of trying to figure things out, and then I had another dream. My mother had a charcoal portrait made of me as a six-year-old child that I now used to cover an eyesore on one of the walls in my apartment. In this dream, I was forced to sit up in bed. There was someone standing in the doorway, holding the portrait, telling me, "You are not a child anymore." The next morning I awoke and after some coffee, it all started to flood back to my consciousness. I had still been unable to come to terms with deep-rooted wounds left from my childhood. That dream caused me to go to God and talk to him about these issues in detail. I already knew that I had been forgiven for all of the horrible sins I committed against heaven. Nonetheless, the hurt and pain of my past had caused me to retreat from letting the Holy Spirit help me mature into the adult I needed to be. For years now, I had been going to the cross to be forgiven, being set free, and yet all the while, I was building a wall around my heart to shield me from the hurt that was still evidently there. Kit had done a lot for me in softening my heart, but I knew what I was being told and wondered how God would finally turn me into the adult I needed to be.

In August of 2007, through prayer and much fasting, I continued to seek guidance from the Lord about the ministry. God had permanently placed five people around me to complete this task which I took very seriously. The Holy Spirit revealed that we needed to reach out with a teaching web site but to present material in a simple and clear way. I could teach the multitude from a venue that would be accessible twenty-four hours a day. More importantly, anyone could receive information at no cost to them whatsoever.

Step by step and through individuals that God specifically placed in my path, the Web site was born. After it was up and running fairly smoothly, the Holy Spirit spoke to me and said, "It is time to complete the book." So once again, I restarted work on the book with one of the ministry partners.

The more I seemed to step out in faith for God trying my best to be obedient, the more severe the warfare increased. Over the years, Satan attacked me in every possible way to try and shut me up but I wouldn't give in. I had begun feeling very ill over the last year or two, not telling anyone. I stood on my faith for my health but clearly, something was wrong. I developed a disorder from years of breathing in foul nail liquid, dust from nail files, and tons of hair products. I was so sick at times it was all I could do to function, but I never quit. Each time I thought I couldn't go on any longer, thinking it would be better if God would just go on and bring me home, someone would deliver a word that would keep me going. Each time I thought I would just throw in the towel and give up, the Holy Spirit would speak gently to me and tell me to tune in to one of two individuals on Christian TV. One was Jentzen Franklin and the other was Mark Chironna. At my greatest times of distress, I would listen with my spirit and know that God was ministering to me to keep the faith, keep going and stay focused. I was tired, worn out, and so sick, I just didn't know if I could face living anymore. But I also knew that if a word was given, then the rest would be up to me to act on it. My motto and self-talk was, "Don't quit; don't stop, no matter what! Get up! Move forward!"

A ministry board member came to one of the weekly meetings in the spring of 2009 and handed me an envelope with $755.00 in it. She told me that God told her to give it to me so I could go to the doctor. For years, I have had no insurance and have had to stand on faith for my health and my finances but evidently this time the illness was going to have to be treated by a doctor. I made the appointment *knowing* I was very ill. I would awake each morning wet with perspiration not hardly able to get out of bed. But I didn't complain, and I didn't tell anyone how ill I really felt. I continued to quote the same scripture I had used when God had kept my gallbladder from poisoning me to death. When I would eat, there would be sharp pains as I would try to swallow and I had became very nauseous. This had been going on for about two years by now but had become progressively worse. I had prayed, fasted and offered all along to the only one I knew who could help me, but I was out of time and I knew it. The chest x-rays came back clear, much to my relief, but the problem was in my esophagus. One morning while sitting on the edge of my bed feeling hung over—not from alcohol—I heard a voice. At first, I was uncertain whose voice it was because I had been so sick. I soon realized it wasn't *the* voice; this voice was a jeering, sneering voice that stated, "Do you actually think I am going to let you have this book published?" This affront from Satan made me fight even harder for my health. My resolve and belief that God really had ordained this book and ministry to come into the light were furthermore bolstered. Many times, I have told God that people would never understand what I have gone through to accomplish his will. His reply is always the same, "You will have to be content in knowing that I know." Through continued prayer and prescribed medication, I believe I am healed. I had decided long ago that I would be "The Terminator" when it came to Satan. The only way I would ever stop doing what I was doing was if the very life of me was sucked out of my body. One day, I sat down after exercising and heard *the voice I knew* say, "Lucifer hates you." I replied, " I know, good." I then dropped it and did not invite Satan to "come and get me" like I had done years earlier.

Shortly thereafter, I was awakened in the middle of the night by a loud banging on my front door. I got up out of bed and walked into the living area finding the front door bowed. There was a fierce, glaring, uninviting light all around, as if it was going to burst the door open. The pounding became louder and more fierce. I stood firmly, pointing my finger at it, repeating over and over, "I plead the blood of Jesus Christ over this home. I command you get out of here, Satan, in Jesus' name." Finally the pounding stopped. I saw a dark cloaked figure walk past the window. The next morning as I was leaving my apartment, I took notice of my front door. About ten inches up from the bottom, it appeared as though it had literally been burned. The rest of the door looked as if fire had been splattered all over it. Then a thought occurred to me to go look at each of my neighbor's doors for comparison. Nothing was wrong with them. I knew it was only the blood of Christ and the words of my testimony I had spoken the night before that had saved me (Revelation 12:11).

THE FACE OF CHRIST

Right before the summer of 2009, I was walking around in my apartment and the Holy Spirit spoke to me saying, "You are going to be given an apparition." I had no clue what I was going to see or how it was going to manifest.

The ministry group was disbanding one Monday, and one of the attendees picked up a see-through frame that contained several different progressive sonograms of my yet to be born grandson, J.C. For weeks, these pictures had been sitting on the table and I would show them to anyone who was interested.

This particular attendee stood there staring and said, "Have you noticed the face on this photograph?" I took a closer look. It took me a few seconds but a face came into view and it was burned across the left side of the baby's most recent shot. That face had not been there previously. My heart was racing as I told the group that the Holy Spirit had spoken to me of an apparition. I was dumbfounded, to say the least. Upon further inspection of the picture, I saw another face burned on the right side that looked like a pig's face. I took in a deep breath and didn't say anything at first glance. Then I said, "This looks like a demon to me."

The woman who had pointed out the first face said, "I saw it too, but I didn't want to say anything."

I was in complete shock and stood there for a few more moments unable to move. I gathered my things and left with everyone else to run some ministry errands. I got into the car, buckled up, and the Shroud of Turin came on my heart. I had no doubt what I was being told. I could hardly wait to get home and get on the Internet. It didn't take me long to find a site with a picture of the Shroud on it. I downloaded it and took a deep gasp. The face was elongated and similar in appearance to the picture on the front of J.C.'s sonogram. The following week, I really couldn't wait to show everyone who had become a part of this ministry. They too agreed it was the same face. The face was the face of Christ.

Knowing full well those two faces were not on that particular photograph when Dara had given it to me, I was still somewhat in shock. Through prayer, I was given instructions by the Holy Spirit to go to my daughter's house to reveal my discovery. Dara is not easily moved by anything spiritual, but after looking at this particular sonogram picture, she couldn't deny seeing the face on the left side of the picture and seeing the demon face. I then delivered the word I was given by God to tell her about J.C.

> Then the word of the Lord came to me saying: "Before I formed you in the womb I knew you; Before you were born I sanctified you; I ordained you a prophet to the nations."
>
> Jeremiah 1:4

Now by the authority that has been given to me by God Almighty, I issue a degree in the earth: "I call forth J.C. as a prophet to the nations."

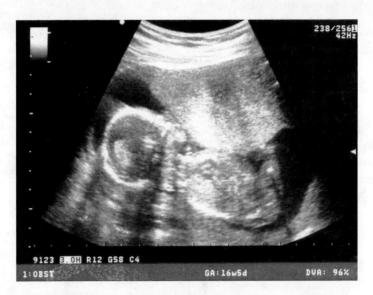

J.C.'s Sonogram

EPILOGUE

For the Son of Man has come to save that, which was lost. What do you think? If a man has a hundred sheep, and one of them goes astray, does he not leave the ninety-nine and go to the mountains to seek the one that is straying? And if he should find it, assuredly, I say to you, he rejoices more over that sheep than over the ninety-nine that did not go astray. Even so it is not the will of your Father who is in heaven that one of these little ones should perish.

Matthew 18:11–14

I didn't arrive home from the trip to St. Albans, with a thunderbolt experience of why I had to go sit in the church sanctuary where I was raised, in the fall of 2007. The revelation of the stained glass windows took time and prayer to "see" the mystery of the multicolored lights in the dream I was given prior to my return. No one ever told me that a man who had been born in a stable, in a manger, two thousand years ago could give me answers to help fix my mess of a life. All people ever did when it came to religion was preach to me and it left me cold. I didn't want to hear them or the message they carried. No one told me Christ was really real. I was truly a wild stallion that had to be broken by the Lord ... I was the *one* he came to save in the mountains of West Virginia.

Fear crippled me mentally most of my life, keeping me from attaining what God had waiting. Discovering the fact that Satan is real and learning how to fight him helped me conquer the demons that were trying to stop my life and destiny from coming to fruition. Knowing it is solely the anointing of Christ that will deliver and set an individual free revolutionized my state of existence. Then God used the fear of him to help keep me on his path, even though there were times that I still made mistakes.

When I set out to unlock the mystery once and for all of whether Christ actually existed or not, I had no idea what lay ahead of me. There were times in the beginning of the journey I thought I just might stop, but then this thought would pop into my mind- "What will you have if you quit?" I began journaling in 1997 and penned this late one evening: I was thinking today about writing a book, *My Testimony, Saved by Grace*. When I think back on my life the only explanation for my still being alive is Jesus. What a turbulent life I have had. I heard that sometimes lives like mine happen so that I can be compassionate and help others since I have experienced it. Oh—how true. The list is endless. It's made me tuff, too tuff. Life is a long time you cannot make it through without Christ.

The spiritual aspects of my life are interesting, to be certain. But I began to see that the dreams, visions, and *the voice* of the Holy Spirit were given to me to help teach and direct me so I in turn could help others. They continued only as I was obedient to stay connected to the Lord. I have walked solely by faith, not knowing where I was going, even with all that I was being shown. It was many years into my journey with God before I realized that he was actually ordaining every step I took so that he could use me to "bring heaven down to earth one rung at a time" in the lives of his children if I could but stay obedient.

Deliverance for me manifested in different ways and did not come all at once. Heaven has dictated when and how it has come. Some of it came instantaneously and some issues are still being addressed to this very day. The Holy Spirit is careful for this *one* to guide me in the way I can handle it. I learned that I cannot cope with all of my issues at one time. The process would be too overwhelming for my heart to bear. The fact that I am still here after all I have endured is only because of the hand of the living God. I am set free, delivered, sane, still have my memory intact and am relatively healthy, *only* because of his unfailing mercy and grace.

And Dara? She will be twenty-nine on May 20, 2010. She graduated from a four-year college on December 10, 2005. She then went on to obtain her real estate broker's license. She has had but one full-time job in her life. When she met her husband, he cleaned carpets for a living. Through prayer and intercession, he is now doing what he has dreamed of since a child. He is now a detective on a police force in North Carolina and a member of the SWAT team. Both of them walk with Jesus.

At fifty-four years old, my heart is at peace. My mind doesn't reel on and on like it used to. I have learned that being settled is a state of mind, not a physical address. Although I have lived at the same address now for the past seven years. I have finally been able to mature into the adult God needed me to be but it wasn't easy. The walk I have walked I would not wish for anyone unless they have been called by God. This was my purpose, destiny and the reason I was born to give glory to the Lord (Jeremiah 29:11).

The true miracles of my life? First, I received a second chance from God. He listened to and answered my prayers the night I raised my hand to him after all the years I spent living in defeat. But, he did it on his clock, not mine. Second, my one and only daughter's life did not end up like mine. Last, but certainly not least, Dara loves and trusts me … and that is worth it all. And the answer to the question that was posed to me in 2006 by the Holy Spirit right before I took *Get Nailed* to the stage still remains the same today … "Yes, Lord, I would die for you so that others might live."

The one stained glass window of the woman in a prostrate position holding on for dear life to the cross of Christ was *the answer* God had tried to get to me years ago at my grandmother's funeral. Satan had kept the multicolored lights blurred so I couldn't bring them into focus, but now I see clearly that the woman in the picture is me. I was *the one out of the ninety-nine* he needed to rescue.

AFTERWORD

I stepped out into the unknown to the edge of a mountain to begin the journey that God had ordained just for me in 1996 to finally discover if God was really real. Fourteen years later, I hold in my heart a peace that truly surpasses human understanding and a belief in knowing that, yes, God is really real. There is no way to recount every instance of alcohol, drug or sex abuse. I came to the conclusion by the end of the writing of this book, that not all things are meant to be exposed for everyone to read, but knowing I have humbled myself before God and repented for each and every sorted detail of my life, I now have been given great solace. Through prayer and fasting, I enclosed within the covers of this book what I believed the Holy Spirit guided me to share. The rest of what I have done and what I have been shown only heaven will know.

While embarking upon this task, I was taken back in time to feel the same emotions I originally felt. There have been many tears, much heartache, and much pain behind these written words. No one will ever know the depth of my regret of blindness to the Lord.

Jesuswithoutthejunk became a 501© *(3) tax exempt entity* July 5, 2007.

I have listed below an overview of what this ministry of five people, who began with nothing, has been able to accomplish so far for God's purposes. The figures reflect the time of July 5, 2007 through June 30, 2010:

- $ 8,196.08 was sown into several worldwide ministries

- $ 8,196.49 was sown locally into the lives of the needy at Christmas, Easter, and Thanksgiving. In addition, several hundred of these dollars were used to help underprivileged children purchase back to school supplies

- $1500.00 was used to fund our Heart of Hope T-shirts. Fifty percent of the profit made from shirt sales is donated to domestic violence shelters

- $3985.50 was used to produce this book, which will be used as seed to reach the multitudes with the gospel of Jesus Christ

The above money does not account for monies used to begin a ministry from the ground up but know this, each and every penny that has been sown into this ministry has been accounted for legally.

Even after all the waste and near destruction of my life, the Lord still wooed me to his bosom and washed my stains away with the blood of the Lamb. It is the only place he knew I would find a safe haven and rest for my weary soul. Life is hard, but hope is waiting for you at his feet. It is now the expressed will of the Father to pose this question to you and to the churches at large: If five everyday people can come together to accomplish so much for the kingdom, aside from our full-time lives and jobs, then why can't you?

The wisdom of all the ages is within you.

Molly Malvern Painter

FOR MORE
INFORMATION

For more information on *Jesuswithoutthejunk,* please contact:

Jesuswithoutthejunk
P.O. Box 16491
Wilmington, North Carolina 28408

Or email with any requests, feedback or prayer concerns to:

Jesuswithoutthejunk.com